Presentations for Decision Makers

Third Edition

Marya W. Holcombe and Judith K. Stein

JOHN WILEY & SONS, INC.

New York   Chichester   Weinheim   Brisbane   Singapore   Toronto

Copyright © 1996 by Strategic Communications®.
All rights reserved.

Published simultaneously in Canada.

This publication is designed to provide accurate and authoritative information in regard to the subject matter covered. It is sold with the understanding that the publisher is not engaged in rendering legal, accounting, or other professional services. If legal advice or other expert assistance is required, the services of a competent professional person should be sought.

Library of Congress Cataloging-in-Publication Data:

Holcombe, Marya W., 1944-
  Presentations for decision makers / Marya W. Holcombe and Judith
K. Stein. — 3rd ed.
    p. cm.
  Includes index.
  ISBN 0-471-28765-2
  1. Business presentations.   I. Stein, Judith K., 1935-
  II. Title
HF5718.22.H647   1996
658.4'5—dc20   96-32249
                                                                              CIP

Printed in the United States of America.

10 9 8 7 6 5 4 3

Contents

5   Putting it all together   63

Crafting riveting beginnings and actionable endings. Making storyboards to ensure effective transitions and determining appropriate visual support. Increasing the impact of the presentation by
choosing the best medium. Designing a computer presentation and
considering options for multimedia.

6   Creating compelling visuals   95

Designing visuals to support the message. Using color appropriately. Producing polished overheads, slides, flipcharts and handouts. Using computer presentation features effectively.

7   Setting the stage   153

Taking responsibility for staging and arrangements. Briefing the
audience. Working out procedures and managing the details. Preparing for a computer presentation and selecting output hardware.

8   Rehearsing and delivering the presentation   173

Getting ready to present with confidence. Delivering the message.
Using visuals effectively. Presenting with a computer. Evaluating
the presentation.

9   Managing the audience is like "herding cats"   201

Preparing for questions. Learning to read the audience and to listen. Encouraging positive discussion while remaining in control.
Handling questions and objections. Dealing gracefully with interruptions.

What's On the Disk

Chapter 6 of this book, "Creating Compelling Visuals," provides numerous guidelines for the kind of visual support that can help make a successful presentation. The disk included with this book is designed to give you a jump-start toward creating those visuals for yourself. Aimed specifically at users of Microsoft PowerPoint, one of the most popular presentation software packages for both Windows and Macintosh, the included files can be opened and edited by users of PowerPoint for either platform.

The disk is DOS/Windows formatted but can be opened on any Macintosh that uses Apple's standard "PC Exchange" system software. Files on the disk include:

VISUALS.PPT — Microsoft PowerPoint 4.0 file

This file contains effective visual examples from Chapter 6 of "Presentations for Decision Makers" in PowerPoint format.

- All charts are fully editable by the user (new figures can be fed into the datasheet to produce new graphs)

- New user-created charts will default to standards recommended in this book

- PowerPoint "Auto-Formats" conforming to standards suggested in the book are included, and can be applied to any chart

- All visuals can be copied and pasted into other presentations

- A customized color palette has been created for this file; all new graphics will default to the provided color scheme

- All new slides created within this file will default to a customized master slide template

- New presentations can be created using the provided file as a template; all of the defaults for color, text, and charts will then be included in the new presentations

COLOR.PPT — *Microsoft PowerPoint 4.0 file*

This file contains examples showing effective and ineffective use of color.

- Template examples show how ill-advised use of color for backgrounds, text, and graphic elements can distract and interfere with the message of a slide, and how color used effectively on a template can support that message. Separate examples show different uses of color for on-screen presentations and for overhead acetates.

- Visual examples show how to use (and not to use) color within a visual

- Palette examples give pointers on how to create an effective color scheme for a presentation, using PowerPoint's color system in combination with a color wheel

- Switching to "Notes" view in PowerPoint provides pointers on use of color and design elements for each slide

PCX and PICT file examples

We are aware that many readers of this book are not users of Microsoft PowerPoint. Unfortunately, while there are many other excellent software packages available, lack of disk space means we're unable to offer additional files for other presentation programs. Some presentation programs may be able to import the PowerPoint files and edit them up to a point.

For readers who have no way to open the PowerPoint files, we are also including some color files in PCX format for Windows, and PICT format for the Macintosh. PCX files can be displayed in many Windows programs, including the Paintbrush program included in the Windows accessories set. PICT files can be imported into many Macintosh programs, including the standard SimpleText program that is provided with the Macintosh system software.

README. TXT — text file

This plain text file can be opened by any text editing program, such as Microsoft Write or Notepad for Windows, SimpleText for Macintosh, or any word processor. It provides full instructions on how to use the PowerPoint and PCX/PICT files included on the disk. To open the README.TXT file, insert the disk in your floppy drive, open your text editing program, and open the text file using the "Open" command under the "File" menu.

Strategic Communications® creates customized disks for its clients and for customized bulk orders. Please call 203 481 4438 for more information.

Acknowledgments

We are deeply indebted to our friends and clients who took the time to read and comment on sections of this book. Special mention goes to Judith Bauer, who contributed to the sections on the use of the MBTI (Judith is our MBTI-certified instructor), and to Lalana Green, who contributed her insights to the chapters on negotiations and on global presentations. Lisa Kamemoto, Lisa Dickinson, Kerry Holcombe, and Susan Smith supplied anecdotes and insights from their years of experience communicating cross-culturally. Ron Osso of the Caribiner Group read the chapter on videoconferencing, and Dennis Perkins of the Syncretics Group read the team presentations chapter. Both gave us helpful feedback and positive support with these new chapters.

Nicholas Appleby, the computer guru of the Strategic Communications team, has been living with this project for over half a year — providing vital advice and research on the chapter on visual support as well as the chapter on videoconferencing. Nick also created the camera ready copy for the book, and with valuable help from Bret Logan, prepared the content for the accompanying disk. Pat Korngiebel, our administrative genius, has lived through two editions of this book and kept us together during the process. Pat and Nick have pursued this project with unrelenting good humor and patience. We could not have done it without them.

1
Every Communication
Is a Presentation

Every time you open your mouth you are selling — yourself, ideas, or a product. And every time you are selling, you are making a presentation. Since we first started helping people improve their written and spoken presentations, the pace of communication has accelerated beyond all expectations, and the choices of media have multiplied. Developing and delivering presentations in this changing environment will require
- Understanding the new demands
- Setting individual goals to meet those demands

The World Is Changing
But Some Truths Remain

The Internet affords people access to a vast array of information instantly; presentations come over the fax, on a computer disk, and by video as well as by traditional means. Voice mail provides each of us with the opportunity to make a sound-bite presentation many times each day.

The increased pace at which information is exchanged and decisions are reached has made all of us more insistent that everyone who talks or writes to us tell us immediately what they want and why. Exposure to high-quality, visual support material has made us critical of anything less. We communicate across cultural boundaries as we used to communicate across town, and to be successful we must be aware of and honor differences.

This book will help you meet the demands these changes in timeframes and expectations have created. It will assist you in creating well-structured, persuasive content using any medium, for any individual receiving the communication. It will help you produce compelling visual support that "sells" ideas, and deliver spoken messages smoothly.

In our experience, and that of the thousands of people with whom we have worked, the most critical component of a presentation is the content. Presenters throughout an organization must sell their ideas and proposals in order for anything to happen. Even people who think they are not making recommendations must support conclusions. Presenters who think they are being asked merely for data are fooling themselves. Information is readily available — ideas and conclusions require the presenter to think.

Because most of us are visual thinkers, the quality of visual support and its ability to reinforce messages is probably second to strong content in importance. Delivery, while important, is last. Weak delivery may cause good content to go unheeded. But even the best delivery cannot save vapid content in a business setting. This book therefore addresses the components of an effective presentation in order of importance — content first.

Use a Systematic Approach to Developing Content

The first four chapters of the book describe a system for structuring content that has stood the test of time. (See Exhibit 1.1.) You begin by learning what questions to ask yourself about the audience in order to meet that audience's needs — whether the audience is one person or many, whether the presentation will be heard or read, whether it will take place as a meeting, a videoconference, over the phone, or as voice mail. In today's environment, "personal power" (and by extension persuasion) is more important than "positional power" or the authority of

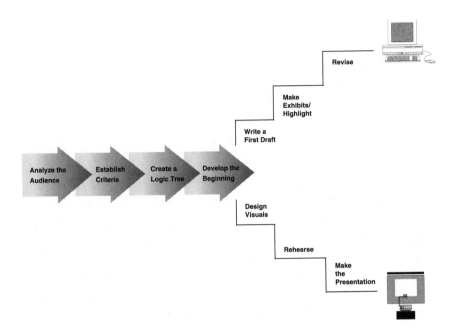

Exhibit 1.1. A systematic approach to developing content

command, so our insistence on crafting a presentation to meet the needs of the audience is crucial. The audience analysis section provides new techniques for discerning the decision maker's thinking styles, as well as methods for coping with situations in which your credibility has yet to be established or has been damaged in some way.

Next, you will learn to turn the audience's concerns into criteria so that you are truly selling benefits, not features. The concept of criteria — the standards people use to judge whether or not they agree with you — is a powerful one in deciding what to include in a presentation and what to leave out.

A logic tree is a picture of your argument. It serves as a tool for testing your logic before you begin to put slides or pages together, or before you begin to speak. Many consulting firms use the tree as a project management tool. We show you how to support a recommendation or conclusion, and how to use it when you must consider alternatives or options in your presentation.

Use Technology to Your Advantage

Ten years ago a business person who was a technological Neanderthal could still succeed. That's no longer true. In Chapters 5 and 6, we provide you with the information you'll need to cope with changes in presentation technologies, organizational shifts, and global settings. In addition to discussing how to craft a beginning that keeps people riveted, and showing how to use storyboards to check the flow of a presentation, we discuss methods for working with outlining software, provide guidelines for choosing the most appropriate medium and technology, and consider designing a computer-based presentation, including use of interactivity, multimedia elements, and transitions.

You will learn how to design templates for different media — what works and what doesn't; how to develop the best text, conceptual, and graphic visuals; and how to work with clip art to make it look professional rather than silly. You'll get guidelines and checklists for selecting, using, and troubleshooting hardware.

Deliver the Message Professionally

Even though presentations today are often more informal than they were ten years ago, speaking in public remains high on the list of fears. Increased informality also means that presenters are interrupted more frequently than they used to be, making control a big issue. Chapters 7-13 of this book address managing nerves and getting ready to present with confidence, as well as discussing techniques for looking calm and cool when you don't feel that way, whether you are standing before a large group or sitting across from your boss, client, or customer.

Increasingly, as more and more work is done by teams, presentations are made by several people, yet good teamwork doesn't always translate into smooth team presentations. In Chapter 10, you'll learn what to look for and how to make dry-runs effective.

To remain in control while encouraging positive interchange, you need to understand how different thinking styles lead to different styles of participation (why some people have to "talk to think," why some people won't answer a question right away, for example). Handling questions by following a sequence of listening, clarifying (probe, re-state), answering, and checking builds rapport. Dealing appropriately with objections and hostility helps you bring a meeting to closure.

We consider the similarities and differences between informal and formal meetings, one-on-one conversations and addresses to large groups, face-to-face meetings and video-conferences and give you help in all these situations.

Present Successfully to Those from Other Cultures

Each culture has its own norms. Even if you currently do not travel on business, your work is dependent on dealing with associates and cus-tomers from other cultures. As the global economy becomes a reality, knowing what's expected when presenting to people from another cultural background will be crucial. In Chapter 14, we discuss com-mon pitfalls and provide methods for dealing with audiences for whom English is a second language, including word choice, use of backup materials, visual support, and the like. We also suggest ways to get the best results when using an interpreter.

The material covered in this book can be of most help to you if you read it with a specific goal in mind.

Start by Setting Specific Goals

Thinking about what you personally want to achieve by reading this book will help you get closer to your goals. If you are already looking for something specific, write it down at the end of this chapter. Make sure your goal is stated in behavioral terms. Vague goals like "I want to improve my presentation skills" won't work. You won't know whether or not you've achieved such a goal because you have no measurable criteria. Ask yourself: "How will I know whether or not I've achieved my goal? What will I be able to do differently?"

When we start our presentation training sessions, we always ask participants to tell us their goals, and what they hope to gain during the time we'll be working together. Some of these goals, such as a desire for feedback from the instructor and the group on individual delivery skills issues, can't be addressed directly by a book. However, this book can address some of the goals that surface frequently. For example:

- I want to get action
- I want to reduce preparation time
- I want to increase my self-confidence
- I need to know when and how to use visual support
- I want to keep the audience's attention
- I need techniques for "crowd control" — managing discussion and disagreement

I want to get action

All too often, a presenter fails to focus on what he or she wants the presentation to accomplish. Sometimes (although not nearly so much as in the past) presenters even say they are merely "providing information." However, unless the presenter calls for action or asks for the sale, chances are nothing will happen. The system we describe in this book forces you to focus on both the decision maker and the decision, an essential preliminary to getting action.

I want to reduce preparation time

If this is one of your personal goals, ask yourself, "What's taking me so long? Is it procrastination? Inability to manage the team? Getting caught up in a reviewing process that degenerates into wordsmithing or ceaseless carping on style versus substance?" If it's something you have total control over, like procrastination, you can use our system as a time management tool. Breaking the preparation process into parts means you can trick yourself into getting started by saying something like, "Well, I'll just do the audience analysis first and worry about the rest later."

If others are involved, your main concern will be to start preparing early enough so that you can reach agreement. Oddly enough, the greatest deterrent to efficiency is allowing insufficient time for the organization and production of the presentation. The result is a flurry of misdirected activity, in which team members scurry around trying to find support for a contention they know is right (but they didn't research) or fighting over minor wording changes to relieve anxiety arising from lack of belief in what they're saying. You can get others involved by going through the process we outline here, or at least by asking some of the same questions we raise throughout. If your time is being wasted by the editing and revising process because team members can't agree on what they want or can't decide what to include and what to leave out, the material on team presentations can help.

Similarly, getting your manager to sign off on the structure of the presentation before you create your visuals or pages will greatly reduce last-minute changes. We can't promise that the system will eliminate changes, of course. For one thing, if you are preparing the presentation but the manager will have to deliver it, making changes may be necessary for the deliverer to "own" the presentation. For another, the manager's greater experience may mean that he or she sees holes you simply couldn't see. Being flexible and learning from changes is the keynote here.

I want to increase my self-confidence

As we'll discuss in Chapter 8, the most vital technique for controlling nervousness is the presenter's shift in focus from "How am I doing?" to "Are they agreeing with my message?" People get nervous because they try to protect themselves from their terror by turning inward. As a result, they lose touch with the audience and start watching themselves present as if they were an external (and very demanding) observer. Worse still, they start criticizing themselves: "Ohmigod, I'm using too many ums, I'm rooted to one spot, I'm gasping for air like a beached bluefish," and so on. The only way to avoid this is to tailor your message to your specific audience and then focus on communicating the message to that audience. Our system helps you do just that.

I need to know how to create and use visual support

Because so many people think visually, this goal is especially germane today. Audience expectations are much higher than they were even three years ago. For example, using color in visuals, once viewed as squandering resources, is becoming standard practice. Chapter 6 will provide you with specific guidelines to help you create text, conceptual, and graphic visuals that will support your message rather than steal your thunder.

I want to control the group

Because of the increasing emphasis on participation in presentations, presenters have to encourage group contributions to gain consensus. Nevertheless, they must also ensure that no one person dominates. Again, controlling the group means having a good handle on your message. You can't keep people on track unless you know what the destination is. We have added a great deal of new material on ways to ensure interaction (managing the process means setting guidelines for audience participation early in the presentation), and also substantial advice about using different kinds of questions - open, focused, closed - to prime the pump.

These are a few behavioral goals — you may have others. Decide what is most important to you and then think about these issues as you read. You will get the most out of the book if you have a presentation to work on as you read the first six chapters.

SUMMARY

To present effectively, you'll need to

- Understand that audiences demand well-organized, crisp presentations, bolstered with professional-looking visuals, and delivered smoothly
- Set goals and use this book to learn how to meet them

2
Focusing On
the Audience

As we said in Chapter 1, the first step in the process for developing content is analyzing the audience. This chapter will show you how to
- Identify the decision makers
- Refine the main point
- Recognize concerns
- Determine knowledge, thinking styles, and willingness to hear the message

For a presentation to be successful, the audience must understand the content and believe the presenter. Addressing the above issues and using the information to create content will ensure that anything in the presentation is something the decision maker cares about or can be made to care about. In addition, audience-focused content will help the audience understand and believe.

Many presentations fail because the presenter, in haste to tell all, forgets that not all audiences are the same and that a presentation must address the concerns of the audience. For most internal presentations, you'll know the people in your audience. Occasionally, if someone else has arranged the presentation, you'll be talking with people you've never met. Make sure you are aware of everyone who may be coming to the presentation. Nothing is more unnerving than a walk-in appearance by the executive vice-president when you had planned an informal session with a few colleagues and subordinates. For external presentations, you may not have met all of the people who will be in the room or who will be given copies of the presentation.

Filling out an audience profile (see Exhibit 2.1) helps you to take the needs of your audience into account when you're developing your presentation. It may also alert you to a recycling point. That is, as you think about your audience and its attitudes, you may realize that your preliminary attempts to build consensus have been inadequate. If

---

Audience Profile

Who is the decision maker? (There may be more than one.)

What primary question did or should the decision maker ask?

What is the answer to that question?

What are the decision maker's concerns about the issues surrounding that answer? In other words, what does the decision maker care about?

How much does the decision maker know about the subject?

What is the decision maker's thinking style?

How willing is the audience to hear your message?

Who else is involved in making the decision? (What are their concerns?)

Exhibit 2.1. The audience profile

you discover that members of your projected audience disagree on the need for change or are locked in apparently irreconcilable conflict, you may be able to defer your presentation until you have a better chance for success.

Sometimes, of course, you can't defer, and decision makers are often seemingly inaccessible or perceived as too exalted to be contacted. This is especially true with new-business presentations or other presentations to external clients where group decision-making is the rule. When you don't have enough information about the decision makers, ask people you know. Better yet, overcome your reluctance to call the decision makers and ask them directly. We once sat in on a presentation to a CEO who took the presenter to task for not calling him the day before to check the agenda. "You had my phone number," he thundered. "I fully expected you to take five minutes and discuss what I wanted to achieve in the meeting. Instead, you came in and started to tell me what I should care about. Asking would have gotten you much farther." Some people feel that the advance work the CEO was requesting represents too great a risk. What if, they say, the decision maker is interested in something we can't provide? Most people would think it a greater risk to not ask and waste everyone's time. If you can't get the information you need, making educated guesses is your only recourse.

Deciding on the Decision Makers

The person who called the meeting or asked you to speak may not be the most important person in the room.

Who is the decision maker?

Ask yourself: "Who needs this information to take action?" That's the person or people to focus on. Everything you say or do will be aimed at meeting their needs.

If you immediately come up with the name of the decision maker, and he or she is someone you know well, your job is infinitely easier.

But for most major issues, you'll have several names, and some of them will be unknowns — your boss's boss, for example, or someone you have not worked with in the client organization. Frequently, for all the major decisions related to a project, some decision makers remain constant (the CEO who hires the consultants, for example), while for individual presentations, the role of decision maker shifts to others — for example, the people who will have to implement a recommended change or the people who will sell your ideas in the organization.

If you have any doubt about who is making the decision, ask the person who set up the meeting, or ask anyone else in a position to know. If you feel that asking a direct question will put someone on the spot, say something more open-ended, like "Could you tell me how the decision will be made?" or "How are decisions generally made around here?" The worst thing that can happen is that people refuse to tell you the information you need, and that is also valuable information about the organization and the way the presentation is likely to play out.

Refining Your Main Point

It is helpful to think about every presentation as the answer to a question. But it is often hard to narrow that answer to one sentence that the decision maker can carry away as a recommendation or conclusion. In fact, refining your main point may be the most difficult step in developing a presentation.

What question did or should the decision maker ask?

If you have been asked to present, the person making the request usually asked a question. The question may be stated: "How can we increase sales?" Or the question may be only slightly disguised. For example, "What are this month's figures?" usually means "Why are we above (or below) plan, and what are you doing about problem areas?" Unfortunately, however, because many managers don't know how to give assignments, you may have been asked to "Give me a progress report on the X project," or "Be prepared to talk about market research issues in our staff meeting." Neither of these requests is particularly helpful — in fact, they invite the presenter to do endless research and then dump all the data on the audience. If you get one of these marshmallow assignments, do a bit of delicate probing: "Could you tell me a bit more about what you're interested in?" Usually, people respond well to this questioning, since you're trying to save them time in the long run.

There's always the occasional person, however, who believes it is a subordinate's obligation to read his or her mind. Keep asking questions, or — if all else fails — ask yourself, "If I were in this person's position, what question would I really be asking?" Remember that managers have a bias in favor of taking action. Undigested analysis and philosophical ramblings leave them cold, so even if the assignment was "Tell me about what's going on in the plant," the real question was probably more specific — for example, "What should we do about the absenteeism problem?" If you think the decision maker only wants to know about the problem, not how to solve it, ask yourself whether you are merely avoiding sticking your neck out. Completed staff work, in business as well as military terms, means not only identifying the problem but also solving it.

If you are presenting because you have an original idea, you will have to plant the question to which your idea is the answer. You will do some planting before the presentation and some in your beginning. (See Chapter 5 for more on planting questions.) For now, answer, "What question should the decision maker ask?" Presumably that question is either "Why should I do …?" or "How should I do …?" Management questions are almost always why or how questions.

If you've called a meeting to inform subordinates of a decision already taken, you're answering a different question: "How does this affect me?" It may be hard to conceive of your subordinates as decision makers, but to the extent that their wholehearted cooperation or indifference can affect the implementation of a decision, that's the way to view them.

If you're making a sales presentation, the question really depends on what stage of the relationship you're in. If it's the initial meeting, the question is, "Why should we keep on talking to you?" or "Why should we let you give us a proposal?" Only when you're getting near the close is it, "Why should we hire you?" Answering that question before you've earned the right through preliminary steps is a sure invitation to disaster. (See Exhibit 2.2.) Be sure you specify what the decision maker wants to know. "Why should I agree with your idea?" is vague. "Why should I spend $10 million to expand the galoshes factory?" is specific. The more specifically you state the question, the more likely you will be able to address the decision maker's concerns.

Most often the question you've been asked is the question you will want to answer. Sometimes, however, if you've been asked to do some troubleshooting, you may find that the decision maker has asked the wrong question. For example, he may have asked, "What should we do to reduce our head count?" After working on the problem, you decide the question should have been: "What can we do to cut costs?" In another example, an entrepreneur asked, "What's the best way to take the company public?" when the right question was this: "Is the timing right for an IPO?"

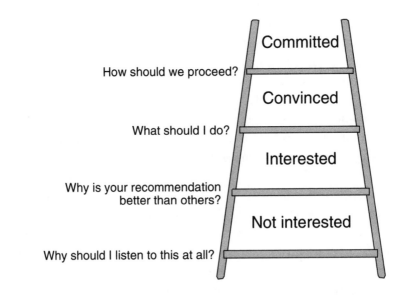

Exhibit 2.2. Which step are you on?

Getting the right question is vital, because the main point of the presentation is the answer to that question, and every presentation can have only one main point. If the decision maker has truly asked the wrong question, you'll have to work hard to change his or her mind in advance of the presentation itself, perhaps by holding a series of meetings to discuss what the decision maker is trying to achieve, or why he or she is asking the question that way. When you present, if you haven't been able to reorient the decision maker's thinking, you'll have to deal with the original question early on, or the decision maker will be spending valuable time wondering when you're going to answer the question. This is far from the ideal situation, however, as most decision makers don't like surprises.

One caveat here. Sometimes consultants (and internal staff) are engaged to provide support for a decision that has already been made (even if that fact is not necessarily conveyed to the would-be presenters). If your probing questions fail to establish what the decision maker is trying to achieve, or if people seem evasive when you try to check, be wary. You may not have the scope you think you have in generating alternative answers to the question. It's best to know that in advance.

What is the answer to the question? What do I want the decision maker to remember? to do?

The main point of any presentation is the answer to the question you want to address. It usually involves an action, since most presentations are action-oriented. A good way to think about what you want the audience to remember is to assume that the decision maker couldn't come to the presentation but sent an associate. After the presentation, he or she will ask the associate, "What did Charlie say?" What, in a short sentence, do you want the associate to answer?

Boiling your main point down to one sentence is often extremely difficult to do, but it is critical to the success of the presentation. The main point must be an assertion, not a phrase or a category. "How we market," for example, is a phrase that provides no definitive statement. People remember best ideas that are grouped in support of one major assertion. Can you always boil your message down to one point? Most of the time, yes. But occasionally that point would be so broad as to be useless. If you truly have several equally important points to make, it may be that you actually need to make several presentations. Some presenters make the mistake of trying to do too much, because they feel that as long as they have the decision maker's attention, they might as well bring up everything that's on their minds. We call this "trashcanning" and it is not advisable because the decision maker will lose focus. It is better to achieve a smaller goal than to lose everything by asking for too much.

Marketing people often ask whether they can answer the question "What's your recommendation?" as well as the question "Are you the right firm or company to do this for us?" Although we recognize how difficult it is to get in front of the client or customer, we still believe that you need to come to closure on your recommendation before you've earned the right to make the case for engaging your company to do the work, unless the reason to hire you is the quality of the recommendation. The only exception is when the client or customer already knows what he or she wants to do, and the presentation is a true "shoot-out" or "beauty pageant." Even then the focus should be on what you can do for the client rather than how great you are.

If you must, you may have three critical points, but absolutely no more. Think about what happens when you give your spouse one item on the "to-do list" (for example, pick up food for dinner on the way home from work) and, once on a roll, list everything that needs to be done for the week. A presentation structured in this way has the same effect on the audience that a seemingly endless list of chores has on your spouse — it causes overt tune-out or subconscious sabotage.

Recognizing Concerns

People do things for their reasons, not yours. Therefore, understanding the decision makers' concerns helps you ensure that you address the issues that are important to them.

What are the decision maker's concerns?

Think about the decision maker's concerns both in broad business terms and in terms of the issue under discussion. For example, does she always ask about cost first? Is he the "keeper of the flame" as far as the organizational culture is concerned? Does she worry a great deal about control issues because the outside accountants have said the company needs to tighten up? Does the phrase "quality products" have a very specific meaning to him? Is she under fire, simply wanting the complaints to stop? The more ideas you can jot down at this phase, the better. If you know specifically what the decision maker is after, you're well off. Don't be satisfied with "risk" as a concern — determine how the decision maker defines risk.

If you don't know the decision maker, first question someone who does — asking such questions isn't presumptuous; it's part of doing your job. One way to tease out relevant information is to throw out suggestions like this: "Many companies in this situation are concerned about litigation. Is that one of the things on your mind as you are making this decision?" Don't be tempted to start discussing solutions at this stage, though, because your true goal is to find out how decisions are made, not to get people excited about specific recommendations. People under pressure may hop on a solution without thinking it through, and that always backfires later.

If all else fails, you can speculate; a director of internal audit is concerned with a whole constellation of issues that are vastly different from those of a plant manager. The CEO hired to "clean house" will have different concerns than the CEO who's been in charge for twenty years and reaches retirement age next December. If your presentation deals with an issue that has been under discussion for some time, someone can fill you in on the history of the problem and the decision maker's concerns or preconceptions about the issue. If you don't know the concerns and can't find out what they are, think about the questions he or she has asked in prior meetings. Make educated guesses rather than easy assumptions. The most common assumption — "The decision maker cares about exactly the same things I do" — is always wrong.

Determining Knowledge, Thinking Styles, and Willingness to Hear

The most important questions are those we have already raised. But in order to know how much to say and the detail you need, the answers to these next questions are important.

How much does the decision maker know about the subject?

Knowing how much the decision maker knows is essential to prevent either his befuddlement because he doesn't have enough detail, or his irritation because you've given him too much. Remember, we said earlier that every presentation is the answer to a question. What keeps people listening to you is that when you answer a question, that answer raises another question. When you say something that raises no question, you have said enough on that topic. Therefore, considering how much the decision maker knows is important in determining what questions you have to answer.

If you're addressing a vice-president with an accounting background, you won't have to define FASB-5. On the other hand, if you are talking to a vice-president of marketing about an IRS regulation, you may have to explain the technical terms. If you and your boss have been wrestling with a quality control problem for the past six months, you can skip the history of the problem. If you're a consultant presenting to the CEO of a privately held corporation, you won't start out by saying, "As the CEO of a privately held corporation, you already know that ..." and go on and on about things that, indeed, she already knows. If you're talking to subordinates, they need to know enough about why you did something to be convinced that you know what you're doing and that they can trust you.

From the audience's point of view, any presentation is, in a sense, an imposition. Everyone feels he or she has left an important project in order to be present and, consequently, will view unnecessary detail with irritation. On the other hand, if members of the audience don't understand something and you don't go into enough detail, they have only two options: they can tune out, or they can interrupt you and ask for clarification. It's unlikely they'll interrupt, particularly if the audience includes people at different levels in the organization. The reasons for their reticence? They don't want to be considered uninformed ("I should have known that") or stupid ("I should be able to understand this").

In most cases, especially in presentations that represent the culmination of a long problem-solving process, the people involved already know a fair amount about both the problem and your approach to it. In the consensus-building stage, you talked to most of the decision makers, found out what they knew, and kept them informed of your progress. Although you can't assume they will remember the details of these preliminary discussions, you can be sure they will remember the general drift.

The most difficult problems arise when you're dealing with something fairly technical or when the decision maker is new to the organization and doesn't know the genesis of the problem. In such cases, a preliminary briefing to bring the nontechnical people or the new decision maker up to speed is a necessity. You can't hope to educate listeners during the presentation — you don't have time.

What is the decision maker's thinking style?

Management theorists have beaten style (as opposed to substance) issues to death, but it's worth thinking about how the people involved in making decisions think and how they like to deal with problems and people in order to decide how much detail to include and how to put ideas together.

Trying to delve deeply into the decision maker's psyche isn't feasible when doing a preliminary audience analysis. But you can attempt to determine how the decision maker takes in information and what he or she pays attention to when confronted with a new situation. There are several instruments that are helpful for doing this. One, the MBTI (Myers-Briggs Type Indicator) is used worldwide. Our discussion uses

MBTI terminology to help you recognize specific behavior and respond to it. Remember that these "categories" are really just preferences, and that people may act one way in a business environment and another way socially. Even though you can't tap into the many facets of analysis on this level, you can discern a few things that will help you plan (and, as you will see later, deliver) your presentation.

Sensate or intuitive? Some people prefer to approach the environment through their five senses and pay attention to what is "real." Others tend to prefer to look for possibilities and concepts and pay more attention to internal cues. For the first kind of person, the "sensate," a presentation that does not provide sufficient hard data to support each contention will be unsatisfactory. Sensates will tend to ask questions like "where did that number come from?" and to quote other studies on the same point.

A heavily numeric presentation with little conceptual framework will bore the second kind of person rigid. These "intuitives" will constantly seek the big picture and need to have the significance of facts highlighted. They will need to be fed a constant stream of ideas and may also wish to contribute their own new ideas as the presentation progresses.

The challenge, of course, is when you are confronted with decision makers who have different styles. You always do your homework so you'll have the data to support your case. However, you may wish to beef up the pre-presentation briefing so that you can raise the comfort level of the sensate person. In addition, you should pay particular attention to the beginning (see Chapter 5) and explain in detail how you will proceed throughout the presentation. "Road maps" are especially important for sensates. Chapter 9 includes more on thinking styles.

How willing is the audience to hear the message?

It is helpful to think of a presentation as a triangle connecting three points representing logic, credibility, and willingness to hear (see Exhibit 2.3). If the audience is not going to like your argument, you will have to increase either the credibility angle or the logic angle.

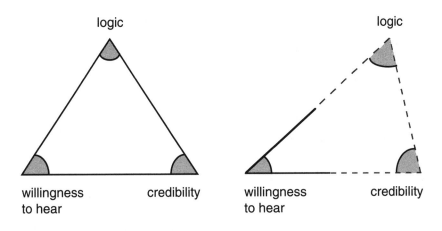

Exhibit 2.3. The size of the willingness angle determines what you say

Credibility can come from many sources — your position in the organization, your experience at other companies, your technical expertise, your informal influence with key people, or your knowledge of how things work in the organization. If the decision maker will find the message unpalatable, and you do not have built-in credibility, you may need to build some for yourself by outlining the work you did. Methodology sections, after all, usually have little purpose except to build credibility. But don't get caught front-loading a presentation with credibility builders if they are not necessary. The best place for technical information is in an appendix. In fact, you'll note that none of the angles is labeled "information" per se. Presentations are not data dumps, and undigested data is useless. Knowing how willing the audience is to hear your message also helps you decide how to structure the content, as you will see in Chapter 4.

Who else is involved in making the decision?

Even if they're not decision makers, other people involved in the success of your proposal must be considered. What are their concerns? Knowing what the people involved care about allows you to address their concerns in the presentation itself and to continue to check as implementation proceeds (for an internal proposal) or the relationship develops (for a client or customer). For example, if one of the people involved is the corporate director of public relations, you'll want to deal with image considerations, even though that's not at the top of the decision maker's list of criteria.

If you present regularly to the same people, you know the answers to most of these questions intuitively. But even if you are preparing for the weekly status meeting, you need to think seriously about the answers to the questions in bold on the audience profile. For anything less commonplace, answer all the questions carefully before you start to write.

Once you have a clear understanding of your audience, you can begin to construct a message that will lead to the action you want. Techniques for deciding how to convey that message are the subject of the next chapter.

SUMMARY

To design an effective presentation, you must satisfy the needs of your audience.

- Identify the decision maker
- Refine the question the presentation is answering
- Answer that question concisely
- Recognize the decision maker's concerns
- Determine how much the decision maker knows about the subject, his or her thinking style, and willingness to hear
- Recognize who else is involved in the decision

3
Criteria For Solving the Problem and Conveying the Message

People listen to a presentation because the presenter is interesting. In other words, they listen because the presenter raises and answers questions that the audience wants to know more about. Most of the time, in a presentation, you raise the question "why?" For example, "Why is that true? Why should I do that?" You may raise the question "how?" ("How do I do that?") or "what?" ("What is it?, Describe it"). But since most presentations are intended to move people to action, the presenter is usually trying to prove something with reasons.

By definition, a criterion is a standard on which a judgment or a decision is made. Using criteria, or as consulting firms call them, "critical success factors," is the key to being persuasive. The only valid reason is a reason based on the decision maker's criterion. This chapter will show you how to

- Establish useful criteria
- Use criteria to
  - Evaluate and choose among alternative solutions
  - Set the structure for your presentation

"My people don't present clearly because they solve problems haphazardly." In our interviews with managers, comments like this crop up repeatedly. To these men and women, proper problem-solving means analyzing a situation to find the parts or the cause of the problem, evaluating alternatives, and making realistic recommendations. Clarifying the decision maker's criteria or convincing the decision maker he or she should have a certain criterion, is challenging. But if you establish criteria carefully, you will avoid wasting time on unnecessary research and will produce clear and coherent presentations that focus on issues that matter to your decision maker.

We use criteria in every decision we make. For example, if you are shopping for a new car, you probably have set some criteria that the car should meet: "The car should have bucket seats," for example. Unless you are very lucky, you won't find a car that meets all your criteria, so you will have to compromise and make tradeoffs. The same concept applies in solving management problems. How do you know when something is wrong? Only by knowing the criteria for what is right. How do you know which alternative is best? Only by knowing which best meets your criteria. How do you persuade people that the solution you recommend is the best? Only by showing them how it meets their criteria.

Establishing Criteria

To be useful, criteria must be
* Stated as assertions against which alternatives can be measured
* Based on the problem solver's, organization's, and decision maker's standards
* Limited in number

State Criteria as Assertions

Good criteria should be written as complete thoughts that include *should* or *must*, and that use specific language. It's tempting to try to juggle vague criteria in your head, especially if you like to operate on intuition, or dislike being pinned down to details. But only by disciplining yourself to write your criteria as complete thoughts will you be sure they define your standards of measurement and the desired result. By including "should" or "must," good criteria indicate the result you want and, if stated specifically enough, they allow you to measure how well they are met by an option. For example, when asked, "What are your criteria for your next job?" most people come up with a list that includes words or phrases like "good salary," "location," "opportunity for advancement," and "opportunity to use my skills." But these generalizations are not useful in evaluating options. To one person, for example, a "good salary" might be $50,000; to another, the figure might be $250,000. Similarly, what does "location" mean? City or country? Sun Belt or East Coast? Ten minutes walk from the office or an hour commute by car? How fast does advancement have to be? What skills must be called upon in the job? Imprecise criteria usually reflect fuzzy or incomplete thinking and ultimately lead to poor problem-solving and weak support for your recommendation.

Most people start with a generalization or a category (like location), and refine that category until it is a criterion. Look at these criteria for evaluating job offers:

> The position should pay a salary of at least $70,000.
> The position should include benefits of at least $25,000, including stock options.
> The position should be with an organization located within half an hour of the St. Francis Yacht Club.
> The position should guarantee review for a major promotion after two years.
> The position should enable me to use my analytical skills and strategic planning experience.

Not only are all these criteria precise enough to allow a choice among job offers, but they are all stated positively. Positively stated criteria are easier to work with than negatively stated criteria, and the arguments based on them are likely to be more persuasive. Consider these two criteria:

The marketing campaign should allow us to meet our plan goal for 1997. The marketing campaign should prevent us from falling short of our 1997 plan goal.

Which one appeals to you? Even highly risk-averse people respond better to positive appeals.

Consider All Three Sources of Criteria

Criteria come from three sources: you (the problem solver), the organization, and the decision maker.

Your criteria

As the person asked to solve a problem, you are expected to know, or to establish, the standards by which you will define the problem and select a solution. (In addition to the criteria you set as the expert, you may also have personal criteria. Some of these, such as, "The solution should help my division meet its goals," make sense for the organization. Others, such as, "The solution should make me look like a hero," are best left unstated.)

Organizational criteria

The organization for which you work may have specific criteria for making a decision, such as "Any property should provide a return on investment of X," or "Any project must exceed the hurdle rate of Y." If you're lucky, you're part of an organization in which people at the top articulate precise goals and objectives that can be used to develop standards for any decision. If the CEO has been quoted frequently as saying, "We want to produce the best widget in the world," you can count on quality being an element in your criteria when you're looking for a solution to the production problem at the widget factory. If you are dealing with a client or customer, use every possible source of information to discern the organization's criteria — public record, competitors, your own firm's experience. If they fired your firm ten years ago, find out why. If their decision was based on a criterion you can now meet — lowest price, for example — make sure they know it.

The decision maker's criteria

When you are making a presentation to people high up in an organization, criteria may be based on what they believe will promote the success of the overall organization. But even senior managers have biases and preconceptions that may indicate to you some personal criteria or, at the least, which of the objective criteria for solving the problem are most important to them. Check the audience analysis. How did you assess the decision maker's concerns or views of the subject? You probably wrote down items like "budgetary concerns," "feasibility," "state-of-the-art technology," "increased control," and "security of EDP operations." You may have jotted down issues of personal concern to the decision maker ("wants to make her mark on the organization") or pure biases ("hates consultants"). Anything you've written down should be examined carefully and, if possible, restated as a standard. For example, "budgetary concerns" might be "should not cause us to exceed our annual training budget of $xxx."

Don't give up if you don't know everything about the decision maker's criteria, especially if the decision maker is your client or customer. It's perfectly appropriate to ask what the criteria are. Most people will answer a direct question to the best of their ability, and you'll learn an enormous amount. One presenter, who believed a major advantage of his product was its high-level customization, was astounded to find that the customer viewed that as a detriment because it required his valuable time to help in the process. The criterion, which was originally stated, "The product must be tailored to our company's needs," became, "The product must be tailored to our needs with little in-house effort."

Ask about the decision maker's criteria tactfully. If you need clarity or feel you need to identify the underlying criterion, ask a probing question like "What are you trying to achieve by meeting or exceeding this criterion?" Suppose you are preparing a marketing presentation. If someone states that "we want to hire the number one firm in the field," asking what they will gain by that may reveal that their main concern is that the firm have the resources to get the job done, and they have naively assumed that size is all that counts. If you feel asking will reveal that the decision maker lacks sophistication, however, you can ask focused questions. Be prepared to back off if the person resists answering questions such as, "What is your budget for this?" or "How much risk are you willing to assume in this portfolio?"

Decision makers often don't know what the criteria should be. If the decision maker gives you little information about criteria, you will have to sell the criteria you believe are important before you can sell the reasons. It is often possible and helpful to review your criteria with the decision maker. If you sense resistance when you test a criterion, recheck. Every once in a while, a dramatic change in the environment or even a change in the decision maker's personal life will so alter the decision making landscape that the entire issue must be revisited, especially if you are making a sales presentation.

Group Criteria

It is important to group related ideas together in a way that is meaningful. Criteria can provide that grouping because the only important information is information that supports important criteria. But even the number of criteria must be limited. Research has shown that although people can keep in their minds only five to nine separate pieces of information at a time — and most of us are at the five end of the scale — they can retain more information if the ideas are grouped as subsets of a higher-level concept. By grouping criteria that address similar issues, you limit the number of reasons you give and therefore provide better focus.

You probably noticed earlier in the chapter that the first two criteria the job applicant put down had something in common — they both related to total compensation.

The position should pay a salary of at least $70,000.
The position should include benefits of $25,000, including stock options.

By combining those criteria into one, the problem solver achieves greater flexibility and therefore a more useful criterion:

The position should offer a total compensation package of $95,000.

After all, if the salary component is sufficiently large, the applicant can purchase benefits to compensate. Conversely, if benefits are vital, an impressive pension plan and health insurance may compensate for a lower salary.

Using Criteria to Evaluate Alternatives

If the problem is evident and you did not need to use criteria to isolate it, it is very tempting to get on with finding solutions — to "brainstorm" for options and then come up with the reasons why one is better than the others. Some people believe that setting criteria before they generate options inhibits their creativity. Coming up with alternatives before you establish criteria, however, may very well inhibit your objectivity. Once you have a favorite option, you may become so enamored of it that you forget an important criterion. For example, a friend recently told us this story:

Le Grand Restaurant sounded like a super place for an important business lunch I had scheduled. It serves my companion's favorite souffle, the service is impeccable, it is quiet enough to carry on a serious conversation. But I really did myself in; I forgot that Le Grand doesn't take credit cards and I had $2.50 in my wallet.

Since the major criterion was "must be able to pay with credit," the alternative chosen was a disaster. Establishing criteria first saves time spent chasing weak alternatives. Organizational behavior expert J. Rohrbaugh reports that groups that establish criteria first come up with solutions that are as good as those the most experienced member of the team arrives at alone. Groups that simply discuss alternatives and personal preferences tend to sink to the level of the least experienced member of the group. Making criteria useful for evaluating options requires

- Distinguishing negotiable from nonnegotiable criteria
- Weighting negotiable criteria

Be realistic — rarely do you find an alternative that meets all your criteria. Good problem-solving requires tradeoffs, and to make tradeoffs effectively, you must know what is most important to you.

Distinguish Negotiable from Nonnegotiable Criteria

Nonnegotiable criteria are criteria that must be met. You can avoid wasting time studying options that will surely be unacceptable by determining early which of your criteria absolutely must be met. A word of caution: people tend to cast a great many negotiable criteria as nonnegotiable. To illustrate, "A project must be within our budget" is rarely nonnegotiable: if your proposal will bring in large infusions of money, management is often prepared to spend more than the amount budgeted. If you allow yourself more than one or two nonnegotiable criteria, you will severely restrict your options.

Technically speaking, "Any proposal must be feasible" is a nonnegotiable criterion. But since you would not propose anything that was not feasible from a technological or organizational point of view, you would use this criterion in your problem-solving but not when structuring your presentation.

Weight Negotiable Criteria

All the job applicant's criteria for a job cited earlier included the word *should*, which means they are all negotiable criteria — standards the applicant would like met but is willing to forego if necessary. For negotiable criteria to be useful, you must know which are most important to you. We use a scale of one to five (with five being most important) to weight criteria, because it allows distinctions but does not force very fine comparisons.

Let's look at the criteria listed by a staff person whose boss asked for a recommendation on where to relocate a key plant. The decision to move had already been made. In this case, the writer did not find any nonnegotiable criteria but did establish three negotiable criteria:

Negotiable Criteria
The site chosen should be the cheapest available.
The site chosen should have the best access to a skilled labor force.
The site chosen should provide the easiest access to our markets.

These are decent criteria, but you would get a more useful first criterion if you asked "Don't you have any price limit?" The other two criteria also need work. What is "best access to a skilled labor force"? Do the workers already have to live within commuting distance to the plant or should the location be in such an attractive location that workers could be recruited to relocate? How many workers with what specific skills are required? What is "easy access to markets"? Within a certain distance of major population centers if the product is shipped by truck? Close to a major airport? In the middle of a city? By asking these questions, the presenter can either make the criterion more specific or generate subcriteria that will allow him to measure how each plant site stacks up to that standard. He might have revised these criteria this way:

Criteria	Weight	Reason
The plant should not cost more than $5 million: $1 million for site $4 million for construction	2	Costs are less significant than location and labor.
The plant should be located within 12 hours of the major market, door to door.	5	Our business is based on immediate availability of parts.
We should have a pool of 8,000 skilled workers who can run our equipment.	3	We need some to start but can train technical-school graduates.

Note that the problem solver was able to give a reason for the weight of each criterion. Writing down the reason for the weight encourages you to be objective. You may even choose to include the reasons in the presentation itself. But most often, for the presentation, it is sufficient to rank the criteria in order of importance. People expect you to present your ideas starting with the most important, so be sure you meet that expectation.

Checklist for Criteria

- Is each criterion written as a complete thought? (Does it contain a verb?)
- Can the decision maker measure precisely how well an alternative meets the criterion?
- Have I grouped related criteria together under a higher-level criterion that covers the entire grouping?
- Have I separated criteria into nonnegotiable criteria (those that must be met) and negotiable criteria (those that are desirable)?
- Have I reduced the number of negotiable criteria to five or fewer?

Assess Alternatives Against Criteria

After you have established criteria, spend the first part of your thinking time just generating alternatives. Unless it's a "go/no go" situation, or the alternatives have been established for you, you have some latitude in developing alternatives to solve a problem or capitalize on an opportunity. Save the evaluation for later and don't reject any solution out of hand because it seems absurd. Devotion to the status quo can blind you to workable alternatives. Even some ideas that seem ridiculous may be adapted to become workable or may lead to other good ideas.

Be systematic about assessing the alternatives you've generated. Policy analysts have developed a quantitative technique for assessing alternatives that assigns each alternative a value (on a scale similar to the one used to weight criteria) and multiplies the value by the weight you gave the criterion. Using this system, you can develop a picture of how well each alternative meets your criteria. The manager trying to decide on a location for the small-parts assembly plant did it this way:

Criteria	Weight	x Value	= Score	Reason for Value
	Location A			
Within 12 hours of major market	5	5	25	10 hours maximum distance
Pool of 8,000 skilled workers	3	5	15	10,000 potential workers ages 20-65
Cost less than $5 million	2	1	2	Most expensive location — $7.2 million
	TOTAL SCORE:		42	

	Location B			
Within 12 hours of major market	5	1	5	15 hours from market
Pool of 8,000 skilled workers	3	3	9	7,000 potential workers
Cost less than $5 million	2	5	10	Least expensive location — below $5.5 million
	TOTAL SCORE:		24	

This formal assessment provided the manager with a "score" for judging each alternative against the others and helped him to organize his thinking.

Using Criteria to Structure Your Presentation

Having used criteria to solve the problem, you are ready to use them to structure the presentation. If you are making a recommendation or offering a conclusion, your main point probably raises the question "why?" A reason is a statement of the way an alternative met a criterion. We should move the plant to Location A (main point), because Location A is within ten hours of our major markets (reason based on a criterion), and because it offers a pool of 10,000 potential workers (reason based on criterion). (Location A does not meet the cost criterion; we'll discuss how to deal with that problem in Chapter 5.) Reasons will become the topics for the sections of your presentation. (See Exhibit 3.1 for an example of how the wording changes. Chapter 4 includes a discussion of how to actually lay out multiple options.)

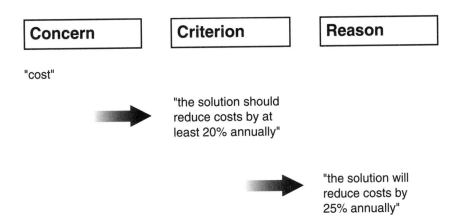

Exhibit 3.1. Converting a concern into a criterion and a reason

You are now well on your way to creating a presentation structure, which is the subject of the next chapter.

SUMMARY

Thoughtful, organized problem-solving leads to logical, well-supported arguments. Establishing and using criteria will make your task easier and quicker. To be useful, criteria must be

- Stated as assertions
- Based on the problem solver's, the organization's, and the decision maker's standards
- Limited in number

Criteria should be used to

- Evaluate alternatives
- Structure your presentation

4
Building a
Logical Structure

Analyzing the audience and establishing criteria take time, but you should do those steps before you ever sit down in front of the computer or sheet of paper. With the main point and criteria clear in your mind, you have the overall structure of your presentation as you saw at the end of Chapter 3. Now, by making a diagram of that structure, you can test your logic before you start to write notes, pages, or slides, increasing the likelihood that your presentation will be successful and saving yourself the time and effort of revision. In this chapter, you'll learn how to

- Create a logic tree to show the structure of your presentation
- Use that tree to check the support for your main point
- Turn the tree into a presentation
- Use the tree as a project management tool

When you have given presentations that "really clicked," your sense of success probably came from being comfortable; and unless you had an unassailably positive message ("sales are up 50 percent over last quarter" or "your bonus will be $30,000"), that comfort probably resulted from a tightly structured message, one in which you supported all the important points and covered all the decision maker's criteria.

Every effective presentation has a structure that answers the decision maker's mental questions. Sometimes experienced presenters can create that structure intuitively. Most of us, however, need a systematic approach, especially when the subject is complex. Some presenters use the linear outline they were taught in fifth-grade English, others shuffle notes in search of a comfortable order. We believe that the logic tree (see Exhibit 4.1) is the most useful tool for structuring ideas, because it forces you to focus on the audience's questions and because it shows how ideas relate to each other.

Using a Logic Tree to Create the Structure

If you learned to outline in grade school, your teacher probably encouraged you to think in terms of individual topics or categories. A report on Nicaragua, for example, would include I. Introduction; II. Geography; III. Political System; and so on until you reached the Conclusion. You didn't have to focus on your audience while planning for the outline to work. Of course, the teacher may have entered your mind once or twice, but probably only in relation to such questions as

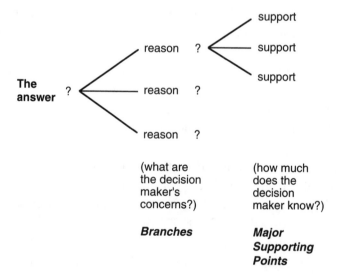

Exhibit 4.1. The logic tree is based on the audience analysis and shows relationships

"Will this outline give me enough topics so I can write five pages (or ten or twenty)?" Because you can use an outline to structure a presentation without referring to a specific audience, continuing to use this form tempts you to "tell about" the topic rather than answer the decision maker's question (typically "What should we do?") with a crisply stated main point. The logic tree, in contrast, forces you to know your main point. By continually asking yourself, "If I say this, what will the decision maker ask?" you will create enough support to meet at least the decision maker's needs.

The tree also makes it much less painful to change ideas and structure. Once you start creating visual support, you're committed in some way to your phrasing (after all, it's there in writing, so it's done) and you look at pages one at a time rather than thinking about the story line. As a result you may let fuzzy thinking and inadequate support stand rather than take the time to revise. You want so badly to be done that you may not even listen when others try to give you suggestions. Since a logic tree is only a plan, not a final product, most of us are willing to make changes. You may, therefore, listen with an open mind to someone else's comments.

Because of its flexibility, the logic tree is a valuable tool for mapping out a team presentation. If you merely divvy up the assignments in the usual way ("Harry, you look at the cost figures. Joyce, you get the data on the competition. I'll take care of the market research."), each team member will wander off to research a topic and create an individual mini-presentation on that topic. Sadly, you are likely to find yourselves at 3:00 a.m. trying to glue the unrelated pieces together or even arguing fiercely about the main point. Or you'll agree on what you think it means, and then find that you are missing valuable support because no one stumbled onto a particular major discovery while there was still time to get the data. If you agree on the overall structure first, you'll be much farther ahead. (More on this in Chapter 10.)

For both individual and team presentations, using a tree provides the best defense against procrastination. Many people find actually beginning quite difficult. They stare at a legal pad or computer screen, unable to go forward with the presentation because they have no idea of their main point, and thus have no way to focus. Once everything is mapped out on a diagram, however, the beginning, body, and ending come easily.

As you'll see in Chapter 6, we feel that any modern presenter should consider reinforcing his or her argument with powerful charts, graphs, and conceptual visuals. The tree helps do that as well, because it lets you lift appropriate headings and subheadings directly from the major support points and supporting details or evidence. Even more important, the tree forces you to omit any charts or graphs that, however important they were in solving the problem, are not necessary to make your point. The time savings, both for you and for your audience, is incalculable.

To create a tree, follow these steps. Be sure to use complete declarative thoughts (subject and verb), because questions and sentence fragments will not let you check your logic.

Start with the Main Point

On the far left of the tree, fill in the one statement you want the decision maker to remember or do: the answer to the decision maker's question. (See your audience profile.) Remembering to refer back to the audience analysis will save you from insipid and passive main points like this one: "You have four key issues." That main point is only acceptable if the decision maker asked "How many key issues do we have?" Often presenters fall back on this kind of mush when they are desperately seeking a link to the ill-conceived research and problem-solving they did. Don't fall into that trap.

Here's a forthright main point: "We should buy the Gemini spreadsheet program." It's a full sentence. It's specific (that is, you'll know whether or not it happens). And if your decision maker doesn't have time to come to the presentation, grabs your arm in the hall, and asks "What are you going to say at the meeting tomorrow?" you can state it without um-ing and uh-ing and tripping over your tongue. Not all main points are this easy, of course. Sometimes you have a main point like this: "We should adopt a new investment strategy." That says what you want the decision maker to do, but it's not specific enough to be either memorable or actionable. Now is your opportunity to revise it to something like this: "We should shift 50 percent of our portfolio into long-term fixed-income investments."

Remember that we're still in the planning stages. The main point is not usually the first statement out of your mouth during the actual presentation. Beginnings must include the main point, but you'll say other things first, as you'll see in Chapter 5. So don't be frightened by a forthright statement of your actual recommendation or conclusion. In fact, the only way you can get what you want is to decide what it is, and then provide reasons why you should get it. You can always tone down the language if necessary when you create visuals or when you rehearse. A word of caution here. Try to avoid using the words "only" or "unique" in the main point. It's tempting to do so, particularly when you are in the selling mode, but it's almost impossible to defend claims to uniqueness.

What if you're fairly sure that your decision maker will be unwilling to hear the main point or won't agree with it? Your news may be unbelievably grim, the decision maker may have a preferred solution to the problem at hand, or your recommendation may fail to meet a cherished criterion. Presumably, for anything of major importance, your final presentation will be the culmination of a series of meetings. Therefore, your main point won't come as a shock, and you will have some sense of what wording is acceptable before you commit yourself. If you haven't been able to lay the appropriate groundwork, though, the phrasing of the main point is crucial. There's a world of difference in the impact of a main point stated as "Your programs, as you have designed them, will fail" and a main point stated as "You should redesign your programs to …." And yet, they are logically equivalent and can be supported with the same arguments. People naturally resist being told not to do something, especially if you do not give them a positive alternative. When in doubt, choose the most positive phrasing possible. Similarly, try to work around the natural human resistance to change by saying "We should refine our existing system to …" rather than "We should use a brand-new system." Most systems aren't totally new anyway, and the first phrasing is far more persuasive.

Another strategy to use when you are championing an unpopular course of action is to change your main point from a recommendation to a conclusion. This approach is useful if you intend to present alternatives. For example, perhaps the decision maker asked you to select locations for a new plant. Under most circumstances, you would come back with a direct recommendation like this: "We should move the plant to Lakehurst, New Jersey." However, if you know that alternative is going to be extremely unpopular with the decision maker, you might hedge with something like this: "Of the three most attractive plant locations, Lakehurst is the best, given the criteria we established." Or, if you don't know or do not agree with the relative importance of the criteria to the decision maker, your main point may be, "The choice of locations will depend on how you view the relative importance of the decision criteria." You will then develop a structure in which you compare criteria and alternatives. (See Exhibits 4.2a and 4.2b. We will discuss when to use each of these structures later in the chapter.) For now, let's consider how to support a direct recommendation or conclusion with reasons.

Develop the Major Supporting Points

On the branches of the logic tree, write the major supporting points. These should be complete thoughts, and they all must answer the one question the decision maker will be asking silently when he or she hears the main point. For example, if the main point is a recommendation or conclusion, the question is probably "Why?" and the answer is a series of reasons, all of them based on the way the preferred alternative met the criteria. If the main point either is very broad ("We should change our strategy") or sets up a procedure, the question is "How?" and the answer is a series of steps. If the main point is the description of an analysis, the question is "What?" and the answer is parts of the whole.

For the main points we have been discussing (recommendations or conclusions), the decision maker's immediate question starts with "Why?" Why should we select the Gemini spreadsheet program? Why

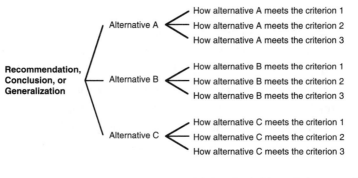

Exhibit 4.2a. Structure comparing criteria against each alternative

should we redesign our programs? Why should we move the plant to Lakehurst? Because "Why" questions are the hardest to answer, we'll spend most of our time discussing how to create the reasons that answer them. If you have already sold the decision maker on why, then you may be answering a "How" question like this one: How do we go about moving the plant to Lakehurst? If the recommendation is broad, the first question may be "How?" but the next question is likely to be "Why?" If, on rare occasions, you're in a technical problem-solving presentation with your peers, and they're asking "What?" you can prob-

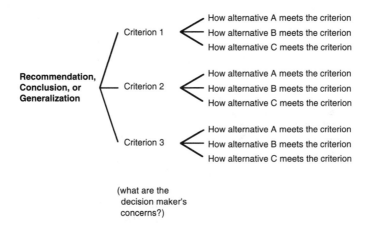

Exhibit 4.2b. Structure comparing alternatives against each criterion

ably answer by describing the parts of the whole or the components of
your analysis. Remember that the question may change often during a
presentation; but you can only answer one question at a time.

In most presentations - internal or external - you anticipate some
action; therefore, we'll start with examples of recommendations and
explain later how to use the same rules for building logical support for
other types of main points. Support for choosing the Gemini spreadsheet program might be developed as shown in Exhibit 4.3. The major
supporting points are all reasons for the recommendation; we assume
they all reflect the decision maker's concerns or criteria — what he or
she does or should care about. And, because the reason relating to cost
is first, we assume it reflects the most important criterion. The second
reason presumably reflects a criterion that "Any proposed spreadsheet
should provide us with essential capabilities." The third criterion is a
bit tougher to deduce from the reason as stated on the tree. It might
be, "Any proposed spreadsheet should be up and running within two
months," or "Any proposed spreadsheet should be up and running in
the shortest possible time." If the criterion was "shortest possible time"
and if Gemini doesn't quite meet that criterion as well as the other
alternatives, the supporting reason represents a tradeoff.

Although this tree has three major supporting points, there can
be as many branches as there are important criteria, although there

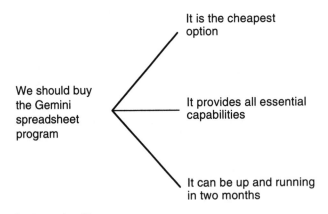

Exhibit 4.3. Example of basic structure

usually won't be more than five. If there's only one branch, you may have overlooked a criterion, or, far less likely, the decision maker only has one concern, in which case you can build that criterion into the main point (for example, "This strategy will enable us to achieve 25 percent ROI"). Your support, then, relates only to meeting that ROI criterion.

Because most recommendations do not meet all the decision maker's negotiable criteria exactly, you'll have to deal with the downside somewhere, either by rephrasing the reason, as in the Gemini example above, or by showing that it lacks importance, perhaps in the beginning. (See Chapter 5 for a further discussion of this concept.) Rephrasing sometimes feels like a hedge. For example, suppose the criterion was "Whatever we propose should not involve layoffs," and there was no earthly way to meet it without massive infusions of non-existent cash. Stating the reason as "the proposal will involve minimal layoffs" is more truthful than ignoring the criterion.

Choose Parallel Support for the Basic Structure

There are two ways to build support. With parallel support, which we've just described, independent statements support the generalization. With chained support, statements are linked together. (See Exhibits 4.4a and 4.4b.) We believe that parallel support is a better form of support for the main structure of your presentation than the various forms of chained logic for two reasons:

- Parallel support is easier for listeners to follow
- Parallel support is less risky for the presenter

Parallel support is easier for listeners to follow

Even with well-constructed text visuals to guide them, listeners are at a disadvantage compared to readers. They must grasp what you are saying quickly; they have no time to digest your points and ponder them at leisure as a reader can. Because the relationships among the major points in a parallel argument are all the same, the argument is

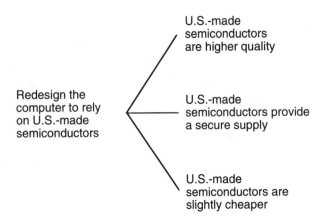

Exhibit 4.4a. Example of parallel support

easy to follow. With chained support, the listener must try to discern whether an argument is cause and effect, process of elimination, or deductive, and, once he or she has identified the form, must check the logic.

Even though chained arguments are legitimate and sometimes the only way to build support, they can be difficult to follow. If you must use them, be sure to represent them graphically on a page or slide,

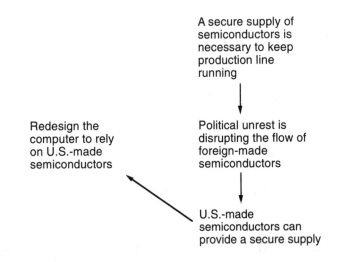

Exhibit 4.4b. Example of chained support

since use of a list as visual support implies parallel structure to an audience.

Parallel structure is less risky for the presenter

Remember the adage "A chain is only as strong as its weakest link"? Compare the structures in Exhibits 4.4a and 4.4b. These arguments have the same main point and the support for each is logically valid, assuming that each point can be supported with evidence. However, the chain (Exhibit 4.4b) requires that you work your way to the conclusion. What if the decision maker interrupts you halfway through to contest your point that the flow of semiconductors is being interrupted? He has worked with a Korean supplier for ten years, he says, and the supplier has never let him down. At that point, the presentation cannot proceed. You must either fight it out with the decision maker or pack up your transparencies and go home. If, on the other hand, you are working your way through the parallel argument (Exhibit 4.4a) and the decision maker makes the same objection, you can suggest leaving that discussion for later and focus on the contentions that U.S.-made semiconductors are slightly cheaper and that their quality is superior. Those two reasons may carry the day, even if you and the decision maker continue to disagree on whether the supply is secure.

Other Pitfalls to Avoid

Avoid emphasizing risks

If you want people to follow your recommendation, you'll have to show them how it provides them with a benefit or enables them to avoid a risk. This is another way to look at the whole idea of reasons based on criteria. Because positive messages are generally more persuasive than negative messages (unless the threat is immediate and personal, as in "Watch out for that truck!"), you should spend more time on benefits. If a large portion of your professional time is devoted to focusing on risks - for example, you are a compliance officer or an internal auditor - you'll need to monitor this especially closely and turn problems into opportunities whenever possible.

Avoid description (features) masquerading as reasons or benefits

Stating facts as if they are reasons for a point of view is one of the most common problems for first-time logic tree makers. Almost everyone knows the basic sales precept, "sell the benefits, not the features," and yet you will find numerous marketing "trees" in which the support is sheer description.

Consider the tree in Exhibit 4.5. This tree certainly appears acceptable when you read it, probably because you hear this stuff all the time, but let's examine the connections. Why are each of these points important to the decision to hire the firm? Presumably, having offices in all these countries is a good thing, and the statement is indisputably true. But what does it have to do with the ability to help sell the subsidiary? Does it mean you know more willing buyers? Does it mean that you can execute the deal more quickly? Make the connection absolutely clear and you'll be more persuasive. Again, how about the issue of expertise? What about your expertise means you ought to be hired to sell the subsidiary? Does the fact that you have it mean you can get a

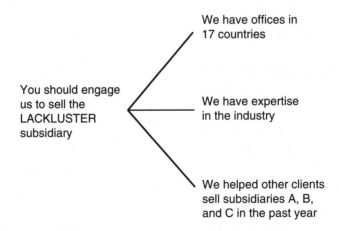

Exhibit 4.5. Example of description masquerading as benefits

better price? Does it mean that you can help smooth the transition? Be specific. And, finally, does the fact you've done it before mean that you did it well? Does it mean you can do it for me? You get the general idea. Using the decision maker's criteria to form the branches will help you avoid listing features.

Avoid treating your logic tree like an outline

When you first try to make a logic tree, you may fall into the category trap. In other words, you may decide that the tree is just like an outline and, instead of using Roman numerals, you'll just slot in topics on the branches. Exhibit 4.6a is an example of such a tree.

The tree in Exhibit 4.6a is far from useful. What is the presenter going to say about XYZ reports? Does he recommend them? Should we discontinue using them? There are two problems here. The first is that a sketchy tree lets the presenter be intellectually flaccid — anything he says about timeliness will "fit." And he cannot test whether his assertions answer the question in the decision maker's mind. The second problem relates to the presenter's working time. How many of us have the luxury of working on one project at a time? If the presenter were to put this tree aside and go on to something else, he would have a difficult time remembering what he meant by each supporting point.

The second tree (Exhibit 4.6b) is a major improvement — these sentences tell exactly what points the presenter is making. With this

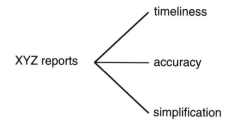

Exhibit 4.6a. Example of a tree that is too sketchy to be useful

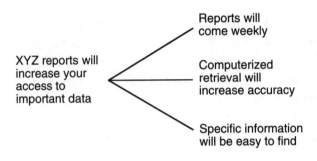

Exhibit 4.6b. Example of a useful tree

diagram, there's no place to hide. The presenter knows exactly what support she needs and she can test whether she is answering the right question.

Create Further Support by Using either Parallel Support or Chains

Once you have your basic structure, it's unlikely you can rest on your laurels. Take the Gemini spreadsheet program tree (Exhibit 4.3) as an example. Do you have such immense credibility that you can persuade the decision maker by simply making these four statements? You'll need to look at each supporting point and decide if the decision maker will

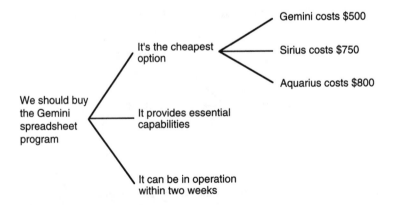

Exhibit 4.7. Example of basic structure with further support

be convinced without further evidence. Take the first one. Is Gemini truly cheapest? You'll need further support, as shown in Exhibit 4.7. You'll keep building support for each assertion until you believe the audience has no more questions. Only then is no further support on that point necessary. You can check the amount of detail you need to include by referring back to your answer to the question "How much does the decision maker know?" on your audience profile (Chapter 2).

Checking Parallel Support for Logic

To test a parallel argument, make sure it follows these rules:
- All branch statements must answer the same question. "Why?" is answered by reasons. "How?" is answered by steps. "What?" is answered by parts of the whole.
- All branch statements must be independent of each other. Say something only once. If you repeat words or two words with the same root in two different branches, you may be making the same point in different words. Also check that no branch is support for, or a subset of, another branch.
- The main point, or point to the left, must be fully supported. If you assert that a process is efficient and ensures quality control, you must prove both "efficient" and "ensures quality control."

Logic flaws are far easier to pick up on the tree than on a complex overhead. Here are some examples:

In Exhibit 4.8, can you insert "because" between the branch and the supporting points and have it make sense? In other words, do all the supporting points answer the question "Why"? Although the last statement provides information about the recommendation, it is not a reason for it. Answering more than one question at a time confuses audiences.

In Exhibit 4.9, you've got lots of support, but are all the points independent of each other? The statement that the legal department will understand your special needs is probably tied to the assertion that it will provide specialized patent and trademark help. The tip-off is the

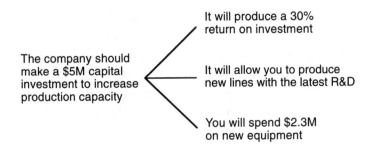

Exhibit 4.8. Example of flawed support — a nonsupporting point

repeat of "special" and "specialized," indicating that the second point is probably support for the first.

Remember being told, when you learned to outline, that every point needs at least two pieces of support? Look at Exhibit 4.10. The evidence the writer provides is not adequate to support the point that financial projections are reasonable.

It is much easier to make these changes at the planning stage than to discover, the night before the presentation, that you have an argument that won't hold up.

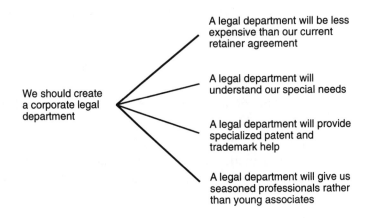

Exhibit 4.9. Example of flawed support — an overlap

| Financial projections are reasonable | ———— | Cash flow projection is consistent with similar set-ups |

Exhibit 4.10. Example of flawed support — incomplete evidence

Checking Chained Support for Logic

Suppose you have to support your message with chained logic because you are benchmarking, because the audience needs to understand the cause to accept the effect, or because you don't have enough evidence to build a more imaginative case. Here are a few basic rules for the different types of chains.

Causal chains

Causal chains are usually based on the premise that if event A did not take place, event B would not happen. For example, in Exhibit 4.11 we're asked to agree that the supplier is the cause of our delays and lost income. If we cancel our contract, our troubles will be over. This assertion may be valid, but only if it follows these rules for causal chains:

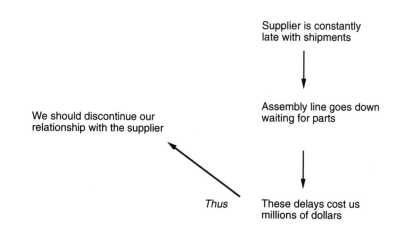

Exhibit 4.11. Example of a cause-effect chain

- *The first cause stated is the **ultimate** cause of the problem.* In Exhibit 4.11, you'd have to be positive that discontinuing the relationship with the shipper would save millions of dollars. You would do that by asking questions: Does the supplier get orders far enough in advance to deliver on time? Do the orders contain all the information needed? Ask yourself, "If I do A, will B necessarily happen?" One way to be certain you have the ultimate cause is to eliminate all other possible causes. The key word is "necessarily."

- *There are enough links for the audience to understand the connection.* Presenters who understand clearly how to get from A to C may forget that the audience can't make the same leap of faith. The presenter, therefore, may say something like "High interest rates will be good for independent carpenters" and go on talking, leaving people in the audience trying to figure out how she made that connection (see Exhibit 4.12). Go back to your audience profile and consider the decision maker's level of knowledge.

- *You can insert **as a result** between each item on the chain and **therefore** before the main point.* A word of advice — don't confuse corre-

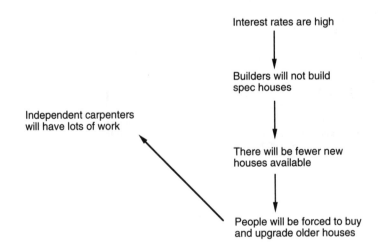

Exhibit 4.12. Example of chain with sufficient links

lation with causality. Just because one event happens after another, it doesn't mean the first is the cause and the second the effect. In the days when football was a fall sport, one humorist "proved" that football caused winter. After all, didn't winter always occur after the start of football season? When the season was over, didn't the weather soon warm up? And so on.

Deductive chains

There are numerous forms of deductive chains. The example in Exhibit 4.13 is one of the most popular. The chain has a major premise, which must be supported with evidence, a minor premise that repeats one part of the major premise, and a conclusion. Deductive chains assume only one criterion. In the case of this example, the criterion is: "We want to be the gold standard." If the audience agrees with your major premise and your minor premise, the conclusion is inescapable. But never underestimate an audience's ability to poke holes in a deductive argument, especially if the individuals making the decision don't want to accept your conclusion.

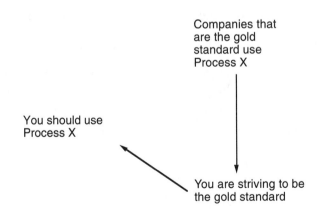

Exhibit 4.13. Example of a deductive chain

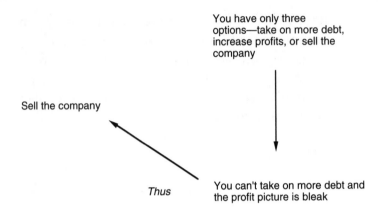

Exhibit 4.14. Example of a process-of-elimination chain

Process-of-elimination chains

Process-of-elimination chains, intended to trap the audience into agreeing with the presenter, often trap the presenter instead. Consider the process-of-elimination chain in Exhibit 4.14.

If there are truly only three alternatives and if two of them have been foreclosed, the decision maker really must take the third alternative. But it's an uncreative decision maker who can't find more alternatives than the ones you suggest or, failing that, can't find reasons why the two alternatives you've eliminated will work. Furthermore, this kind of chain is especially tricky if you're presenting internally (as opposed to relying on your knowledge as an outside consultant). It sounds very much as if you're telling the boss how to run the business, and the boss quite likely knows far more about the business than you do.

Trees based on conclusions

So far, all of our examples have been based on recommendations. Exhibit 4.15 shows how the tree works if you are supporting a conclusion instead of a recommendation. Apparently, the presenter didn't feel comfortable enough to say what the decision maker should actually do. Instead, the main point is a conclusion, probably responding to a spe-

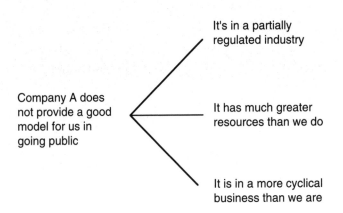

Exhibit 4.15. Example of support for a conclusion

cific question from company B, such as "Should we follow company A's example when we go public?" The supporting points are all the same sort of statements, but instead of reasons for a recommendation, they are all ways in which company A differs from company B. Providing that company B has agreed that any model selected must be similar to it in these three respects, and the presenter can prove that company A is different, the support is adequate.

Trees comparing alternatives

Go back to Exhibits 4.2a and 4.2b. Both these structures compare alternatives using criteria. Exhibit 4.2a, in which the alternatives are the branches, is the format to use when the alternatives are roughly equal in weight, or when the decision maker will determine the weight. Do not use this format when the decision maker has a preferred alternative (and it's not the one you are recommending), because the presentation is likely to become confrontational. Instead, compare all three alternatives using one criterion at a time (Exhibit 4.2b). You'll be emphasizing the things everyone already agrees to (the criteria, because you will have cleared them in advance) and showing how the preferred alternative is best in the case of each criterion. A pros and cons or advantage and disadvantage structure makes it extremely hard to make comparisons and impossible to see how criteria are ranked. Presenters often forget the importance of using the same criteria in reviewing each alternative. A criteria tree is useful in showing the audience the tradeoffs a choice requires.

Turning the Tree into a Presentation

The tree provides the structure for your presentation. As you can see by comparing the shadings on the tree and the presentation figure in Exhibit 4.16 (we'll discuss openings thoroughly in the next chapter), each branch of the tree forms a major section of the body of the presentation. You support the first branch fully, then summarize briefly what that branch was about, preview what the next branch is about, support it fully, and continue the process until you have presented all the branches. If at any point the decision maker indicates, either verbally or through body language, that he or she agrees and wants to proceed, you can cut short the more detailed discussion and proceed to the next branch or the end, whichever is appropriate. Before going on, check your logic tree using this checklist.

Checklist for a Logic Tree

- Is the main point the one concept the audience should remember?
- Do the branches all relate to the main point in the same way (do they all answer the same question)?
- Do the supporting points all relate to the branches in the same way (parallel or chained)? If parallel, are they all independent, without any overlap?
- Is each branch fully supported?
- Are all the statements on the tree written as full thoughts?

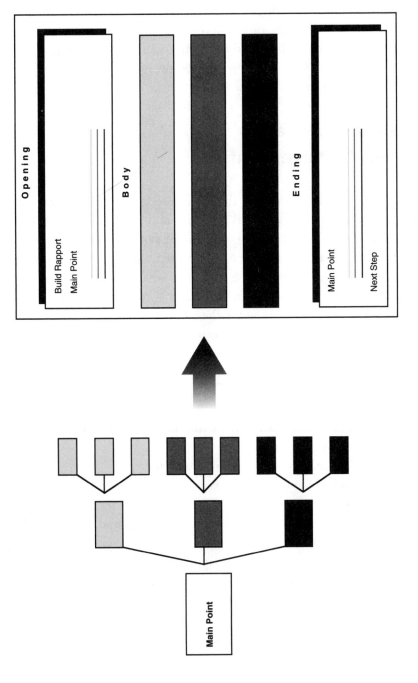

Exhibit 4.16. Turning the tree into a presentation

Because you're now confident you have a strong argument for your recommendation or point of view, you're ready to create a riveting beginning, a punchy ending, and relevant visual support, all of which are covered in Chapters 5 and 6. But before going on, think of the usefulness of the tree in organizing your work.

Using the Tree as a Project Management Tool

We have discussed the value of the logic tree for writing a presentation, assuming you have done all the work and know all the answers. The tree is also valuable in laying out the research. You usually have a hypothesis about the main point, or you have several possible main points. You can use the logic tree to lay out what needs to be true for that main point to be true — the criteria that it must meet. Then ask yourself what needs to be true for the audience to believe each assertion at the branch level. You now can test your hypotheses without wandering aimlessly through reams of data.

SUMMARY

A logic tree provides the structure of your presentation. To create one,
- Start with a specific main point
- Develop major supporting points (branches)
  - Use parallel support whenever possible
  - Check for logic flaws
- Continue to develop support until the decision maker will ask no further questions
  - Use parallel logic whenever appropriate
  - Select chained logic (causal or deductive) if the point can not be supported any other way

Once you're satisfied with the logic of your argument as displayed on the tree, use the tree as a guide for the body of the presentation, and let it help you structure your research.

5
Putting It
All Together

To convert a tight argument to a persuasive presentation,
- Craft an appropriate beginning and ending
- Make storyboards to
  - ensure effective transitions
  - determine the best place for visual support
- Choose the right medium for the presentation

Up to this point, developing a spoken presentation has been much the same as developing a written one. You have analyzed the audience, established criteria, and constructed a logic tree. Now, before you begin to put the parts together, you should take into account the differences between readers and listeners. Unlike readers, your listeners are totally dependent on you, the presenter, for focus. They have only one opportunity to grasp your message. They cannot reread or look ahead in the text for clues, and they cannot drift off into fantasy and hope to pick up the argument later. Therefore, you need to use special techniques to hold their attention. A compelling beginning, an action-oriented ending, and an effective blending of words and visual support are the components of a powerful presentation.

The design of the presentation depends on the medium you use. In the second part of this chapter we'll give you guidelines for making the right choice based on the needs of your audience and your resources. Let's take an example to review what we've covered so far, and to see how you proceed from here. As the new product manager for Star Polish Co., you developed a dry towel that, when dampened, became an all-purpose polishing cloth for various metals. Because the market research on that towel did not produce the raves you had hoped for, you subsequently tested, with better results, separate toweling for silver and for stainless steel. Since Star Polish already makes liquid cleaners in these categories, the dry towels will be line extensions. Although you really liked the idea of an all-purpose towel, you are now prepared to abandon that product based on the test results and the potential cost saving in bringing out line extensions. Exhibit 5.1 shows your tree. Because you know that senior management originally had a bias in favor of the all-purpose towel, you developed the presentation in a way that compares the options rather than making a simple recommendation. You find WHAT your presentation is about (your main point) on the tree as well as HOW you will develop it (the branches). You write a note to yourself above the tree noting WHY it is important: We have an opportunity to build both volume and profits. You check your audience profile to reassure yourself that the tree includes everything the audience needs to know to understand the presentation and that you have touched on everything the audience cares about by comparing alternatives in the body of the presentation. You are now ready to think about the beginning and the ending, to decide on the medium you will use to deliver the presentation, and to put the pieces together.

Crafting the Beginning

Just as the "logic tree" is the skeleton of a presentation, the words you actually say provide a way to bring the message to life, and the words you choose to say in the beginning are the most important.

What Goes Into a Beginning

A good beginning is one that sets the stage for the rest of the presentation by establishing rapport and a personal connection, creating a sense of urgency (why listen), and providing a road map.

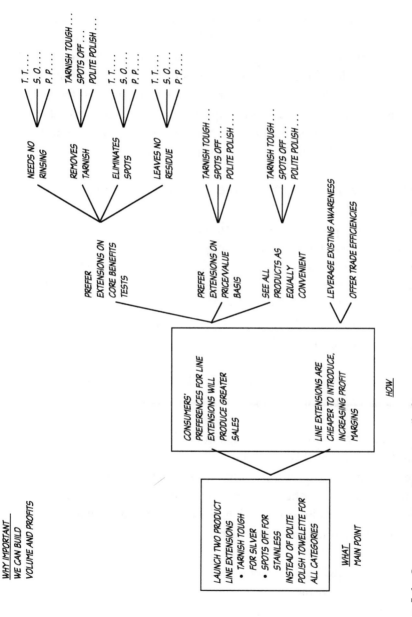

WHY IMPORTANT
WE CAN BUILD
VOLUME AND PROFITS

CONSUMERS'
PREFERENCES FOR LINE
EXTENSIONS WILL
PRODUCE GREATER
SALES

LINE EXTENSIONS ARE
CHEAPER TO INTRODUCE,
INCREASING PROFIT
MARGINS

LAUNCH TWO PRODUCT
LINE EXTENSIONS
• TARNISH TOUGH
FOR SILVER
• SPOTS OFF FOR
STAINLESS
INSTEAD OF POLITE
POLISH TOWELETTE FOR
ALL CATEGORIES

PREFER
EXTENSIONS ON
CORE BENEFITS
TESTS

PREFER
EXTENSIONS ON
PRICE/VALUE
BASIS

SEE ALL
PRODUCTS AS
EQUALLY
CONVENIENT

LEVERAGE EXISTING AWARENESS

OFFER TRADE EFFICIENCIES

NEEDS NO
RINSING

REMOVES
TARNISH

ELIMINATES
SPOTS

LEAVES NO
RESIDUE

T. T. . . .
S. O. . . .
P. P. . . .

TARNISH TOUGH. . . .
SPOTS OFF. . . .
POLITE POLISH. . . .

T. T. . . .
S. O. . . .
P. P. . . .

T. T. . . .
S. O. . . .
P. P. . . .

TARNISH TOUGH . . .
SPOTS OFF . . .
POLITE POLISH . . .

TARNISH TOUGH . . .
SPOTS OFF . . .
POLITE POLISH . . .

WHAT
MAIN POINT

HOW

Exhibit 5.1. Structure comparing options (looking at options against each criterion)

Establish a personal connection

Don't forget to introduce yourself unless everyone already knows you or someone else has introduced you. If you have an unusual name, you might want to mention it again even if someone else has done the introductions. In addition, use the names of people present as soon as possible. Thank the person who introduced you by name. Refer to someone in the group who has been helpful to you by name. Several studies have shown that using names gets the audience's attention and helps establish a bond between the group and the presenter.

Tell them why they ought to care about what you say

All too often, presenters do not think about how they are going to get started, and fall back on something vapid like "Today, I'd like to talk about …." An audience who hears this will be led to believe that the whole presentation will be a rambling description of a topic. What you need instead is a "hook statement," a sentence or two that tells the audience why it is urgent that they listen to your presentation today. A "hook" can be dramatic, like this one:

> When we ran the numbers, we were shocked to find that we were actually losing money on over 30 percent of our products.

A "hook" can also be a "relationship bookmark," a statement that reminds people that this presentation is part of a larger project or a segment of an ongoing relationship. Don't assume that everyone in the audience realizes either of these facts. Most of them do not devote much time to thinking about these issues. An example of a hook that is also a "relationship bookmark" would be this one:

> As you recall, three weeks ago we came to closure on the mission for the research department and agreed to meet today to work out the criteria for judging alternative strategies.

A "hook" like this puts everyone on notice that they are accountable —
not only for the process, but also for paying attention to the presentation.

The same idea works for a sales presentation:

> Last time we met, you asked us to work up a proposal for customizing en-
> gines for your robot painting machines. Today, we are pleased to provide ...

It's always worth reminding the customer that you are responding to a
specific request. A hook can also tie the topic to current concerns. For
instance, if the department budget is due next week, beginning a presentation with "Mr. Thomas asked me to discuss our new training program," will not cause many decision makers to stop thinking about
columns of budget figures, even if Mr. Thomas is the CEO. On the
other hand, consider this opening:

> Because we have 10 percent fewer managers than we had only three years
> ago, we must increase productivity. We have budgeted to provide all manag-
> ers with a laptop computer and the software they need to ... Our next step
> is to provide training so that they can use the software appropriately. An
> essential part of our budget decision depends on the actual design and deliv-
> ery of this presentation.

People will be more apt to listen because this beginning makes the
connection between the training program and the budget quite clear.

State the main point

Once you have everyone's attention, you should give them insight into
your message. It is difficult for your listeners to concentrate on your
subject if they don't know specifically WHAT it is about. In other words,
if you say, "Today I'm going to tell you about computerized inventory
systems," they won't listen. No one in the room is interested in a generic discussion. If you don't have a message, you shouldn't be pre-

senting. The main point on the tree is a message:

> We should institute a computerized inventory management system by the
> end of the fourth quarter.

Listeners appreciate having your recommendation or conclusion up
front, and it may be enough to establish the importance of listening.
They then know where you're headed and can better follow the logic
of your argument. In those rare instances when you have to lead up to
a recommendation or risk the audience rejecting it out of hand, you
must still be specific about the subject.

> In deciding whether or not a computerized inventory management system
> would be effective, we must consider potential changes in turnaround time,
> anticipated cost savings, and initial price. Today, we will look at each of these
> factors in order to move forward and make a decision.

If you are to get and hold your audience's attention, you must, within
the first few minutes of your presentation, indicate specifically what
you will discuss and why it is important to everyone in the room.

Provide a road map

A good beginning must tell the audience HOW you intend to develop
your presentation. A beginning is akin to the table of contents or the
executive summary of a written report. Without the HOW, the audience will spend time trying to decide what direction you will take next
and when you will finish, instead of thinking about your ideas. If your
listeners can mentally check off your points as you make them, they
will be able to focus on the content more easily.

Some presenters believe they are providing guidelines when they
say, "I will talk about four things today." They then proceed to the first
item, and create a transition by saying, "That's the first point. My second point is ...." Although this approach provides categories, it does
not help listeners follow the flow of the presentation and understand

the relationship among points. A better approach is to use the branches from your logic tree as the road map:

> We should hold our annual meeting away from headquarters for three reasons. First, off-premises meetings produce better problem-solving. Second, our staff needs the break an enforced trip entails. Finally, we need to bring our new executives together in a relaxed setting. Let's look at these reasons one by one.

After hearing this beginning, the audience knows the skeleton of the discussion and, for the remainder of the presentation, can listen to the support for these major points.

Check it out

Depending on the setting, you should plan to follow your beginning with a check statement to make sure you are responding to the audience's concerns and that your planned agenda is the one you want to follow. A check statement can be straightforward. For example, you might say something like this:

> Is there anything else we should be discussing?

or this:

> Are those still the points you'd like to cover?

Note the use of the word "still" in the last question. It implies that you've already cleared the agenda by calling in advance of the presentation, a practice we heartily recommend.

Checking seems risky to many people, who wonder "What will I do if I ask the decision maker whether this is the appropriate way to proceed and he or she says, 'Well, actually, something has come up and we'd like you to talk about the recent developments (in the market, in the political arena in X country … etc., etc.) as well.'" We know the feeling of being asked about something we hadn't prepared to discuss — it's far from pleasant. But ask yourself: When is it better to know that the decision maker wants to talk about something else? Right away? Or after an uncomfortable thirty minutes when you can see he or she is not involved with the topic and is thinking about something else?

Others object because they feel check statements imply they haven't done their homework. Actually, it's the opposite. Because no one can know everything, checking is actually a sign of confidence. If you ask, and the decision maker wants to add an issue to the discussion, adjust your presentation to allow for it. If the issue is one you do not feel prepared to address, and it is crucially important to the decision maker, ask whether rescheduling is the best course. Either way, you'll look responsive and you'll get the results you want more readily than if you were to force people to sit through what you've come prepared to discuss.

Confine yourself to relevant information

You will notice that we have not yet mentioned a standard component of many beginnings — the background of the problem. That's because most times the discussion of background is superfluous. A beginning should include only what the audience needs to know in order to understand and follow your presentation and to believe you. Consult your audience profile to assess people's knowledge of the subject. Then look at your logic tree to determine whether you've assumed too much technical expertise or experience in any of your support points. Rather than filling the beginning with detail, provide whatever is needed to understand a point at the time you discuss it. If the audience needs general information about past experience with a situation or problem, then include a limited discussion of the history in the beginning, but be conservative. Nothing puts an audience to sleep faster than a rehash of information everyone already knows.

Build credibility

People at a presentation respond more positively to a presenter whom they trust and whom they perceive to be an expert on the subject of the presentation. Check the audience profile. If you know the members of the audience and they understand why you're making the presentation, and are willing to hear your message, you won't need to go to special lengths to establish your credentials. If, however, the audience doesn't know you or is likely to disagree with your proposal, you, or the person introducing you, must convey your qualifications to speak on that topic to the audience.

Talk to the person who will introduce you before the presentation begins. Introductions are usually much too long. No one is interested in a detailed discussion of your career. An audience will, however, respond to a simple statement like this one:

> Susan Thomas is an attorney on our corporate legal staff. She has several recommendations concerning the company's risk management program based on her review of the impact of the new law.

If you're introducing yourself, you can use the same approach:

> I'm Samuel White of the legal department. I've reviewed the federal legislation in detail and want to outline the four major areas we need to target to ensure compliance.

It is not enough, however, to be an expert. People trust speakers who understand their point of view. In preparing your beginning, check your audience profile to see whether any members of the audience are likely to reject all or part of your message and whether you have ignored any criteria that may be important to the decision maker. In dealing with a potentially antagonistic audience, make it clear to your listeners that you understand their position. For example, you might say:

> I know you are concerned principally with the cost of any program we undertake. Although our current backlog of orders makes cost a crucial factor, we should give primary consideration to training our workers on the new equipment ...

Since your purpose is to arrive at a common perspective on the problem, state why you chose your criteria if they are different from those of the decision maker. If you don't acknowledge people's concerns, they are likely to think about your apparent lack of understanding when they should be focusing on your logic.

Guidelines for an Effective Beginning

- Build rapport
- Provide a "hook"
- State the main point
- Provide guidelines for the discussion using the branches from your logic tree
- Check it out
- Confine yourself to relevant information
- Build credibility if necessary

Weak Opening Statements

Some people try to start a presentation with some topical device designed to get attention. These devices rarely work.

A forecast of doom

"Your current strategy of diversification will guarantee bankruptcy within two years." Exaggerated statements like this will attract attention, but they may arouse hostility, at least among those members of the audience who helped construct the strategy you are attacking. Skip the theatrics unless you are certain the audience is predisposed to accept your idea. If you do choose to begin this way, always follow up with a solution before you take a deep breath.

A personal experience

"The other day, I was talking to George and we agreed that our inventory ..." or "The other day it took me five hours to get a count of the lumber in Warehouse 3." No one in the audience cares about what you did. Concentrate on the problem and its solution.

A rhetorical question

"Do you know how long it takes to get a printout of the last week's sales figures?" A rhetorical question snidely suggests that the presenter knows something the audience doesn't know but should — not a good way to establish rapport. In addition, there are times when someone in the audience actually tries to answer a rhetorical question, creating an embarrassing moment for everyone.

An overworked quotation

"As Ben Franklin said, 'A penny saved is a penny earned.' We can save and earn $40,000 a quarter by computerizing ...." Beginning with a quotation makes your presentation seem more literary than managerial, and a tired maxim like this one insults the audience's intelligence.

A planned joke

We all love humor. Unfortunately, not only do most planned jokes sound contrived, they are often funny only at someone else's expense.

An apology

"Time didn't permit me to do the kind of research I would have liked." Instead of gaining the audience's sympathy, such excuses alienate and irritate. "Poormouthing" at any point in a presentation is ill-advised — as an opening line it can be fatal. If you haven't done your homework, you are not an expert. Why should anyone listen to you?

A definition

Dictionary definitions, "Webster's defines oligopoly as ...," remind everyone of elementary school reports. In a management setting, starting with a definition is not only boring, it is condescending.

Creating an Ending

The ending of a presentation provides a last opportunity to persuade the audience and reach agreement on the course of action. Endings should cover three elements:
* the recommendation or conclusion
* a brief restatement of the major supporting points (branches)
* the steps required for action

The function of the ending is to reinforce understanding of the main point and to come to closure on the next step, whether it is acceptance of your recommendation, agreement to continue the relationship, or the process for implementing your recommendation. It's important that you actually ask the decision makers for their agreement. "Closing" does not only apply to sales; it is an important element in making people feel that their time in the presentation was well spent. If people feel nothing happened as the result of the presentation, you can imagine how happy they will be to come to the next one. Asking for closure, again, feels risky to people ("What if they say no?"). Our response is this: You'll find out whether they say no sooner or later, and if you ask them when you are face to face with them, you'll be able to find out why more easily, and perhaps allay their concerns. The amount of material you include in an ending depends on the audience's commitment to your position — the more committed the audience, the less you need to say.

Making Storyboards

If you were writing a report, you would, at this point, begin to write the first draft. In developing a spoken presentation, storyboards can serve as a first draft. They provide a mechanism for developing transitions, checking the flow of the argument, and designing rough visuals to support your messages. If you are putting together a team presentation, or if a group has done the work leading up to the presentation, storyboards provide a good vehicle for reaching agreement on flow and visuals.

In the standard box storyboard (Exhibit 5.2), you write the key message at the top of the box, select the visual form, sketch the visual, and add a transition. (If you don't know much about creating visuals, you might move on to Chapter 6 at this point, and then come back. Or

Exhibit 5.2. A blank box storyboard

read this section for the sense of how you use storyboards, but be sure to reread it after you have read Chapter 6.)

Using the Star Polish Co. situation again as an example, this is how the system works. Start with WHY, your statement of significance: "We can build volume and profits." You think this can stand alone, so you move on to WHAT and HOW. You write the main point and the branches in the first box of the storyboard (see Exhibit 5.3). You might create a conceptual visual, but for now you have a text visual that serves as your first visual and may also serve for transitions between sections. You then move on to the first branch, "Consumers prefer line extensions." You have examined how each product meets three criteria for accepting a new product: provides core benefits, provides value for the price, and is convenient to use. Your conceptual visual shows that consumers find that line extensions deliver on all three criteria while Polite Polish delivers on only one. Because you don't plan to go into detail on convenience, you discuss it without a visual as a transition to your next visual. You write that transition on the storyboard because it is important. You then go on to show, visually, how Polite Polish does not deliver core benefits. You continue creating visuals and adding transitions based on the supporting points of the first branch until you believe you have answered all the questions the audience would ask on that subject. You then return to a summary visual and move on to the second branch. You continue this process until you come to the end with a visual that includes next steps.

Developing Transitions

Transitions are critical in management presentations, not only because they link sections and emphasize relationships, but also because they sum up what's already been said and forecast the next section. Judicious reviewing signals to the audience the conclusion of each major portion of your discussion, increasing comfort that the presentation is marching along as planned. Repetition increases the likelihood that the audience will remember your ideas. Transition words and phrases like "however," "therefore," "as you can see," and "in conclusion" guide the

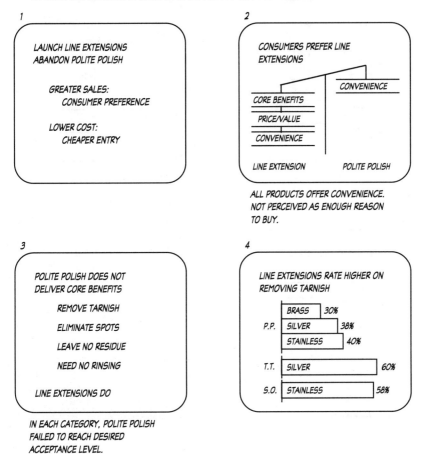

WE HAVE AN OPPORTUNITY TO INCREASE SALES AND ADD $750M TO THE BOTTOM LINE

1

LAUNCH LINE EXTENSIONS
ABANDON POLITE POLISH

GREATER SALES:
    CONSUMER PREFERENCE

LOWER COST:
    CHEAPER ENTRY

2

CONSUMERS PREFER LINE
EXTENSIONS

CONVENIENCE

CORE BENEFITS

PRICE/VALUE

CONVENIENCE

LINE EXTENSION   POLITE POLISH

ALL PRODUCTS OFFER CONVENIENCE.
NOT PERCEIVED AS ENOUGH REASON
TO BUY.

3

POLITE POLISH DOES NOT
DELIVER CORE BENEFITS

    REMOVE TARNISH

    ELIMINATE SPOTS

    LEAVE NO RESIDUE

    NEED NO RINSING

LINE EXTENSIONS DO

IN EACH CATEGORY, POLITE POLISH
FAILED TO REACH DESIRED
ACCEPTANCE LEVEL.

4

LINE EXTENSIONS RATE HIGHER ON
REMOVING TARNISH

	BRASS	30%
P.P.	SILVER	38%
	STAINLESS	40%
T.T.	SILVER	60%
S.O.	STAINLESS	58%

Exhibit 5.3. Box storyboard based on Exhibit 5.1

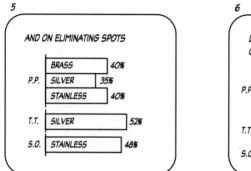

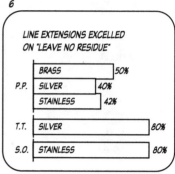

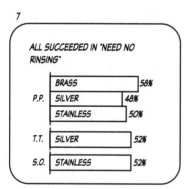

BUT POLITE POLISH SUCCESS IN LAST 2
CATEGORIES WAS NOT ENOUGH TO
CREATE BELIEF IN CORE BENEFIT.

IN ADDITION, ITS COST HURTS
POLITE POLISH

Exhibit 5.3. (continued)

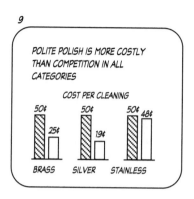

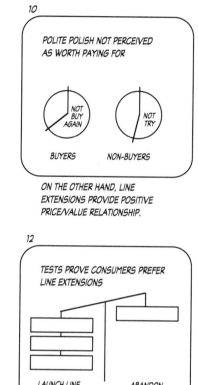

ON THE OTHER HAND, LINE
EXTENSIONS PROVIDE POSITIVE
PRICE/VALUE RELATIONSHIP.

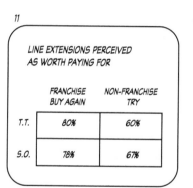

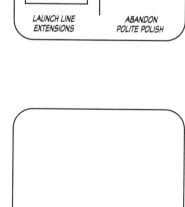

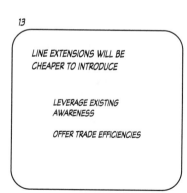

Exhibit 5.3. (continued)

listeners through your presentation. If done well, a transition can provide subliminal cues that make your message more persuasive. Be sure, however, that you use transition words correctly. If you say "however," the audience expects an opposing view. "Therefore" indicates that what you are about to say follows from what you just said. If you misuse these words (and many do), you'll confuse the audience.

Spread the storyboards out on a table or pin them to a wall and read through them to see whether your ideas flow smoothly. Although you checked the logic tree and determined an order before you designed the storyboards, formulating transitions may suggest changes, particularly in the order of your messages.

Determining the Best Place for Visuals

As you create your storyboards, make a rough sketch of the visuals you'll need on the boards themselves. During the problem-solving process, you may have made rough charts and graphs. Look at your presentation with a fresh eye now and revise those visuals that help make your point, reject those that don't, and sketch new ones as needed. Your message headings determine the visual content, not vice versa.

Working with Outlining and Structuring Software

Most current presentation software packages offer the option of working in an outline mode. Here you can view and edit the text of your slides without getting involved in the look of the actual slides. (Some programs allow you to see formatted text; however, you always have the option of reducing the text to its most basic, unformatted form if you wish.)

Outlining software helps you focus on the structure of your presentation without being distracted by considerations of design. If you have structured your presentation using the tree system, the outline is the interim step in getting your message on-screen. An outliner won't provide a structure for you, however — it's just another tool to use in the whole presentation process. If you feel more comfortable working with your favorite word processor than with a presentation program, you can usually work on your outline as text, then import it into the presentation program when it is complete. You just need to check how to format your text so that the presentation software can read it correctly.

The real magic of outlining software comes when you are ready to move from structuring your content to creating your visuals. Once you have set up your visual templates the way you would like them (see Chapter 6), one click of a button transforms your outline into slide form. Your branches become message heads; your supporting points are the bullets. A little editing, then all that remains for you to do is to add graphic elements, such as charts and conceptual images, and your presentation is ready to roll.

A feature provided by some presentation programs is a form of precooked presentation. You start by opening a new presentation file, then you simply answer a few questions, and the program provides you with a readymade outline for your presentation. The message that is coming across here is a good one — the structure is the first step toward the finished presentation. However, a readymade structure can never be as effective as one that has been specifically tailored for a specific presentation to a specific audience. Your software can make your life easier in a multitude of ways, but it can't analyze your audience for you.

Choosing the Appropriate Medium

This section shows our bias. We're assuming that you'll choose to use some form of visual support for your presentation. Whether you believe the research or not, you know intuitively that a presenter who only talks to you is harder to follow than one who uses visual support, and that it is harder to remember what he or she had to say. No one in business today would consider making a presentation of any importance without some visual backup. Your choice then revolves around which medium to use.

Visual support, broadly defined, can be anything from a piece of paper to a plant tour. However, most presentations take place in a conference room or an office; although you may bring in a part or a piece of machinery or show a short video, you are most likely to use overhead transparencies, 35mm slides, presentation books, handouts, or a computer presentation system.

During the first half of the 1990s, audience expectations for quality and readability of visual support changed drastically. Before desktop publishing, overheads were often difficult to read and time-consuming to create. Thirty-five millimeter slides were made off premises, at great expense. Audiences understood these constraints and accepted the results. Now, however, anyone with a personal computer is expected to produce elegant graphic visual support. Audiences have become more sophisticated about visuals, and are therefore less tolerant. Your choice of media should be based on the audience's preferences, your purpose, available resources, and the size of the audience (see Exhibit 5.4).

Audience's Preferences

As with every other factor in a presentation, the needs of the audience come first in choosing a medium. Industries and organizations vary in the formality they expect: in some, a stand-up performance is the norm; in others, anything more formal than meeting around a conference table is considered overdone. Some individuals have specific preferences: several senior executives we know always want 35mm slide shows, some want hard copy of the presentation in advance so they can ask questions and focus on what is important to them. If you're uncertain about the decision maker's preferences or the norms of the organization, by all means, ask.

Remember that we often unwittingly train our audiences to expect certain kinds of presentations from us. If you want to try something different, most audiences will be happy for the novelty, so long as you check with them first.

Choose the Medium	Overheads	35mm Slides	Handouts	Flipcharts	Laptops
Desired format	Discussion Information	Information	Discussion Detailed information	Discussion Idea development	Discussion Information
Degree of formality	Informal or formal	Formal	Informal	Informal	Informal or Formal
Design capability	Computer Typeset	Computer Typeset Photography	Computer Typed	Handwritten	Computer
Equipment needs	Projector Screen	Projector Screen Dim lights	—	Easel Chart	Laptop Projector/Panel Screen
Time to reproduce	Negligible	About 24 hours	Negligible	Time involved in writing	Time involved in creation
Costs (beyond design)	Acetates – minimum production costs	Most costly medium (per presentation)	Minimal	Minimal	Hardware Software
Size of audience	Up to several hundred	Up to several hundred	Under 10	Under 20	Up to several hundred

Exhibit 5.4. Guidelines for selecting a medium

Your Purpose

Assuming the audience is open-minded about the medium, consider what you are trying to achieve and what your data demand. Do you want intense discussion? You won't get it with a 35mm presentation or some multimedia computer presentations. A darkened room and a predetermined locked-in order and script create a "me talk, you listen" environment that discourages interruptions. Slide presentations also imply a finished product and are not appropriate for a work-in-progress meeting, unless you prepare "What-if" scenarios to illustrate the effect of different alternatives. On the other hand, a laptop with an LCD panel can increase your control of the meeting. After all, you have the only copy, and as long as you are thoroughly comfortable with the software, you can make changes instantly. This can work well in a small, informal situation.

Are you trying to convey to a client that you're willing to invest in winning his or her business? A polished presentation may help. Do you want the client to think you are down-to-earth and understand the value of a dollar? Skip the full color, professionally prepared visuals. Does the audience need to see how something works? Try a demonstration. If something is too complex to bring into the presentation room, consider video or computer demonstrations.

Available Resources

Time, money, and availability of equipment will obviously influence your decision. Can you produce slides in-house? How long will it take? Do you have the equipment and the technical staff to produce the visuals you want on in-house computers? A surefire way to create errorloaded visuals is to make them yourself at 3 a.m. before a 9 a.m. presentation because the production system failed you. Most equipment for computer presentations is bulky and expensive. Unless you are doing presentations daily or weekly, it may not be a good use of money.

The Size of the Audience

Everyone in the room needs to see the visuals clearly. Although you may like the interactive quality of flipcharts, they are virtually useless in a group of more than twenty. Light-on-dark overhead transparencies with large type are as good as slides for a group of several hundred. Dark-on-light transparencies can work for a large group if the room is wide rather than long — just keep in mind how far from the screen the most distant person is seated. Presentation books and handouts can theoretically be used in groups of any size. However, since it is very difficult to keep people with you when they can turn pages at their own pace, you should limit use of books and handouts to small-group presentations so you can monitor page turning and respond to it.

Once you have settled on a medium for your presentation, the next step in the case of "traditional" media — overheads, 35mm slides — is to create visuals from your logic tree. We'll go on to discuss visuals in detail in Chapter 6, as well as considerations for the specific medium that you have chosen. However, there is one medium which requires considerably more thought than the others at the design stage, because of the increased danger of the presentation technology overwhelming your carefully crafted presentation structure. This is the computer-based presentation.

Designing a Computer-Based Presentation

These days, presenters usually end up using a computer regardless of what presentation medium they finally intend to use. Presentation software has made the process of designing the presentation, as well as producing final output for handouts, 35mm slides, and overheads, a very straightforward task. However, when it comes to producing a presentation which will actually be delivered directly from a computer, there are a number of other possibilities to consider. The key is to use technology only if it *supports your message*.

Using Multimedia

Multimedia is a buzzword which seems to cover a multitude of different concepts, depending on the context. As far as a presentation is concerned, we like to feel that it covers any items above and beyond a regular linear slide show. Multimedia is most common in the case of a computer-based presentation with an LCD panel or projector, though some multimedia elements could be added to a regular presentation, say by using a tape deck or video player along with regular slides or overheads. At present, there are a great number of "ifs" and "buts" involved in using multimedia elements in a presentation; you need to be aware of these before you get too deeply involved. As with pretty much anything in the computer world, however, multimedia is only going to get cheaper, easier, and better — if you're not using it now, you can be quite sure that somewhere down the road, you will be.

Advantages of multimedia

- If you use it effectively, it can make you look terrific. A recent University of Arizona study concluded that multimedia enhancement increased an audience's agreement with the presenters by 17 percent and boosted credibility 27 percent. But watch out — the 3M Institute also made a survey which adds a caveat: "A glitzy multimedia presentation won't help an unprepared speaker impress an audience."

- Sounds and music (as well as video) can have a significant emotional impact. Music can carry you along emotionally — just try watching a horror movie with the sound turned off and you'll get the idea. So a well-placed music clip may actually inspire your audience to take action. Be very aware of your audience and your message, though. While music may be just the thing for a sales presentation to a large group, it could be embarrassingly out of place in a small meeting, or a situation where the logic of your message is the key issue.

- Video can show procedures and places that can otherwise only be vaguely described by a presenter. A complicated assembly process may be best portrayed in the form of an animation. A proposed site may be more effectively displayed in a video clip than with photographs. A roleplay or a simulated client situation could be recorded to reinforce a point you are making.

- You can certainly impress a client by showing how you're up-to-date with the latest technology, just as long as you do it right, and the client cares.

- Multimedia elements can be purchased easily on CD — but be sure you really need an element obtained this way, and, as with clip art (which we'll discuss in Chapter 6), check that your clip media are royalty-free.

Disadvantages of multimedia

- Multimedia is hard to use effectively, and if used badly (as is often the case), will harm your presentation rather than enhance it. A music clip that is too long, or too loud, or a video clip that plays in the background while you present, will inevitably direct the audience's attention away from your message.

- The multimedia version of clip art is now common, with CDs available containing megabyte upon megabyte of precooked video and audio. With today's pressure to appear "high-tech," there is a temptation to grab a video or audio clip from a CD that may only loosely fit your message. Beware — this approach will almost always end up distracting from what you are saying rather than supporting it.

- Multimedia is expensive to do well. Clip media can be useful, and desktop video editing is becoming more prevalent. However, if you want a really high-quality video clip custom made, you'll probably have to contract out for it, and you'll need a top-end computer when you actually deliver the presentation.

- Multimedia is risky. With every new element of complexity you add to your presentation, you have a new collection of things to go wrong — and you should always operate on the assumption that anything that can go wrong, will.

Should you use multimedia elements at all?

Before getting involved in the nitty-gritty of multimedia presentation production, you should consider whether you should be using multimedia elements at all. The model in Exhibit 5.5 may help you make this decision.

A common trap (which we hope you won't fall into if you've read this far) is to get involved in the possibilities of multimedia before you've finished working on the presentation structure. All the multimedia elements in the world won't help you convince an audience of a message which you haven't supported sufficiently in the first place. If your content won't stand on its own, go back and fix your presentation structure before you go any further.

The next thing to consider is whether multimedia would directly support your message. If a video or sound clip is really valuable for the point you are making, then by all means you should consider incorporating it into your presentation. If you can't honestly say that multimedia would *directly support* your message, then you have a few more questions to answer. There may still be a case for using music or video — perhaps to try to give your summary slide a little extra punch at a purely emotional level. Take care, though — remember that multimedia used with the wrong audience can backfire and end up making you look foolish.

Now you have to consider the real ins and outs of multimedia production, which if incorporated into the software you're using for the presentation (the simplest solution for actually making the presentation), can be very expensive. If your budget can support this, great

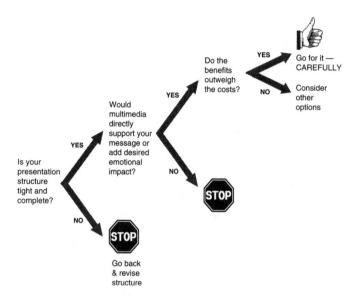

Exhibit 5.5. Should you use multimedia?

— but if not, don't give up; you have other options. Most computer projection equipment provides direct connections for video players, so if you don't mind a moment or so of dead air mid-presentation while you switch projection modes, you can play back a standard video, usually with greater clarity than if you had converted the video clip into a computer movie. Similarly with audio — some presenters even prefer to surreptitiously hit a switch on a portable tape deck than actually have their sound clips run from the presentation. The point is, if you are imaginative, there's no reason why budget restrictions should keep you to a bare-bones presentation, if multimedia is really what you need.

Designing an Interactive Computer Presentation

"Interactive" is another of those buzzwords that are thrown about by just about everyone who is interested in the new technologies of presentation. It is often combined and confused with multimedia. Every presentation is, of course, interactive — the presenter constantly receives feedback from the audience, either in the form of direct questions, or indirectly as body language. But the audience does not have direct control over the running of the presentation. It is the presenter who really has the hands on the wheel.

How truly interactive a presentation is can be determined by how easily the presenter can change gears. If you are simply relying on hand-outs, you have very little chance of any on-the-spot customization. The most you can do is stop to answer questions. With overheads and slides, you can at least reorder, skip, or add slides, and you can annotate overheads to expand on points. Computers, however, offer the true possibilities when it comes to interactivity. As long as you are really familiar with the software you are using, you can take a chart or table that is on one of your slides, and feed in new figures mid-presentation, for example to try out a revised budget plan that a member of your audience has just come up with. Far from looking unprofessional because you are breaking the flow of your presentation, you are adapting the presentation to directly match the audience's needs — true interactivity.

Self-running interactive computer presentations

We will be looking increasingly at a world of "presenterless presentations" — these are currently found most often in the form of kiosks, demo diskettes, and World Wide Web sites. Briefly, these are presentations through which the user can navigate at his or her discretion, usually by clicking on buttons or areas of graphics ("hyperlinks") to move to different pages or slides.

Assembling a self-running, interactive computer presentation offers a new set of challenges. The "presenter" has to consider the usual factors of main point and support, but since interactive presentations tend to be made for wider use or distribution than traditional presentations, analyzing the audience can be an almost impossible task. A good interactive presentation gets around this is by being truly interactive. You can analyze the audience in a limited way by considering what you are offering — a certain kind of product or service is likely to be of interest to a certain type of person, for example. You then need to try to consider every possible criterion of that audience and provide a link to appropriate support related to that criterion. For example, if a presentation is designed to promote a specific product, the first page may provide an overview of the advantages of the product. Buttons can then be provided to link to pages supporting why the product is cost-effective, why the product is efficient, why the product is attractively designed, and so on.

There is another catch. With all the hyperlinks back and forward, the actual setup of the software can get very complicated. If you have developed a good storyboard, this should make your life easier. One way to simplify the setup of hyperlinks is to use a computer drawing program to draw objects corresponding to each page or slide. Then the pages can be reordered, and lines representing hyperlinks drawn between them, to produce a graphic "map" of the final presentation (such as the diagram of the Strategic Communications World Wide Web site shown in Exhibit 5.6). A lower-tech but extremely efficient solution is to use post-it notes to represent pages, which you can then move around any way you wish.

SUMMARY

Beginnings and endings are critical because audiences remember best what they hear during the first and final minutes of a presentation.
- Your beginning must
  - Set the stage
  - Establish rapport
  - Create a sense of urgency (why listen)
  - Provide a road map
- If you have chosen to ignore criteria important to the audience in the body of the presentation, you must deal with them in the beginning
- An effective ending repeats the recommendation and reinforces the need for action

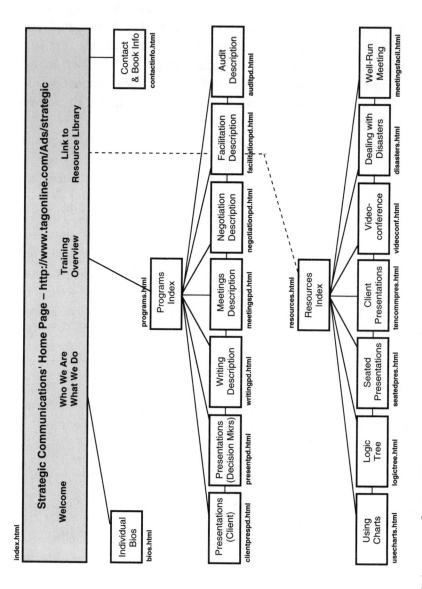

Exhibit 5.6. A map of a World Wide Web site, showing hyperlinks

Storyboards provide a valuable tool.
- Storyboards force you to write transitions and check the flow of your ideas
- If your presentation is the result of a team effort, storyboards enable you to reach agreement on the final version of the presentation
- Sketching rough visuals on storyboards shows you when you need to collect more data and ensures even development of visual support

In selecting the most appropriate medium, consider
- The audience's preference
- Your purpose
- Available resources
- The size of the audience

Be careful when preparing a computer presentation.
- Consider carefully before you use multimedia
- Use only elements that really match the message
- Don't overdo it

6

Creating
Compelling Visuals

Visual support is a critical component of most management presentations, because people remember best what they see and hear and because compelling visuals increase the presenter's credibility. You will increase the impact of your presentation if you

- Design visuals that support your message
- Use color appropriately
- Produce polished materials

Designing Visuals that Support the Message

In deciding when to use visual support in a presentation and what a specific visual should look like, remember that a presentation is an exchange between you and the audience — it is not a picture show for which you provide the voice-over. The purpose of any visual is to increase your persuasiveness — to increase the potential that the audience will understand and believe you in the shortest possible time. Therefore, each visual should add value to the presentation; it must be easy to read, easy to understand and, most importantly, the content must support your words.

Take the heading from your tree – make the message the heading

People read from the top down, and a heading should convey the significance of the visual — "What it means" rather than "What it is." Exhibits 6.1 and 6.2 use the same chart, but Exhibit 6.2 leads much more quickly to the important conclusion that "sales have tripled." Writing the message at the top of the visual also permits you to test whether the visual you intend to use is necessary to support your argument. If you can't come up with a message, you can relegate the visual to the appendix.

Watch out for punctuation in your headings. Slashes and exclamation points can easily be mistaken in poor lighting for letters, confusing your audience. Dashes used to separate words can cause your computer software to wrap the heading text in the wrong place, resulting in headings that look unbalanced. And don't use a period at the end of your heading - your audience subconsciously gets the message "stop here" when they reach a period, and consequently are less likely to concentrate on your support.

Be consistent in the use of design features

Set guidelines for the placement of headings, type size and font, indentation, shading, and color. Consistency indicates care in the design and execution of your visuals, and makes you appear more professional. However, as the old saying goes, rules are made to be broken. If the text looks too crowded because you have more words than usual, leave more space between lines. Your goal is to have an easy-to-read, esthetically pleasing visual.

Most presentation software packages provide a "master slide" setup, which can greatly simplify the process of ensuring consistency throughout a presentation (see Exhibit 6.3). Typefaces can be set up for each of the several levels of headings and bullet points, and recurring items such as horizontal rules and company logos can be placed on the master slide and will then appear in the same place on every slide. Once you have set up your master slide, each new slide you create will

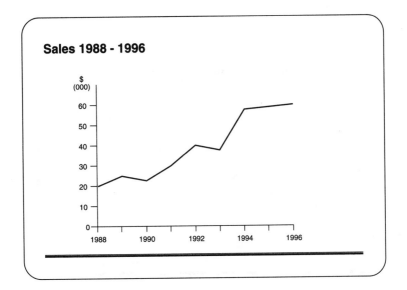

Exhibit 6.1. A topical heading says "what it is."

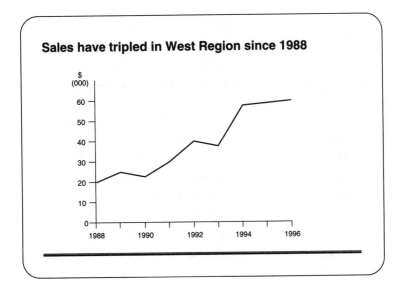

Exhibit 6.2. A message heading says "what it means."

```
┌──────────────────────────────────────────────────────┐
│ ┌────────────────────────────────────────────────┐   │
│ │                                                 │   │
│ │ Click to edit Master title style                │   │
│ └─────────────────────────────────────┘ Title Area for AutoLayouts │
│   ┌────────────────────────────────────────┐         │
│   │ Click to edit Master text styles        │         │
│   │     - Second level                      │         │
│   │        • Third level                    │         │
│   │          - Fourth level                 │         │
│   │            Fifth level                  │         │
│   │                                         │         │
│   │                                         │         │
│   └──────────────── Object Area for AutoLayouts ─┘    │
└──────────────────────────────────────────────────────┘
```

Exhibit 6.3. Example of a master slide

match the master type style, spacing, and so on. However, changing
these settings on an individual slide will not affect the master or any of
the other slides in your presentation. Resist the temptation to create a
master slide with a nonsensical background. We sat through an entire
presentation with a daisy in the background, vainly trying to figure out
the connections. We've also seen world maps and company logos. Nonsensical background images are distracting in the extreme.

Some programs allow you to save your customized charts as chart
format templates, so every chart you produce is guaranteed to match.
Color palettes ensure consistency between charts and text highlight
colors, and some packages also allow you to recolor imported clip art
to match the overall color scheme of your slides.

Once you have set consistent design features for your visual support, you need to choose the best form for it (text, conceptual, or
graphic presentation of data) and design the visual to make it readable
and meaningful.

- Text visuals serve as road maps for the audience. They are most effective in previewing and summarizing information.
- Conceptual visuals use an image to convey a message.
- Charts show relationships and are especially valuable for conveying complex data in an easy-to-grasp format.

Text Visuals Are Your Road Map

Although endless words bore people, text visuals nonetheless have an important place in any presentation. Unlike readers, audiences cannot refer back or peek at the ending to determine how you are going to tell your story. Text visuals, used as a reference throughout the presentation, keep the audience on the right road and remind them where they have just been as well as where they are going (see Exhibit 6.5).

To make sure text visuals convey a readily understandable message and are simple in content and in design, follow these rules:

Use action or message phrases, not topic words or full sentences

No matter how compelling a presenter you are, people's minds will inevitably wander and they will miss some of what you say. A full thought reinforces your message; a topic word does not. (Compare Exhibit 6.5 to Exhibit 6.4.) Limit the number of lines to between five and seven. If the audience has to read a wordy visual, you have two choices: let people read (thereby ruining your pace) or read it to them and irritate them (since they can, after all, read more quickly themselves). (Compare Exhibits 6.6 and 6.7.) The key is for you to retain control and add value by using phrases on the visual and by expanding on the topic as you speak.

Keep lists parallel and in the order you intend to follow

Any series of items on a visual is perceived as a list. People expect lists to be parallel (independent items, same grammatical form) in thought and in form. If they are not, they are difficult to read and to understand

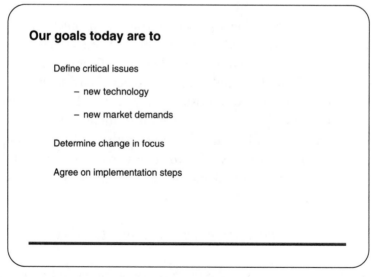

Agenda

    Overview

    Current market

    Competitors

    Opportunity

    Next steps

Exhibit 6.4. By providing only categories, this visual, which is for the same presentation as Exhibit 6.5, tells the audience only that the presentation will be divided into five parts. It does not tell a story of any kind or provide a meaningful map of the presentation.

Our goals today are to

    Define critical issues

        – new technology

        – new market demands

    Determine change in focus

    Agree on implementation steps

Exhibit 6.5. This text visual sets the stage for the presentation by letting the audience know what the presenter expects to achieve and the order in which topics will be considered.

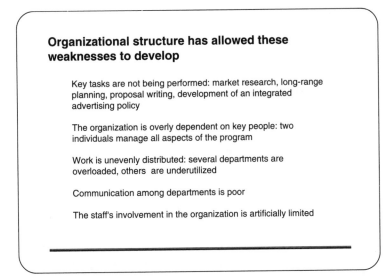

Exhibit 6.6. The text on this slide is too dense, making it visually unappealing and too long. The words tell the whole story.

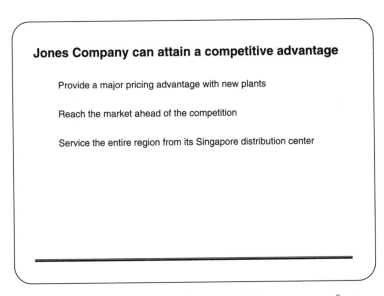

Exhibit 6.7. Phrases let the presenter tell the story. Verbs give a sense of action.

(see Exhibits 6.8 and 6.9). In addition, any list implies an order; it is your contract with the audience and you have an obligation to observe it.

Use upper and lowercase type and a simple typeface

People read by recognizing differences, especially in the heights and "tails" of letters. These differences do not exist in uppercase type, so people must read more slowly. We suspect the common use of all uppercase type resulted from an attempt to use the largest letters possible, but with the range of type sizes and styles available today, it is no longer the best choice. Simple typefaces are easier to read than flowery ones. Although serif fonts (this book uses a serif font) are easier to read on a page of text than sans serif fonts (this is a sans serif font), in large type on a screen the sans serif is clearer for most people. And while you may think boldface will make your text stand out, studies have shown that when people are forced to read large areas of bold text, their comprehension of the material is greatly reduced. In fact, in large quantities bold is harder to read.

Highlight the most important message on the visual

You can highlight text by making it larger or bolder or by using shading or color. The most important text on any visual is usually the heading, which is set in larger and bolder type. You can highlight another part of the visual by using shading, bold face type, color, or an arrow (see Exhibit 6.10).

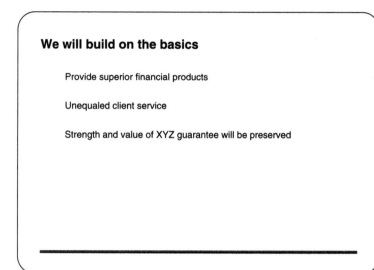

Exhibit 6.8. A list that is not parallel in form is hard to read.

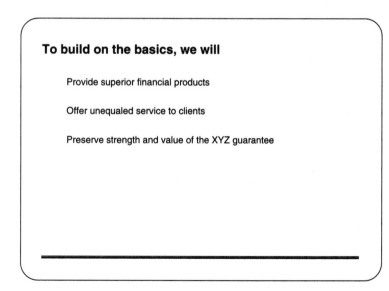

Exhibit 6.9. Strong verbs make good lists.

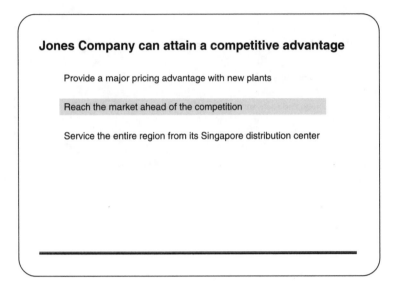

Exhibit 6.10. Since the visual provides the road map for the presentation, it can be used between the sections to remind the audience of what has been discussed and to indicate what will be discussed next. Shading focuses the audience's attention; so does color.

Guidelines for Text Visuals

- Use phrases, not words or lengthy sentences
- Keep lists parallel and in the order you will follow
- Use uppercase and lowercase type
- Highlight the most important message on the page
- Be consistent

Conceptual Visuals Create an Image

Conceptual visuals — visuals that use a picture or design to make a point by analogy or to show the relationship of ideas — are increasingly used in management presentations. We believe this trend results both from a growing understanding that most people think visually (and therefore respond more quickly to an image than to words) and from increased exposure to sophisticated visual images in print and on television. Conceptual visuals may use accepted forms or shapes (such as boxes, arrows, pyramids, etc.) or pictures to convey a message, or they may use analogies or metaphors to clarify a point by putting it in a non-business context that has meaning to the audience.

Getting ideas for conceptuals

In Exhibit 6.11, we provide twelve examples of commonly used conceptual images. You can use these images as a starting point for your own visuals. For other ideas, talk to your teammates and pay attention to the visual imagery your words evoke. One important clue is the verb in the heading because verbs usually describe an action and actions are usually visible (and visual). For example, if you say "Our new, decentralized corporate structure will support our long-term goals," the word "support" suggests a visual (see Exhibit 6.12).

Visuals based on analogy or metaphor are difficult to design and execute, but their value makes them worth the time for an important presentation. These visuals become the focus of discussion, often long after the presentation is over and the recommendation is being implemented. For example, a presenter who wanted his audience to consider whether to focus its marketing efforts on the retailer or the end user used the image in Exhibit 6.13. The term "chicken or egg" became organizational shorthand for the question of where to focus marketing efforts. Talking aloud may help you hear a picture that will work in a visual; brainstorming with others also helps. The more you can say "this is like ..." and the more colorful your language, the more successful you will be. You may also pick up an analogy from the decision

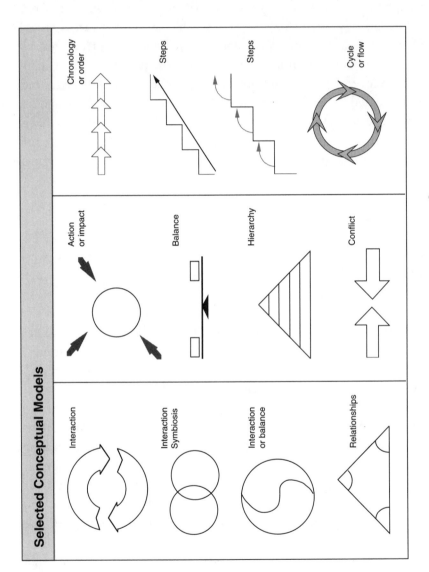

Exhibit 6.11. Here are some standard conceptual models to get your creative juices flowing.

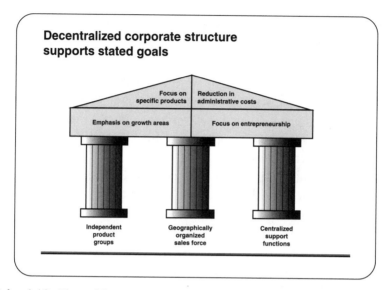

Exhibit 6.12. The verb "support" creates an image. The use of pillars suggests a strong structure. An image that works well for some audiences, this is the kind of imagery we see increasingly in business journals and papers.

Exhibit 6.13. A consulting firm used this image to focus the attention of the client on the question of whether to put out a product first or try to create demand first. The image became the focus for discussion long after the presentation.

maker. Exhibit 6.14 shows a visual suggested by an executive we know who said, "Our presentations sound like someone drove up the truck and tipped it over."

Exhibits 6.15 through 6.18 are slides that use conceptual images to reinforce their message. You can use them, and the examples in Exhibit 6.11, to help you create your own conceptual visuals. The images used in these examples are appropriate for most audiences, and they may suggest other conceptuals.

Some consulting firms are even using cartoonists to generate creative visuals. One consultant told us he used a comic storyboard as a way of presenting; he gets people on their feet and gives them "stickies" to place notes or questions on the storyboards. He claims retention of key messages has tripled!

Some presenters, especially those with less experience, are concerned that the audience will not take them seriously if they use conceptual visuals, especially humorous ones. You must be guided by your

Exhibit 6.14. The image on this visual was based on a comment an executive made to us about presentations in his organization. You may choose not to put a heading on a conceptual visual if the picture tells the story alone or if the picture requires a lengthy explanation.

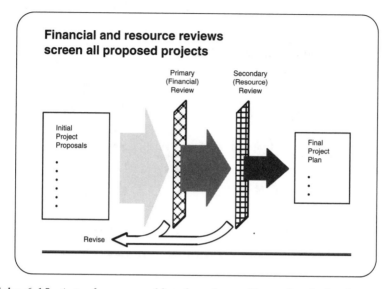

Exhibit 6.15. A simple conceptual based on the word "screen" in the heading

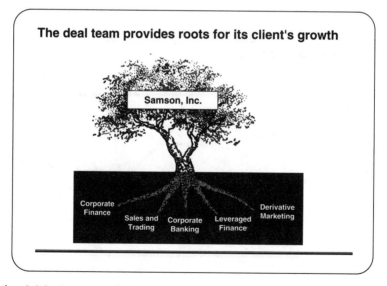

Exhibit 6.16. A conceptual that uses an everyday image

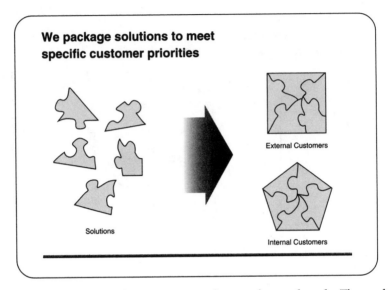

Exhibit 6.17. This visual shows a way to package, with several results. The word "package" can be conceptualized in many ways.

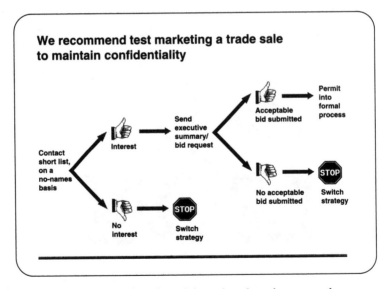

Exhibit 6.18. The conceptual in this exhibit is based on the process the presenter recommends, rather than an image in the heading.

audience and your own sense of good taste. But in our experience, a light touch is a positive addition to a presentation.

Be sure the analogy is meaningful to the decision maker

Some metaphors and analogies are so common that you need not worry about people understanding them. Others may be useful only for specific audiences. An acquaintance of ours likes to talk about cutting the Gordian knot. An audience not versed in mythology will have trouble understanding that he means the problem cannot be resolved by any usual means but needs a bold or radical solution. People react to a metaphor they don't understand with the same discomfort they experience when they are the only one in the room to miss the point of a story. Listen to your audience, not only during a presentation, but in meetings and discussions of all kinds, to get clues to effective analogies to use with that group.

Creating conceptuals

Let's say you have a message that you feel can be reinforced with a conceptual visual. There is one important caveat: You should never have to play with your message to make it better fit an image you would like to use. If you can't find an image which exactly supports your message, then edit an existing image, or create a new one, or don't use one at all. In Exhibit 6.19, the attempt to create a conceptual resulted in confusion at best, and derision at worst.

　　To create conceptuals, invest in a good (preferably postscript) drawing program to edit clip art. Clip art will rarely be exactly what you need to match your message, but you can fine tune it to make it match if you can edit it. You can remove sections of a drawing you don't need, or take parts of different drawings and combine them. You can enlarge and reduce parts of the drawing. You can duplicate, flip, and rotate them. If you are ambitious, you can even change the angle of a figure's arm or the expression on its face. You can recolor images to fit better into the color scheme of your presentation (some presenta-

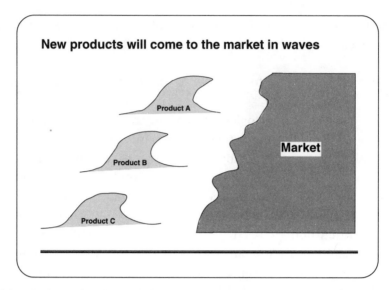

Exhibit 6.19. Rather than suggesting waves, this visual suggests sharks moving away from the market. Instead of making a point, it elicits laughs.

Exhibit 6.20. You can edit clip art to meet your specific needs.

tion programs even have this option built in).

Exhibit 6.20 shows four steps in the process of creating an effective conceptual visual: first selecting pieces of clip art, then ungrouping and rearranging their elements, then regrouping the edited elements, and finally using the updated art on a presentation slide.

If you can't find the clip art you need, and are willing to invest the time, you can use a good drawing program to create your own art. Many good conceptual visuals can be created using basic drawing and shading tools. You can even do basic drawing work with the tools provided with most presentation software packages (see Exhibit 6.21), but a free-standing drawing program gives you better control and fine-editing options.

Many drawing programs (and now also presentation programs) offer an option for distorting pieces of text — either stretching, skewing, or compressing them. This can be a very effective way of creating conceptual images: concepts such as "pressure," "expansion," or "depression" can be portrayed by applying the appropriate effect to the text (see Exhibit 6.22).

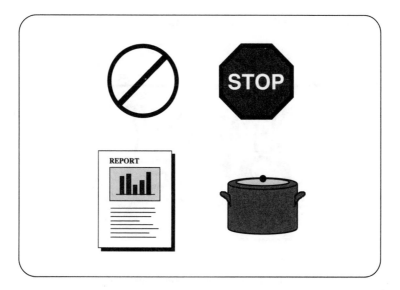

Exhibit 6.21. Many images for conceptuals can be created using the basic drawing tools that come with presentation software packages.

When buying clip art

- Check for the variety of the images in a collection and their relevance to the material you will be presenting.
- Look for clip art you can edit. EPS files can be edited in a postscript drawing program. TIFF and Paint files are harder to edit. EPS files also retain quality when they are enlarged or reduced.
- Check for copyright restrictions. Some clip art collections have no restriction; others require you to pay licensing fees if you publicly display or distribute the clip art.
- Use CD-ROM if you have the option. CD collections are cheaper and more convenient than disks.
- Look for collections with instructions on how to ungroup, edit, and recolor the images. Some collections come with limited editing software.
- Look for collections with files in multiple formats.

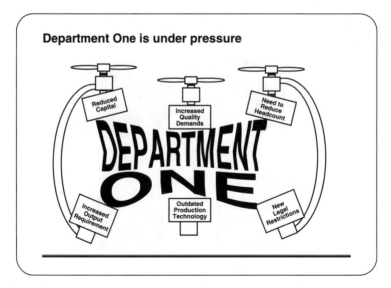

Exhibit 6.22. Drawing and presentation software provide many interesting options, such as stretching or compressing text.

Guidelines for Conceptual Visuals

- Use shapes or pictures to show relationships
- Use analogies that are meaningful to the audience
- Make sure the visual image matches your words
- Create the right image by using a drawing program and clip art

---

Charts Show Relationships among Variables

The graphic representation of data comprises the majority of visuals in most business presentations because decisions are usually based on data. Since you have a number of chart forms to choose from, the first decision you must make is which form best displays your message. Then you must ensure that the content is both compelling and correct.

Most data can be displayed in tabular form. Tables are essential when the audience needs exact numbers to compare a large number of variables. But tables with more than five columns and six rows are difficult to read on a screen and, even if your table is printed on a page, most people do not easily see relationships when confronted with columns of numbers. Tables work well as backup visuals to provide details and prove you really have done the work. They can be effective as handouts, but we suggest you think about creating stronger visual impact whenever possible (see Exhibits 6.23 and 6.24 for comparison).

The message determines the form

Line, bar, and pie charts in various forms and combinations are the most commonly used chart forms in management presentations. Scatter diagrams (or dot charts), diagrams, and maps often play important roles as well. The chart form you choose depends on the message you want to convey. Each message has key words (again, look to the verb)

Dolls are expected to produce greatest sales growth short and long term

	3 yrs	5 yrs	7 yrs	10 yrs
Dolls	17.8%	19.2	22.9	27.8
Trucks	11.3	12.0	13.7	15.9
Guns	9.2	11.6	11.7	12.0

Exhibit 6.23. Tables provide data but do not reinforce messages effectively.

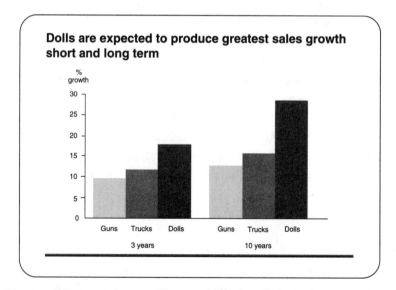

Exhibit 6.24. Although the table in Exhibit 6.23 has been simplified and given a message heading to make it readable, this column chart helps the viewer grasp the relationship of the numbers more quickly.

that indicate the relationship and suggest the most appropriate form.

Not only does each chart form have its own particular function, but each has variations that work particularly well in specific situations (see Exhibit 6.25). Some design concepts are basic to all chart forms; others are specific to a form or even a variation on that form. To avoid

Relationship	Chart form		Function
Exceeds Compares Ranks Equals Falls into Correlates with		Bar chart Column chart	Comparison or grouping of one or several items
Increases/decreases Grows Falls Fluctuates		Column chart Line chart	Change in one or several variables over time
Percentage Share		Pie chart	Relation of part to other parts or whole
Does not vary Varies with Is greatest (least) when Increase (decrease) with		Scatter diagram	Relation of two or more variables

Exhibit 6.25. Guidelines for selecting a chart

redundancy, we will review the common guidelines and then look closely at the function of each chart form, its variations, and the design guidelines specific to each variation.

Design guidelines keep the audience focused on the message

As you consider the following guidelines, remember that your goal is to keep the audience focused on the message, not on the messenger, which in this case is the visual form itself.

Convey one message per chart

Although presenters make many charts in the process of solving a problem, these working charts are not necessarily the most effective ones for conveying the message to the audience. For example, in the working stage you may have manipulated a great deal of data on one chart, from which you learned several lessons. Now you have several points to make. Beware. In your presentation, you don't want your chart to raise peripheral issues that will sidetrack the audience; you want them to focus on the point you want to make.

Let's say you charted sales, manufacturing costs, selling, general and administrative costs, operating income, and earnings before interest and taxes for the last seven years. From this you saw that SG&A costs have risen faster than manufacturing costs over the last three years — this message is important. You also want to show that manufacturing and SG&A are tracking at a consistent rate relative to sales. Abandon the complex chart you made while solving the problem, and make one clear, visually compelling chart for each of your points (see Exhibit 6.26 and 6.27). Fortunately for most of us, our desktop computers will do the charting; we only have to make the decisions, feed the correct data into the computer, and fine-tune the design.

It's permissible to have two charts together (Exhibit 6.28) only if they both support the same message. Some organizations use boxed information at the bottom of the chart to provide the message. (These may be called "tombstones," "kicker boxes," or "takeaways.") Unfortu-

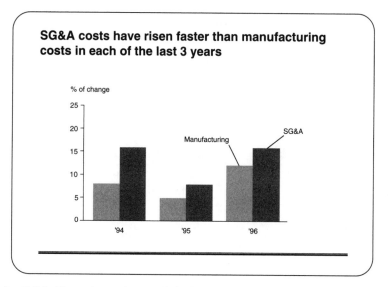

Exhibit 6.26. *This column chart and the line chart in Exhibit 6.27 both came out of one extremely complex chart.*

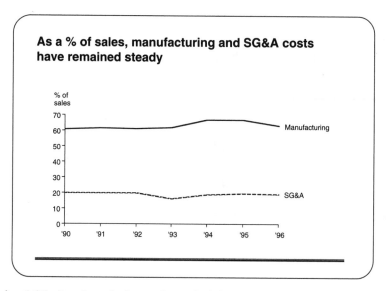

Exhibit 6.27. *Based on the lessons learned while preparing the presentation, these charts clearly illustrate the messages in their headings. Using two charts is much clearer than having the audience wander through a complex one.*

nately, these are sometimes filled in as an afterthought and therefore focus attention on what is a minor detail. If your organization requires use of these boxes, at least make sure that the words truly represent the most significant point that can be made about the chart.

Make the chart easy to read

Label variables on the chart, so the audience doesn't need to look for the key. Label all axes, unless the label is obvious. Make the most important text largest, the most important data lines or sections darkest. Clearly mark any specific goals or other important points on the chart (see Exhibit 6.29).

Convey data honestly

Always respect convention by starting a numerical axis at zero (Exhibit 6.30). Keep differences between quantities equal. Clearly indicate an

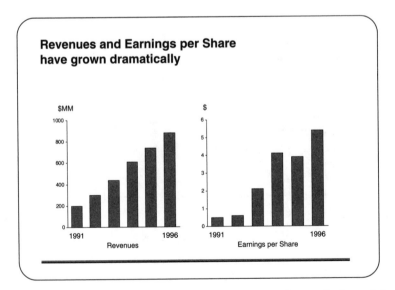

Exhibit 6.28. Two charts are acceptable on one slide when they are both needed to make the point in the heading.

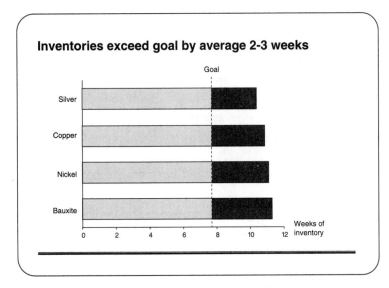

Exhibit 6.29. This chart is well labeled and easy to read.

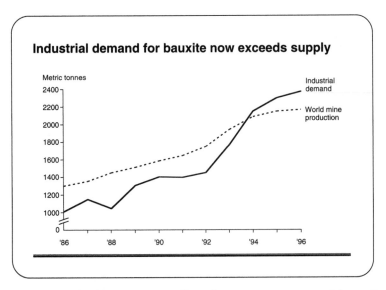

Exhibit 6.30. The break in the Y axis allows the presenter to start at 0 but still create a compact visual.

unequal or unusual break in those differences. Differentiate real from estimated data (Exhibit 6.31). If you are not emphasizing one data item in particular, order variables for easy comparison, as in Exhibit 6.32. Beware of 3D charts, which are the default in many presentation and charting programs. Not only are they difficult to read accurately (Exhibit 6.33), but they can give a deceptive appearance of weight to the section of the chart that is at the "front" (Exhibit 6.34).

Put the least varying bar of stacked bars on the bottom

In Exhibit 6.35, the dotted lines between the columns all suggest a trend upward — even though two of the variables scarcely change from one bar to the next. By moving those variables to the bottom (Exhibit 6.36), the actual trends across the chart are much easier to distinguish. With side-by-side bars, make sure one side shows a trend.

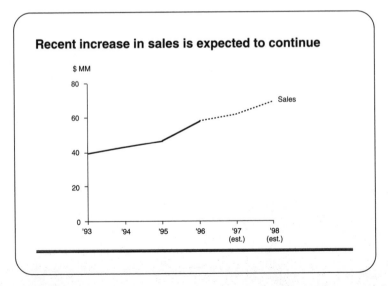

Exhibit 6.31. The dotted line on this chart reinforces the difference between real and estimated sales.

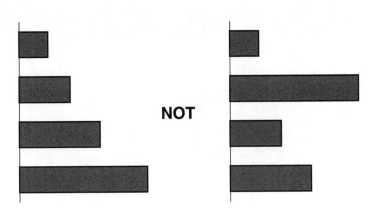

NOT

Exhibit 6.32. Order variables by size (left) to make comparison easier.

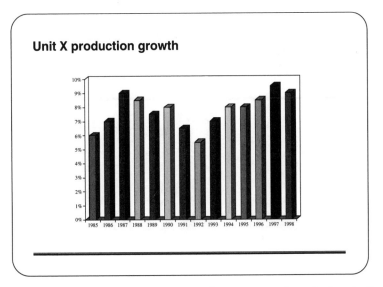

Exhibit 6.33. Three dimensional bars are confusing; it is unclear whether the front or the back of the bar should be read on the Y axis.

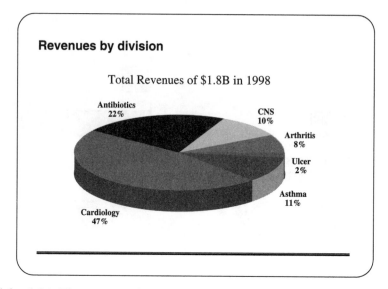

Exhibit 6.34. The sections with a third dimension appear relatively larger than they really are in relation to the sections on the upper portion of the pie.

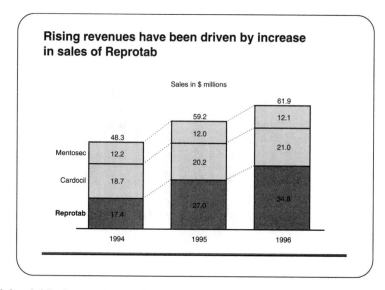

Exhibit 6.35. Because Reprotab is on the bottom, the other variables appear to change more than they really did.

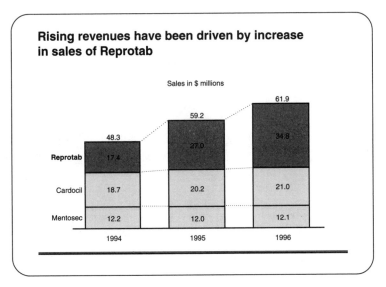

Exhibit 6.36. This chart is a more honest representation of change than is Exhibit 6.35.

Eliminate all unnecessary design details and text

You want to focus attention on the message, not the visual. You do this by keeping the chart simple and by ensuring that most of the ink on the page relates to the message. In other words, don't use a box unless it is necessary, eliminate as many grid lines, tick marks, and data points as possible, and omit extraneous headings and explanations (compare Exhibits 6.37 and 6.38).

Be selective in choice of fill patterns

Before color was common, fill patterns, like stripes, checks, and dots, were often used to distinguish one element from the next. If you are still using them, limit the number in any visual. Choose patterns that can be distinguished from each other easily and are esthetically pleasing in combination. Avoid patterns that "vibrate" (heavily geometric patterns, when viewed, can actually appear to move before your eyes, especially if you have an astigmatism — see Exhibits 6.53 and 6.54).

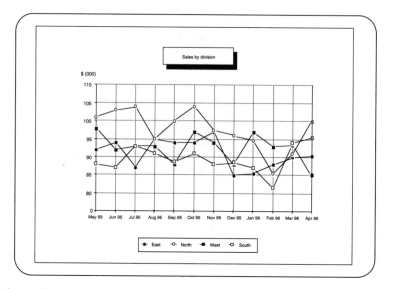

Exhibit 6.37. The heading tells the audience nothing about what to look for on this chart, the grids and boxes detract from the chart, and the key forces people to look away from the chart to figure out what is happening. Because all the data lines are the same weight and criss-cross several times, it is difficult to see the trends.

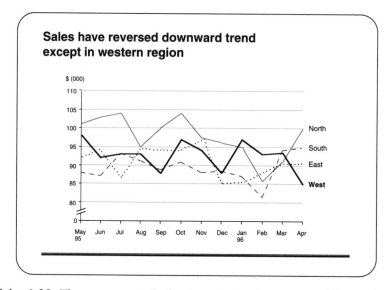

Exhibit 6.38. The message is in the heading, the trends are easy to follow, and, because there is no superfluous ink on the visual, you focus attention on the message.

Guidelines for Any Graphic Visual

- Convey only one message on each chart
- Use action headings that convey the message
- Make the chart easy to read by labeling, focusing attention, and ordering variables for easy comparison.
- Convey data honestly
- Eliminate all unnecessary ink
- Use reasonable fill patterns
- Use design devices to focus attention

Specific Forms Have Specific Purposes

The broad range of variations and combinations available on most presentation visual software makes it especially important that a presenter understand the purpose of each form and how each can be used most effectively.

Bar and column charts are most useful for comparing several variables at one time or one of several variables at discrete points in time. Although they appear to be ninety degree images of each other, and often can be used interchangeably, bar and column charts are not identical twins. Bar charts are more applicable when comparing a number of items at one time because it is easier to put long text labels on bars than on columns (see Exhibit 6.39). At the same time, because the X or horizontal axis is usually equated with time change, column charts work better when comparing variables over time (see Exhibit 6.40). Both column and bar charts permit you to look above and below a base line to separate winners from losers (see Exhibit 6.41) and to look at both a whole and its parts (see Exhibit 6.42).

A Gantt chart is a bar chart that shows a number of processes over time (see Exhibit 6.43).

Stepped bars are often used to show frequency distributions (see Exhibit 6.44).

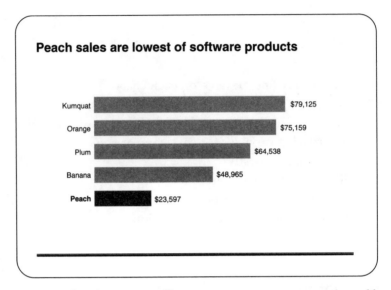

Exhibit 6.39. A bar chart is most effective in comparing one or several variables at one time.

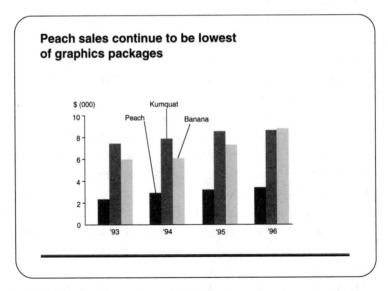

Exhibit 6.40. A column chart is more effective than a bar chart at comparing one or more variables over time. If there are more than six periods, consider using a line chart, which will look less busy.

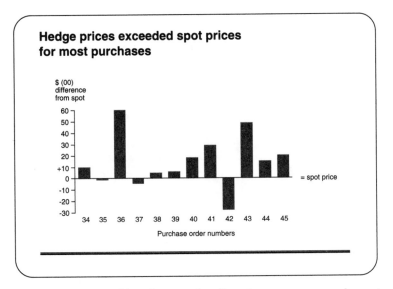

Exhibit 6.41. Column and bar charts work well in showing positive and negative numbers.

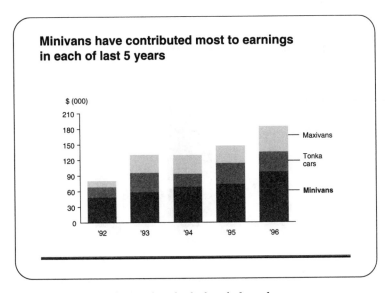

Exhibit 6.42. Divided columns show both the whole and its parts.

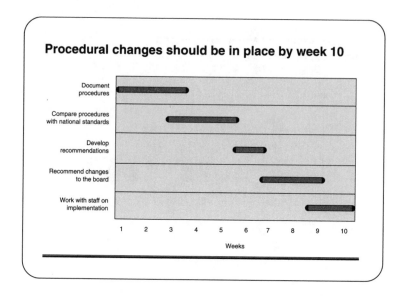

Exhibit 6.43. Gantt charts focus attention on the parts of a process.

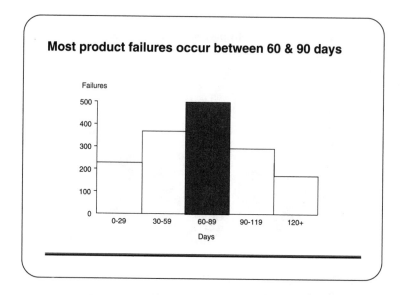

Exhibit 6.44. Step charts are column charts without spaces between the columns. They are especially useful in showing distributions of various kinds.

Waterfall charts are useful for showing all the parts of a whole (see Exhibit 6.45) and for showing cumulative changes over time (Exhibit 6.46).

Guidelines Specific to Column and Bar Charts

- Keep bars and columns wider than the spaces between them to focus attention on the message
- Label bars and columns when possible, instead of using legends and grids (see Exhibits 6.47 and 6.48)
- Group items for comparison (see Exhibits 6.47 and 6.48)

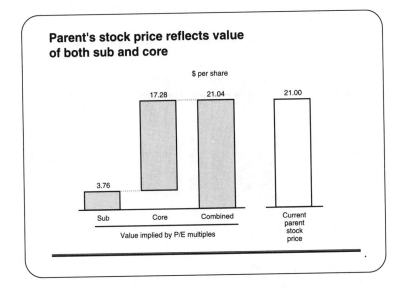

Exhibit 6.45. *So-called waterfall charts show parts in relationship to each other and to the whole.*

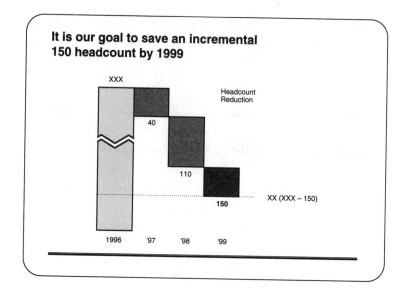

Exhibit 6.46. This waterfall chart shows cumulative changes over time.

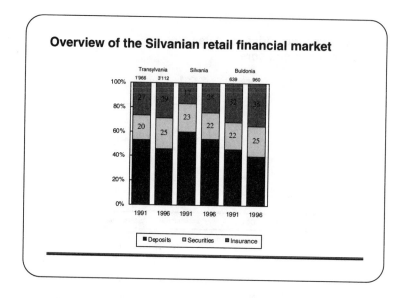

Exhibit 6.47. Using a legend makes it difficult to tell which segment is which.

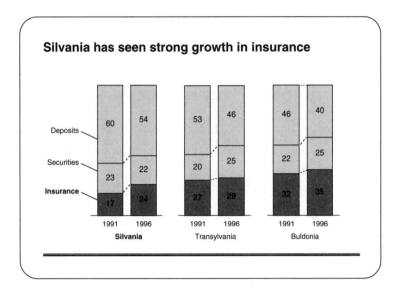

Exhibit 6.48. Labeling the segments this way makes them easy to identify. Grouping makes it easier to understand the comparison.

Line charts show changes over time of one or more variable (see Exhibit 6.38). Line charts are more effective than column charts when you have more than four or five data points and when you are more interested in showing movement than in showing quantity at discrete times. However, do not "smooth" the lines to imply multiple data points if you have only a few. You may prompt questions you are ill-prepared to answer.

Log charts allow you to see relative rather than absolute change (see Exhibit 6.49). Log charts are complex and should be used only with the relatively few audiences that understand them.

Bar charts are often seen in combination with line charts (see Exhibit 6.50). This combination can be effective in showing the relationship of two variables that require different Y-axes. These charts are difficult to read, however, because the line cannot be anchored to an axis. Label the line on the chart and provide careful explanation in the presentation itself.

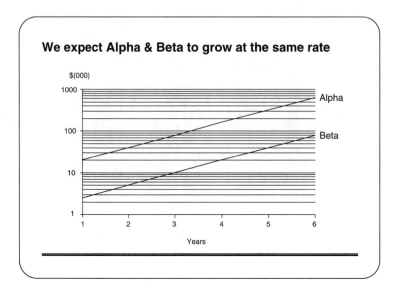

Exhibit 6.49. *Log charts are useful in showing relationships of variables of vastly different size and in showing relative rather than absolute change. Since most people assume that a chart is arithmetic, log charts require careful explanation.*

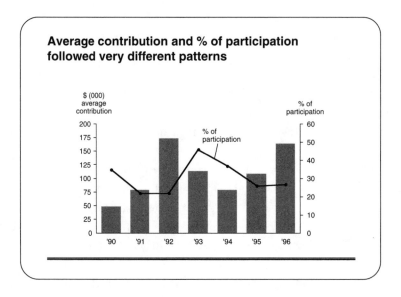

Exhibit 6.50. *Combination charts require careful explanation to ensure that the audience quickly sees which variable belongs with which axis.*

Guidelines Specific to Line Charts

- Reserve the heaviest line for the most important variable or component
- Use a variety of broken lines for other variables
- Anchor the data lines to the left axis
- Label the line on any combination line and bar chart

Pie charts show the relationship of one or more parts to each other and to the whole. They are effective in showing relative change of a whole as well as of the parts (see Exhibit 6.51) and, in combination with a bar chart, two levels of component parts (see Exhibit 6.52). However, relative differences are harder to distinguish in neighboring pie charts than in a bar chart - if exact comparisons are important, either add labels to the pies, or choose a different chart format.

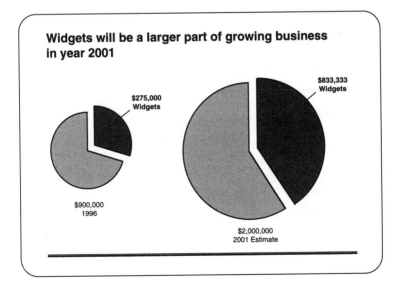

Widgets will be a larger part of growing business in year 2001

$275,000
Widgets

$833,333
Widgets

$900,000
1996

$2,000,000
2001 Estimate

Exhibit 6.51. A pair of pie charts can serve the same purpose as a pair of divided bar charts.

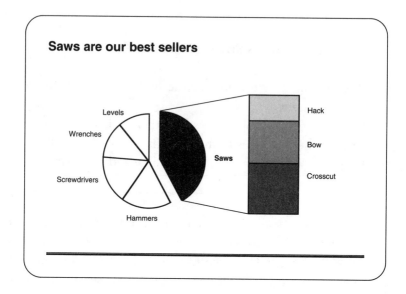

Exhibit 6.52. The bar lets you show the components of part of the whole.

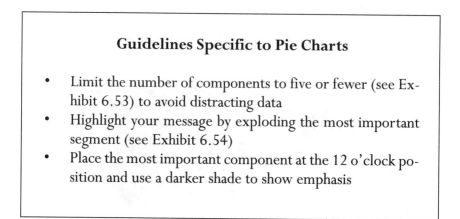

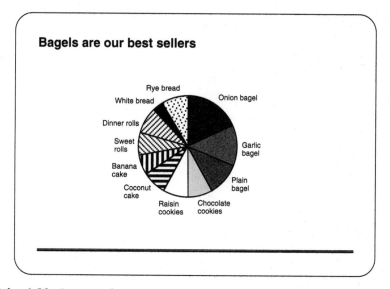

Exhibit 6.53. Busyness obscures the main message. Avoid vibrating patterns.

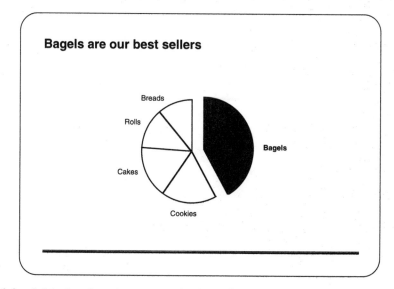

Exhibit 6.54. Based on the message, this simplified visual tells it all.

Scatter charts show the correlation or lack of correlation between two variables (see Exhibit 6.55). Resist the temptation to draw the line regardless of whether there is a true pattern.

Bubble charts are complex scatter charts in which a third variable - size - is indicated (see Exhibit 6.56). Like log charts and column charts that include a dimension of size, the bubble chart is rich in information but must be carefully explained.

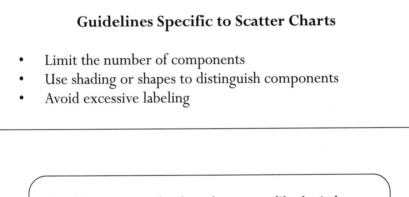

Guidelines Specific to Scatter Charts

- Limit the number of components
- Use shading or shapes to distinguish components
- Avoid excessive labeling

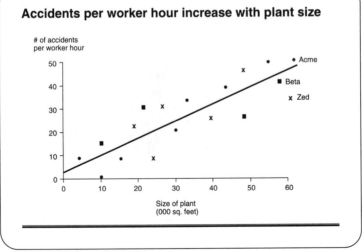

Exhibit 6.55. The different symbols for data points on this chart make it easy to distinguish the components.

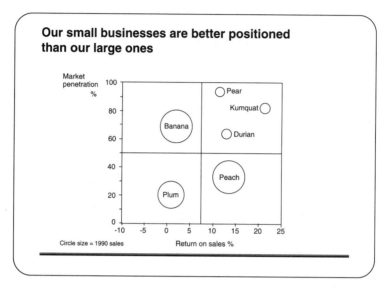

Exhibit 6.56. The third dimension on the bubble chart indicates the relative size of the variables.

Diagrams may be used to show the relationship among the parts of a process or a structure, such as an organization chart (see Exhibit 6.57).

Maps show relationships among geographic areas and distances. They are often used to show relative density of one or several variables (see Exhibit 6.58).

Some Cautionary Thoughts About Presenting Data Graphically

Use presentation visual software with a dose of common sense

While the computer encourages use of exciting graphics, it also allows us to turn something simple into something complex with little effort. Do not let the artistic possibilities interfere with the message. Does the three dimensional aspect of a chart help or confuse the audience? Do lines of little human bodies (often cut in half) really aid the story? Use good judgment. "Cutesy" doesn't communicate.

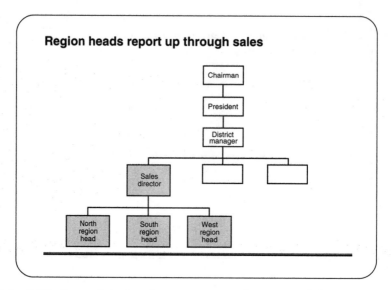

Exhibit 6.57. Size and shading focus attention on the message of this organization chart.

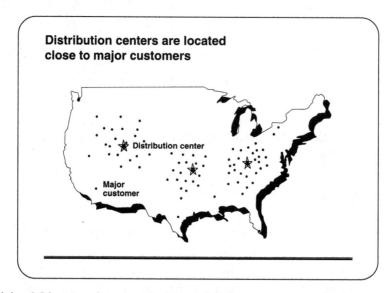

Exhibit 6.58. Maps show spatial relations and density.

Some software programs do not follow the guidelines that make visuals easy to read and easy to understand

Labels are often vertical rather than horizontal; all text and numbers are the same size; headings may not be where you want them; charts may be boxed. If you have time, tinkering with the default mode to improve a visual will justify the effort.

Break any design rules to improve understanding and visual appeal

All the guidelines we have discussed are based on how people think and how they absorb information. A critical eye will tell you when to break the rules.

Proofread everything

... especially the headlines, where typos are often overlooked.

Using Color Purposefully

Color is increasingly available as an option. A degree of caution is advisable, however. Color attracts attention to elements on a page or slide. When you use color simply for the sake of using color, you may draw attention away from the points you want to emphasize. Color can also reduce legibility if used wrongly - brightly colored text, in particular, is very offputting, and greatly reduces reader comprehension. On the other hand, using a light color tint *behind* black text not only is easy to read, but also attracts the reader's eye. The accompanying diskette includes examples of effective and ineffective use of color.

Use color only when it contributes to your message

Reinforcing your message means using brighter colors for the items you want to emphasize, more muted colors, or shades of gray for those you want to de-emphasize.

Beware of conflicts

Some colors, like red and green, "vibrate" when placed next to each other and are difficult for color-blind people to distinguish. A safe solution is to use colors from "triad" groups equally spaced around the color wheel; in other words, use blue with red and yellow, or purple with orange and green.

Use color consistently

If you have a color palette to use, use it; otherwise, pick colors for elements before you begin, then stick with those colors. Using color consistently helps your audience follow the points you want to make and recognize elements.

Keep it simple

Stick to a maximum of four colors on a page or slide — use more and you risk confusing the audience as well as running into color clashes.

Use color combinations that are easy to read and do not appear to "lie"

Some colors stand out more against one color than against another, suggesting greater importance (yellow on blue as compared with yellow on orange). Blue details are often hard to see against a dark background. Be aware that colors look different on different output media; for example, colors that look fine on paper may wash out on an overhead transparency. Always check projection visuals on a screen before using them. And colors look different on the computer screen than when printed out; check your pages in advance, before you send books to the binder. If your screen is color and your printer is black and white, variables may be indistinguishable on paper.

Be aware of color associations

You may think that shading a recommendation in red will make it stand out; however, your audience may read the red shading as a danger warning. Some people can't take seriously anything colored in pink. The colors you use may affect the way your presentation is received; red, orange, and yellow are "warm" colors, suggesting excitement and conviction; blue, green, and purple are "cool" colors, and suggest calmness and objectivity. If your program calls a certain palette the "Casino" color scheme, reflect on whether your serious-minded audience will accept it. Be sensitive to regional differences in how we perceive color — purple means radical in New England, but royal in the United Kingdom. Match colors with the variables, if they are applicable. For example, in showing "Refrigerator sales are higher than oven sales," refrigerators should be blue, ovens red. We saw a major disconnection in a chart where IBM (Big Blue) was represented by a red column, Apple Computer by a blue one.

Break any of the rules we've quoted if the results don't look "right"

With color, esthetics are extremely important. Sometimes you can follow all the rules and the outcome is just ugly. Look at pages and slides carefully — revise when necessary. Software packages are available to help you develop effective, coordinated color schemes, based on your choice of medium and background color. The key is to always remember that the technology is there to guide you, not to take over. If your gut feeling is that the computer's suggested color palette misses the mark, then go back to the drawing board.

Now that you understand how to design effective visuals, you are ready to consider the demands of each medium in order to ensure that your visuals truly work for you.

Producing Professional-Looking Visuals

Because each medium has its unique size, shape, and purpose, each has specific requirements.

Making Overheads

How many times, sitting in the audience, have you squinted in a vain attempt to read an overhead, or simply given up in disgust and tuned out? Because overheads can be easily copied from printed material, some presenters cut corners by reproducing graphics or text from written reports or, worse yet, from computer runs. It doesn't work, as anyone who has ever attended such a presentation can testify. Size of type, placement on the page, and color are all important in making overheads.

Make text large enough to read

Although there are mathematical equations that you can use to determine appropriate letter size, the simplest way to check an overhead is to stand ten feet away from it. If you can read it with the naked eye, your viewers will be able to read it when it is projected.

Use clear or very lightly tinted acetates and dark lettering for management presentations

Avoid brightly colored acetates. They add nothing to understanding and are, especially when combined with dark lettering, harder to read than clear acetates. It is true that light lettering on a dark background — for instance yellow on blue — is easier to read than black type on a clear transparency. However, making light on dark visuals requires special equipment and you cannot use these visuals interactively (write on them, underline, point to particular points) during the presentation. Therefore, we find them appropriate for very large groups, but not for most management presentations.

Work on the horizontal

Although the glass on an overhead projector appears to be square, frames are clearly rectangular. Since the arm of the overhead projector often blocks the bottom of the screen, it is difficult, if not impossible, for people seated directly in line with the projector to see the bottom of a vertically oriented visual. In planning the visual, work within a 7-1/2 by 9-1/2 inch space centered on an 8-1/2 by 11-inch page. Anything outside these borders will not be clearly visible on the screen, and will not show at all if you use frames.

Use frames

Arguably, cardboard frames can be a bother. They take up space in your suitcase and someone has to tape the acetates into them. But the benefits far outweigh the cost and the time. Not only do frames block out extraneous light, but they keep acetates from sticking together, from sliding around on the projector, or from slithering away and falling on the floor. Frames are also a perfect, inconspicuous place to write your notes. We often use removable white adhesive tape to write notes on so we can re-use the frames.

Guidelines for Making Overheads

- Use type large enough to be read by the person farthest from the screen
- Use clear or lightly tinted transparencies
- Work within a horizontal 7-1/2 x 9-1/2-inch space
- Secure transparencies to cardboard frames

Making Slides

In some organizations, and for some decision makers, slides are required. In these instances, you must be especially careful to prepare your material so you have visual support (or blackout slides) at all times, since you cannot turn the projector on and off as easily as you can an overhead projector. When you work with slides, allow plenty of time for artistic and mechanical failures — they are certain to occur. Block out the entire day before a presentation in case emergency revisions are needed. (You should schedule a dry-run that day as well.) When you are designing a slide, work in an area with the 2-to-3 ratio of a slide (6 x 9 inches, for example) to be sure the proportions of the visual fit the medium. In general, follow the same guidelines that apply for making overheads.

Guidelines for Making Slides

- Design enough slides for continuous viewing or create blackout slides.
- Allow sufficient production time
- Design all visuals based on the 2-to-3 ratio of a slide
- Follow the guidelines for making overheads

Making Flipcharts

Flipcharts come in a range of sizes, from small table-top versions to large 30 x 40-inch charts. The primary use of large flipcharts today is in creating visuals during a presentation and as a vehicle for keeping track of ideas generated during a meeting. Pre-prepared flipcharts are sometimes used in training programs. Salespeople and presenters who work with small groups seated around a table often find table-top flipcharts convenient.

If you need to create flipcharts before a presentation, keep in mind the size and shape of the chart and draw your visual to match that shape. The letters must be large enough and dark enough for every member of the audience to see. (For large flipcharts, usually only the darkest colors and the widest felt-tip pens will work.) Test for readability by setting up your chart in a room approximately the size and shape of the one you'll be using. By sitting in the most distant spot where someone might sit during the presentation, you can see for yourself whether every word of text and every line is readable. As a rule of thumb, letters must be 1-1/2 inches high to be visible twenty-five feet away.

As you create the visuals for a flipchart presentation, leave several blank pages between visuals. That way, if you make a mistake, you can draw another without worrying about re-ordering the pages. Just before you give the presentation, remove all but one blank sheet between each of the visuals you've prepared. The blank page assures that the colors from the charts underneath won't show through, allows you to show a blank page when you are speaking about something that has no appropriate visual support, and gives you a page to write on during the presentation.

Guidelines for Making Flipcharts

- Choose a chart size that is appropriate for the size of the audience
- Draw your art to fit the vertical shape of the chart
- Make lettering dark enough and large enough to be read by everyone in the audience
- In the preparation stage, leave several blank pages between each chart to allow for corrections or additions
- Before the presentation, remove all but one blank page before each visual

Making Handouts and Books

Executives sometimes demand advance copies of a presentation. Ostensibly, they want to read them in order to leverage valuable time in the meeting itself; but we suspect that sometimes their real agenda is to increase their ability to control the presentation, to find the messages (in case the presenter is trying to save a zinger for last), and to take notes. The problem is simple. If you deliver copies in advance, some recipients will read them, some will not, and you'll have a hard time keeping everyone's interest during the main event. When the audience does not speak the same language as you do, however, advance copies can be extremely helpful. In order to create effective handouts for use during the presentation, you need to follow some basic rules.

Use large type; limit the contents of each page

Just because you are using handouts in place of overheads, don't assume you can use standard typewriter face or fill the page with text. You still want your audience to focus on you and your message — that means using a large, readable typeface. Furthermore, you need to keep it simple. If you include more than one message per page, the decision maker is likely to be looking at one piece of data when you are talking about another.

Use graphic devices to keep the audience focused

Use headings, just as you do with any other medium. Provide tables as back-up pages to charts when possible. If you find it necessary to use pages that are loaded with more data than you wish (because that is the custom in your organization), highlight important data with shading or with color.

Use summary pages as road maps

Text pages serve as road maps. Be careful not to provide so much information that people stop listening to you in order to read.

Consider adding an executive summary

If the handout presentation is part of a standard monthly or quarterly review in which an established format is required, consider writing an executive summary that highlights the main messages. You may also be able to use headings to focus attention on those messages.

Pages for a written presentation book are usually horizontal. If you have vertical elements (an RFP or letter, for example) place them in the appendix. Appendices and technical backup sections are essential in providing data for audiences who need all the numbers, or for books meant to be read later.

**Guidelines for Making Handouts
and Presentation Books**

- Choose large type; limit the contents of each page
- Use headings and summary pages to make the storyline clear
- Include an executive summary to focus data-heavy presentations
- Use appendices liberally

Working with Computer Presentation Software

Before you get into heavy-duty multimedia like video, consider that even fairly basic slide-show type presentation programs offer some special effects. The rule here, as with true multimedia, is don't distract. It may be tempting to go for a presentation where all your slides arrive with a different transition effect; zooming in from the side, appearing as venetian blinds or checkerboards, then fading out to be followed by others appearing from the center of the screen. The fact is, your audience will spend so much time wondering how the next slide is going to arrive, they won't absorb a word you say. Go for one fairly unobtrusive effect, then use it consistently. This doesn't mean you can't vary your effects at all; it's a good idea to use a different effect to signal the start of a new topic. Or try this for a real eye opener: after all your smooth effects, let one important slide pop onto the screen with no transition effect at all. The contrast will really make it stand out.

Another very common way to apply slide effects is to bullet points on text slides. Like slides, these can be made to appear from all angles, and in all ways — even with sound effects. Don't be tempted. It certainly can be a good idea to have bullet points appear gradually — it stops the audience from reading through the entire slide while you are discussing just one point — but again, if you are determined to use an effect, choose one and use it throughout. A wipe from left can be quite effective, as it makes the text appear in a way which mimics actually writing on the screen.

Graying out bullet points is often another useful option. As you talk through each point, a click on the mouse or remote brings up the next bullet, and all your previous bullets are grayed. This helps the audience concentrate on the particular point you are discussing.

A number of presentation programs now offer the option of adding basic animation to charts — for example, making bars in a bar chart appear on screen as you discuss each data point in turn. This can be an effective way of keeping the audience's attention, as long as you use it only when it is really appropriate. If your program doesn't have this feature, you can still add movement to charts. Copy and paste the same chart into several consecutive slides, then edit each chart in turn, adding another bar or line each time. When you give the presentation, the new bars or lines seem to pop up one after the other on a single chart. Adding simple transition effects can complete the illusion — a wipe bottom-to-top can make a column appear to "grow" from the bottom of a chart.

As for true multimedia — well, if you have used the model in Chapter 5 and decided that you really should be using it, then just make sure you do it properly, or it would be better not to have used it at all. Use video with care — if you insist on accompanying a slide on a new product launch with a video of the space shuttle taking off, then don't be too surprised if your audience doesn't remember much about the product itself when you're done. Audio should be checked thoroughly for volume — one item to add to your equipment setup checklist — you don't want to deafen your audience. And make sure music clips aren't too long, or people will quickly lose interest. Above all, rehearse, rehearse, rehearse, and make sure you do it with the equipment you'll be using for the presentation, or else you're asking for trouble.

Even the best visuals will fail to persuade if used clumsily. See Chapter 8 for a discussion of how best to use each medium.

SUMMARY
Visual support helps people remember your message.
- Design visuals that add value to your presentation
  - Keep visuals simple
  - Make one point per visual
- Use the most appropriate form
  - Text visuals preview and summarize and provide transitions
  - Conceptual visuals use images to reinforce a point or add visual interest
  - Charts show relationships among data
- Follow the guidelines to keep the audience focusing on the message, not the design features of your visuals

7

Setting
the Stage

With all the effort you've put into preparing the presentation, you may be tempted to let someone else take care of the staging. Although a competent aide can help with some of the details, the presenter has ultimate responsibility for

- Briefing the audience
- Preparing the handouts
- Making room arrangements
- Controlling administrivia

Briefing the Audience

Many presentations take place within the context of a meeting. As the presenter, you may be responsible for, or participate in, selecting the people who attend. The quality of the discussion during the presentation depends in large part on how carefully you select, notify, and brief those who attend.

Checking the List of Participants

Before you developed the presentation, you made a list of people who should attend. Now is the time to check that list to ensure that no one important has been omitted and that only those who have a stake in the outcome remain on the list. In too many organizations, the invitation list for a presentation simply duplicates the general distribution list for company memoranda. The danger in this lack of selectivity is that some people attend merely because they don't want to miss out on something. Then they disrupt the presentation with irrelevant questions or self-serving statements. If indiscriminate invitations are the norm in your company and you want to cut back the list to a sensible level, make sure you talk to those you intend to exclude well in advance of the presentation. If you do, you'll find many who will be quite satisfied with a phone call or memo to keep them informed.

Notifying Participants

When possible, the presentation notification should come from the most senior person in the organization who will attend the meeting. As the coordinator, you'll probably have better luck if you draft the announcement for the senior person's signature. That notification should be in writing (in internal communiqués, e-mail is the usual medium these days) and should clearly state the purpose of the presentation. If you can slip in something to get people's attention and generate a bit of excitement for the topic, so much the better. Naturally, participants should be notified well in advance. If available, using a calendar software program to select the time most people can come and to create entries on their calendars is quite compelling. If most of those invited do not know you personally, a comment noting your expertise on the presentation topic may be included. A brief statement like the one below is sufficient.

To: Mike Wylie
From: Jill Howard
Re: October 25th presentation detailing recommendation
          for materials flow changes

On October 25th, Forrest Ross will make a 45-minute presentation to all senior officers detailing the recommendation of our internal consultants that we alter the materials flow in our small motor plant to reduce bottlenecks. Mr. Ross, who has been with Gotham Motors for 15 years, spent six months studying the program at the Iliad Motor's San Antonio plant before heading the consulting team for this project.

Alerting Participants to Advance Work

Although conscientious managers prepare for any meeting they attend, as the presenter, it's your responsibility to tell participants how much advance work you expect them to do. The level of preparation depends on their backgrounds, the norms of the organization, the purpose of the presentation, and the complexity of the subject.

Consider briefing all those who have not participated in earlier discussions of the topic, either by conferring with them individually or by sending them notes of the discussions. These preliminaries ensure that you won't have to explain the basics during the presentation itself.

When substantial advance work is the norm, written evaluation of the alternatives is often distributed before problem-solving meetings. The presentation itself is then used to fill in details and answer questions. If the subject is very complex and those attending have technical expertise, you may speed up the actual presentation by distributing statistical data in advance.

Preparing Handouts

We discussed handouts for use in a presentation in Chapter 6. Take-away handouts present different problems. Take-away handouts are meant as a review, and thus should remind the reader of the major points in your presentation and their significance. You may be tempted to make paper copies of your overhead transparencies (frequently, after a speech or an external presentation, someone may ask you for copies of your visuals), but keep in mind that your visuals didn't stand alone; you elaborated on their meaning as you spoke. The twofold job of visuals that also serve as handouts reminds us of a comment about an amphibious automobile: "In trying to do two things, it does neither very well."You may want to repeat words from a visual as a reminder, but the text must be expanded. (Exhibits 7.1a and 7.1b show what a text overhead looks like after it has been converted into a handout.) Before you transform charts and graphs into handouts, annotate them to show how they illustrate your points. (Exhibits 7.2a and 7.2b demonstrate the difference between a graphic overhead and a handout.)

If you are going to provide take-away handouts, distribute them after the presentation. You will want to announce before the presentation begins, however, that you will provide handouts at the end. This reassurance may allow compulsive note takers to concentrate on your ideas rather than on writing down every word.

Making Room Arrangements

Making room arrangements involves more than finding an empty room. As you plan the presentation, arrange for an appropriate room, check the position of the audiovisual equipment, determine the best lighting configuration, and decide on a seating layout. Always get into the room well in advance of the presentation and check things for yourself. Physically working all the elements will have the dividend of increasing your confidence.

You've seen it happen. The presenter cheerfully sets up the computer to give a presentation ...and the cord doesn't reach ... and the battery is dead. Bulbs blow on the overhead projector. There aren't enough seats for people and some have to lean against the walls (or there are way too many seats and the people who actually came to the meeting feel they are suckers for attending). Careful attention to detail can mean the difference between a well-received presentation and a disaster.

The Right Room

The size of your meeting room has a psychological as well as a physical impact on the audience. Although people will crowd into a room to hear a celebrity, a group of top executives who have to sit elbow-to-

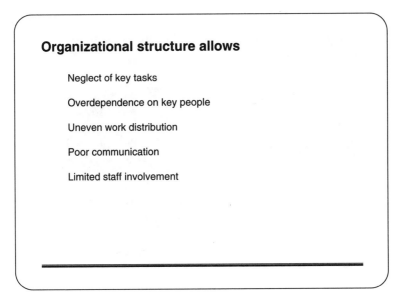

Exhibit 7.1a. A text visual serves as a guide to the direction the spoken message is taking.

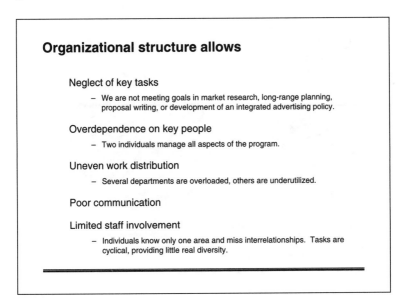

Exhibit 7.1b. A handout must provide enough information to stand alone after the presentation is over.

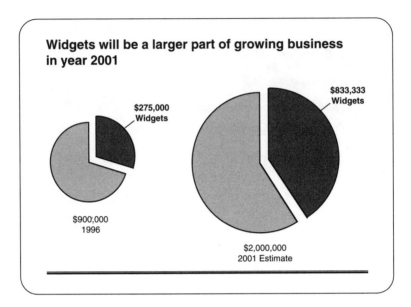

Exhibit 7.2a. An effective presentation graphic must be simple.

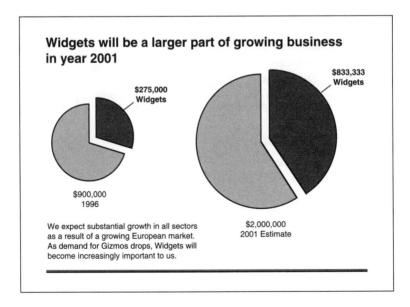

Exhibit 7.2b. A handout must be expanded to explain the visual image.

elbow in an overheated conference room and put up with a presenter who can't find a spot for the overhead will feel insulted and will probably focus their irritation on the presenter. For management presentations, the room should be large enough to accommodate everyone comfortably, but small enough to provide a sense of community. If a room of appropriate size is not available, choose a room that is slightly too small rather than too large. Six people meeting at one end of a cavernous hall are likely to feel uneasy, like members of a primitive tribe huddling around a campfire.

Pay attention to noise level as well. What other activities are scheduled for nearby rooms? If something truly disruptive is going on nearby (one presenter had to confront the sound of the country and western soundtrack of a videotape seeping under the door), you'll need to politely negotiate with the offenders to moderate the sound. Always close the door when you're presenting. Don't wait until a noisy personal conversation in the hall outside steals everyone's attention.

Location of Visual Aid Equipment

In some rooms, the screens are permanently installed and therefore dictate the seating arrangement. In other rooms, think about the location of your visual aid equipment before you settle on a seating arrangement. Ideally, if you are using overheads or slides, place the screen off center and angled slightly in relation to the audience. (Exhibits 7.3 through 7.5 show the placement of screens and equipment for various seating arrangements.) With the screen off center, you can stand in front of the audience without blocking anyone's view. If possible, position the screen so it is slightly above the level of people's heads (you need to be able to point to the messages on the screen, so test the height with that in mind) and slant it toward the audience to create a perpendicular between the screen's plane and the axis of the projector beam. This perpendicular keeps the image a true square or a rectangle. (Many screens can be adjusted by moving the loop that hooks the screen to the upright that holds it.)

Seating Arrangements

The most critical factor in arranging seating is the size of the audience. Within the limitations of room size, door and window locations, and permanently installed screens, choose the seating arrangement that puts the fewest barriers between you and the audience, permits the easiest exchange of information, and allows everyone to see you and the visual aids.

The most effective seating arrangement for a presentation that leads to a problem-solving session is around a conference table (see Exhibit 7.3). This set-up suggests to participants that "We're all in this together." It works, however, only when no one has to turn around to see the visuals and when everyone has a seat at the table. If some participants have to sit in a row against the wall, they will feel distinctly second class.

A U-shaped arrangement (see Exhibit 7.4) accommodates more people and facilitates discussion, as long as all the participants can see each other easily. A U-shape also permits the speaker to move in among

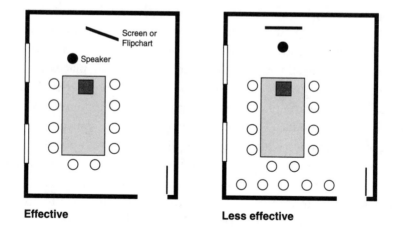

Exhibit 7.3. Conference table seating arrangements. A conference table provides the most appropriate setting for a presentation that will include discussion. In the arrangement on the right, the speaker is blocking the screen, and those not seated at the table are excluded.

participants, increasing interaction.

An auditorium or classroom arrangement (see Exhibit 7.5) is often used for a large audience. This arrangement discourages participation and note-taking and conveys the message, "I'll do the talking; you listen." The audiences for most management presentations are so small that this configuration is not appropriate, but if you must present in a large auditorium, always try to unify the group by having people move forward. If the chairs aren't fixed, eliminate the center aisle, which has a divisive effect.

Regardless of what seating arrangement you finally choose, use these rules of thumb:

- Make sure chairs are comfortable enough for people to sit without squirming, but not so comfortable that they encourage napping. Chairs with arms and firm cushions and backs are preferable.
- Arrange seating so the audience does not face the windows. Not only is the scene outside distracting, but people will have to squint to see the visuals.

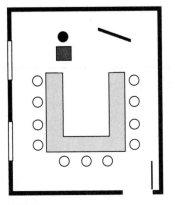

Effective

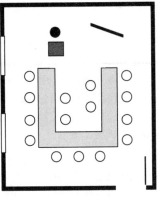

Less effective

Exhibit 7.4. U-shaped seating arrangements. A U-shaped arrangement accommodates more people than a conference table; however, participants should never be seated in the center of a U-shaped arrangement where they cannot see others without turning.

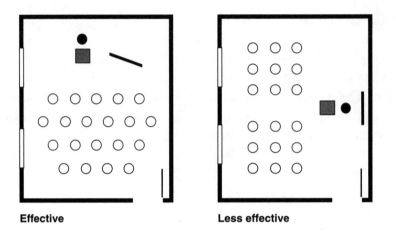

Effective   **Less effective**

*Exhibit 7.5. Auditorium-style seating arrangements. In the "classroom"
arrangement on the left, with staggered seating, every participant has a clear line of
vision. On the right, any exit or entry will create a distraction; the center aisle
creates two groups; and the presenter blocks the participants' view of the screen.*

- Arrange seating so the door is to the rear or the side of the group.
  Once in a while, a participant will have to leave before you're finished. No one can exit gracefully or unobtrusively by walking in
  front of you.
- Monitor attendance so that you have the right size room and the
  right number of chairs for the people you expect. It's better to
  start out with fewer chairs than the number of people expected,
  and then add them as needed.

Lighting

People need light to see you, their notes, the visuals, and each other.
The general light in the room is called ambient light. If there is too
much, people will be uncomfortable, especially if there is glare from
floor to ceiling windows. Too little, and their attention will drift. During 35 mm slide presentations, people sometimes even fell asleep in
the darkened rooms. You're in luck if the room you're presenting in has
separate controls for each section of lighting. If you're using an over-

head projector, dim the row of lights nearest to the screen. Without light reflecting on the screen, the colors will be more vivid and the people in the room will still have plenty of light to take notes. If there is a great deal of outside glare, use the shades or blinds to control it. This is especially important if multimedia is part of your presentation. Sometimes fixed screens are set so they come down in front of windows. On a dull day, this may work. With bright sunlight, you're better off showing your visuals on the wall, providing it's a light colored wall.

Climate Control

Uncomfortable people are inattentive people. Always visually check with the audience for signs of discomfort (people putting their sweaters on, shifting in their seats, clutching their arms). As the presenter, you will be moving around and may be less attentive to physical discomfort because of your adrenalin rush. If you find you usually can't judge uncomfortable temperatures for yourself, have a team member monitor it as well. Thermostats are usually set at 68 degrees. This temperature may be fine if the presentation is relatively short, or people are packed relatively close together, but 70 to 72 degrees is more reasonable for people who must sit for any length of time. Check the thermostat to see whether it can be manually operated (most cannot). Always get the name of the person who can help you adjust the heat or air-conditioning. If something goes seriously wrong, take a short break while it's fixed.

Controlling Administrivia

Presentation pros learn, through years of experience, that attention to apparently minor details is crucial. Many managers develop their own checklists for such logistical elements as the location of the meeting, the person responsible for equipment, and arrangements for messages and refreshments. They also keep a list of the supplies they know they'll need. These needs will vary from presenter to presenter and from presentation to presentation, but keeping track of details with checklists will save you from last-minute phone calls and frantic scrambling. If you use the checklists at the end of this chapter as models and add to them each time you review a presentation, you will ultimately develop lists that cover any contingency you're likely to encounter. In addition, you may want to put together a traveling kit of supplies you use most frequently — ours includes tape, tacks, tent cards, markers for flipcharts, markers for overheads, spare transparencies, a pointer, and extra pens and pencils.

For the typical management presentation, you won't need to allow time for a break, although you will want to see that water is available. For a small group, a water pitcher and glasses should be on the table in front of the participants; for a large group, water should be available at the rear of the room. Any meeting that lasts more than an hour and a half demands a break. As more than one experienced presentation-goer has remarked, "The mind absorbs no more than the seat will bear." Serving coffee or caffeinated drinks as well as refreshments with sugar during the break will help keep your audience alert.

To avoid unnecessary interruption, no message short of an emergency should be delivered in the meeting room; arrange for other messages to be left at a convenient nearby location, or tacked to a bulletin board outside the room.

Preparing for a Computer Presentation

If you are going to be making your presentation from a computer, you have a new range of possibilities to consider. While design of a computer presentation is the same regardless of the size room you will be presenting in, you will have to think carefully about the next steps — such as choosing what type of output equipment to use and keeping the possibility of slip-ups (computer and human) to an absolute minimum.

Choosing Computer Output Hardware

When it comes to making a computer-based presentation, the presenter has the greatest range of possibilities, in terms of media and audience size. The fact is, when linked up to the right kind of output hardware, a computer can provide effective communication from a one-on-one setting right up to an auditorium. The first steps are the same, through structuring the presentation to preparing the "slides;" the difference is when it comes to weighing the quality of the various forms of output hardware against their cost — which can be quite considerable.

There are four levels of computer-based presentation hardware (in ascending order of complexity and expense).

NTSC converters

These are boxes which take the computer's output and convert it into a form which can be displayed on a standard television monitor. A computer can't be plugged directly into a TV because computer and TV monitors have a different number of lines per screen and scan the lines in a different pattern. NTSC converters fix those problems, but they come with problems of their own. One is the lack of consistency between different converters and different TVs. This has led to the joke that the NTSC acronym may stand for "Never Twice the Same Color." Another problem is "overscanning," where the converted output from the computer is actually slightly larger than the TV's display area, and the edge of the computer image gets lost. And once you've dealt with these problems, you still have to contend with the fact that even a large TV monitor will only be useful for presenting to a very small group. Still, NTSC converters are cheap, extremely portable (as long as you don't have to haul the TV), and a handy way of presenting if you can live with the drawbacks. They also give you the option of copying your presentation directly to videotape, so at the end of the day you can leave a real-time playback of your slides for your audience.

LCD panels

These are very popular for computer presentations. They fit on top of a transmissive (bottom lit) overhead projector and are connected to your laptop or computer. The high-end models offer fine color resolution, even brightness, portability, and a moderate price tag. With a good, bright projector (at least 4000 lumens) they are capable of projecting clear, impressive images to small to medium-sized groups. The catch is that unless you bring your own projector and laptop, you can't guarantee what you'll end up with — in which case you may end up with a fair amount of trial and error to get things looking right. And if you bring your own projector, you not only have the extra weight, but also the extra expense, so you're up in the region of the all-in-one projector units — the next option up the ladder.

Projectors

Integrated projectors plug directly into the computer, as do LCD panels, but projectors provide the light source as well. This provides added convenience, an assurance that your output quality will be consistent, and the option of working with larger groups, since projectors are generally brighter than the LCD panel/OHP combination, and can be used in quite large rooms, even with ambient lighting. There are a few catches: increased weight to carry and a heftier price tag; lighter portable units are available, but you'll pay even more for these.

Built-in projection systems

Top of the line, of course, is the kind of system that many large companies now own: a built-in Barco type projection system in a dedicated video viewing suite. Here you have computer output which finally matches the brightness and clarity of a computer monitor, along with the optimum in audio reproduction. While this option offers the ideal situation in terms of output consistency and quality, it is obviously unworkable for anyone who presents on the road.

The one thing that is certain with all of these forms of output is that they will be constantly getting cheaper, better, and more compact. So even if costs prohibit you from using some of the higher end options at present, you may be able to upgrade your presentation quality before too long.

Preventative Medicine for Computer Presentations

Every presenter knows that presentations tend to be prone to Murphy's Law — but not all are aware that the effects of this law appear to grow logarithmically when you start adding electronic items to your armory of presentation tools. Every new electronic gadget seems to increase the possibility of disaster tenfold, so you should take every precaution you can when preparing to make a computer presentation.

First of all, use your own computer and output hardware whenever possible. If you're renting, bite the bullet and rent for an extra day — the extra cost will be more than paid off by the chance to really become familiar with the equipment. And be sure to thoroughly try out the remote that comes with the projector. In addition to learning about some handy features you could use, you could save yourself the embarrassment of finding out mid-presentation that your infrared connection only works when you stand smack in front of the screen.

Whatever computer you're using, do your best to keep it to a bare-bones system. This will speed up software performance and cut down on the likelihood of crashes or freezes or other embarrassing interruptions. This is one of the few areas where the risks are higher when you're using your own equipment — all those screen savers, alarms, and other software "system enhancements" you couldn't resist having on your system can really get in the way of a presentation. We heard of one incident where a would-be presentation wiz was about to close the sale when his calendar program splashed his personal to-do list right across the center of his slides. Right on cue — he'd set a timed reminder for himself and forgotten all about it.

Backup is vital with computer presentations. Always have a backup diskette of your presentation — just in case. Many presenters even bring a full set of overheads or slides in addition to their computer equipment. If you can't handle all that weight, at least make a few hard copy handouts — if all else fails, you can use them to talk through your message.

You should be sure to check the room in which you will be presenting well in advance — on the previous day if possible; at the very least, be sure to arrive an hour or so early to get everything set up. Are tables set up correctly for you, both for positioning and height? You need to be able to get at your computer keyboard easily — but you don't want the computer to be in your way either. You'll need to check for noise, both from your equipment (some projectors have noisy cooling fans) and from outside the room, and you'll need to check that the outlets you'll be using are all working properly.

Lighting can be a real problem in some rooms. You'll want to experiment with how far you need to dim lights to make your presentation clear, especially if you're using an LCD panel. Sometimes you'll find that one light, even when dimmed, reflects from the screen in a distracting manner; in this case, try moving the screen slightly, or remove the bulb from that light fitting. A final thought on lighting — when you have the lights dimmed enough to make the computer image clear, can you still read your notes? Be sure to bring a small flashlight, just in case.

If you're really not sure about the technical side of setting up equipment for a computer presentation, it might be a good idea to bring along a "techie." An extra pair of hands can be a big help in any case, and when things go wrong, it's great to have somebody to troubleshoot the equipment while you concentrate on keeping the show going.

You have much to think about when preparing for a computer presentation, but don't overlook the obvious. Do you have an extra bulb for the projector? An extension cord? (Does your presentation room actually have outlets?) Is the battery in your projector remote getting low? Murphy's Law can have some nasty effects, but if you prepare everything thoroughly (make a list and check it twice), you should get through your presentation with a minimum of stress.

Checklist

Presentation Logistics

Topic _____

Date _____ Time _____

Location _____

Contact Person _____ Phone _____

Presenter(s) _____

Participants _____

Date for sending announcements _____

Person responsible for arrangements ____ Phone _____

Seating arrangement (including # of chairs) _____

A/V equipment (include spare bulbs, etc.)_____

A/V contact/help_____ Phone _____

Speaker's table __ Microphone?__ Lavaliere?__ Flipchart(s)?__

Water/pitcher(s)/glasses _____

Refreshments _____ Time _____

Handout materials _____

Location of restrooms _____

Location of telephones _____

Arrangements for messages _____

Checklist
Supplies

Visuals

Extra projector bulbs

Spare parts for projector

Converter plug

Extension cord(s)

Felt-tip pens (different colors)

Masking tape

Stick pins

Extra eyeglasses

Blank transparencies

Marking pens for transparencies

Pointer

Tent cards

Extra handouts

Extra agendas

Note pads

Pencils

Lozenges

Batteries for computer remote

Backup diskettes/handouts

Computer AC cord

Flashlight

_____

_____

SUMMARY

Always remember that details make or break a presentation.
- Select and brief the audience
  — Limit the audience to those people with a stake in the outcome
  — Notify the audience well in advance
  — Provide whatever information participants need to prepare for the presentation
- Create handouts that are more complete than visuals used during the presentation. Distribute them at the end of the presentation.
- Take the size of the group and the purpose of the meeting into account to choose the seating arrangement.
- Think carefully about audience and room size when you assemble your equipment for a computer presentation, and take a stand against Murphy's Law by preparing for every eventuality.

8
Rehearsing and Delivering the Presentation

Once you've developed your content and your visual support, you are ready to
- Rehearse effectively
- Present yourself with confidence
- Use visuals professionally
- Evaluate your presentation

Rehearsing Effectively

Chances are you weren't hired for your job for your speaking ability. Furthermore, if your early training stressed analytical or technical skills, you may think polished presenters are as silly as performing bears and, for that reason, resist joining their ranks. Your objection, in part, may be a rationalization based on lack of confidence or even resentment that you are asked to do something you weren't hired to do and don't believe you're good at. You may even believe that great presenters are born, not made, and you feel hopeless about trying to "be something you're not."

Rehearsals can help you overcome these feelings. Not everyone is born with a well-pitched, resonant voice, but with practice everyone can develop a speaking style that makes the most of whatever he or she does have. (Clearly, if you have severe speech problems or an accent that you would like to eliminate, you'll need to consult a professional in that field.) Rehearsals help you to develop a sense of timing and to master the material, both of which are vital to a smooth delivery.

If you're not used to rehearsing, speaking to an audience that doesn't exist may seem slightly silly at first. By taking the time to practice in private, however, you will find the presentation itself less nerve-racking. After all, having said it all before, you'll be able to relax, concentrate on the audience, and even have some fun. If the idea of making a presentation is extremely anxiety-provoking, you can go through your own desensitization process, similar to what psychologists recommend for phobias, as you rehearse. Start by visualizing yourself giving the presentation, and then make each successive rehearsal a closer approximation of the real thing. Envision people asking questions and talking to you. The idea is to familiarize yourself with what to expect from the actual situation so that your fears subside and don't get between you and making a good presentation.

Even if you are not particularly anxious about giving a presentation, try to rehearse three times: once alone facing a mirror; another time before a supportive but uninvolved listener; and, finally, in front of two or three friends. If you are not used to using visuals, be sure to include them in all your rehearsals. In your final rehearsal, try to use the room in which you'll be presenting and the equipment you will use during the presentation. When you rehearse with an audience, ask your listeners to raise questions and comment on your style, timing, and professional tone. Because most people are timid about giving criticism, always ask them specific questions: Did they understand the main point? Did they agree with you? Could they repeat your major supporting statements?

Having another person present to react to your rehearsal can help alert you to manners of speech that you may overlook. If you have not had speech training, you may not be aware when you drop endings ("doin'" instead of "doing"), slur words together, fail to pause between words, phrases, and sentences, or pause inappropriately. Be especially careful in pronouncing numbers. Even the most attentive listener can easily mistake "sixteen thousand" for "sixty thousand."

Electronic equipment, which is easy to use and frequently available, can be very helpful during rehearsals. Using a tape recorder, for example, will make you conscious of slang expressions and annoying repetitions that creep into your everyday speech. Listen to yourself. Try making the same point several times in different words. Your purpose is not to memorize the presentation but rather to be comfortable with several ways of getting your ideas out in your own words. This is also the time to practice speaking at different tempos, so you will learn how a good, moderate, easy-to-follow pace feels. Videotaping provides even more specific feedback — your gestures and movements can be very revealing. The final rehearsal is not the time to make your first videotape, however. Although some people are pleasantly surprised when they see the way they actually appear to others, some are shocked. One man promptly shaved off his moustache when a videotape revealed how much time he spent stroking it. To avoid unpleasant surprises that may damage your self-confidence, make your first videotape either a dry run or a rehearsal for some minor talk. Once you've adjusted to seeing yourself as others see you, you'll find videotaping a terrific bonus. Seeing what patterns you fall into when you are nervous will make it easier to correct them — you can't change something you don't know you do.

People often tell us that suggesting rehearsals borders on the ludicrous. With the stringent limits placed on everyone's time these days, the closest anyone gets to a rehearsal is mouthing the words in the hotel room before going out to present. Again, it's a question of allocation of time. It's far more important to sound comfortable and relaxed than it is to do one last minute numerical calculation. And the only way to sound relaxed is to have actually heard yourself say the words out loud prior to the presentation. If you have time for nothing else, at least rehearse the beginning, where you grab the audience's attention and establish a contract for what goes on in the presentation, and the ending, where you summarize and detail the next steps.

Timing the Presentation and Developing Your Pace

During rehearsals, practice your timing so that the presentation fits into the allotted schedule, and develop a good sense of pacing so that you can control the unfolding of your ideas. Some people speed up when they present (usually those who tend to treat stress as a call to action), others slow down (usually those whose response tends to be more possum-like). To get a feel for an appropriate speed, try to read half this page in two minutes (a speed of 120 words a minute is just about right, although anything up to 160 words a minute is acceptable). Although psychologists say that people tend to believe fast-talkers more than those who speak slowly and deliberately, speed has its drawbacks. One presenter, who was allotted thirty minutes for her presentation, managed to whip through it in twenty minutes. However, her audience was so befuddled that the first question was: "What did you say?" Practice can help you achieve a reasonable speed.

Next, check for length. Talk through your whole presentation, then add 15-20 percent of the total time to allow for visuals and discussion. Now you know how long the whole presentation should be. The last step is to break the presentation into sections so that you know where you should be one quarter of the way through, at the halfway point, etc. This will enable you to avoid a last minute flurry to finish. Don't worry too much about having time to fill — except for closely controlled panels or public media events, no one ever condemned a presenter for ending early.

Developing a sense of pacing (that is, knowing when to slow down and when to speed up) is as essential to a well-run presentation as the ability to move from the beginning to the end in a given period of time. You want to give the audience the sense that your presentation is unfolding deliberately, and that you are progressing toward a specific goal. Slow down for an especially important point and vary your pace when you anticipate a change in the audience's involvement. During the presentation, you will want to pick up the pace if you sense your audience is growing tired, and slow down if you sense resistance or lack of understanding. Pacing makes the difference between an alert, interested audience and a collection of distressed people surreptitiously checking their watches. (See "Reading Your Audience" in Chapter 9 for special reasons to vary your pace.)

Mastering the Material

Rehearsals allow you to feel comfortable with your presentation material. If you're rehearsing by yourself, play devil's advocate and ask yourself hard questions. Imagine what you would ask if you were the audience. Roleplay what the decision maker might say. If you find yourself stumbling at any point in the presentation, it may be that you don't truly believe your own point or that you missed some flaw in the logic when you organized the presentation. Go back to your logic tree and check.

Your choice of words also reveals your mastery of the material. Rehearsals will give you the confidence to choose the strongest appropriate words. You won't be afraid to express yourself in clear, direct terms such as "Continuing on this course will be destructive," rather than "This course of action may present problems." Your presentation will have much more meaning and power if you use precise, strong language. Once you've used a good, powerful word, though, don't get stuck on it. Calling three concepts "pivotal" in the same presentation dissipates the force of the word and thus weakens your entire message. Along the same lines, don't exaggerate. Even one exaggerated statement makes an audience suspicious, and a stream of overdone claims will undermine your whole presentation.

Editing the Presentation

Just as you edit memos and reports to make sure your language is precise, use your rehearsals to eliminate weaknesses in your presentation. Although audiences are more forgiving than readers in this regard, careful editing helps you eliminate excessive use of filler words, nonwords, rhetorical questions, jargon, and acronyms.

Filler words

Two favorite fillers are "generally speaking" and "basically." You may find you have other words you slip in when you have nothing particularly earthshaking to say. "I feel that" and "I believe that" are phrases speakers commonly load onto the front of a perfectly good statement, turning it from crisp to sodden. Using "et cetera" or "and so on" suggests that you can't come up with more examples. Because any presentation involves a degree of extemporizing, you can't expect to eliminate all your filler words. But by becoming aware of your favorite filler words, you will automatically use them less; and by your final rehearsal, sheer familiarity with the presentation should have erased most of them.

Nonwords and questions

Inexperienced presenters who are terrified by silence often attempt to fill every gap with "ums" or "uhs" or tentative expressions like "okay?" or "right?" You can, and should, pause to emphasize a point and give the audience time to register what you are saying. As you rehearse, make yourself stop at the end of each sentence; you'll find "ums," "uhs," and "ahs" generally disappear. If you still have trouble, try breathing in when you want to say "uh" — you'll find you can't do both things at once.

Keep in mind, too, that using questioning phrases reveals a subconscious need for permission to continue (because you're uncertain of your argument), or for assurance that the audience is still listening. Rehearsals make you more aware of this pattern and give you the confidence to eliminate such tentative and unconvincing phrases.

Rhetorical questions

Like any device intended to increase verbal interest, rhetorical questions should be used judiciously. When used ritualistically, for example, as a transition device, rhetorical questions can be irritating. One presenter customarily introduced transitions by saying "now what does that imply?" — which he then answered with his next point. Eventually, the audience got so tired of it that they started answering with random statements to throw him off track.

Jargon and acronyms

Jargon and acronyms are permissible only if everyone in the room understands them, and even then should be minimized. Jargon (the special language of your profession or business), in particular, should not be used in any external presentation. As a presenter, you have an obligation to deliver a fresh proposal — jargon kills that freshness. Using jargon, although not devastating to your point, will not advance your cause as much as good, precise English. Furthermore, if your audience includes language purists, such terms will have the same effect as chalk squeaking on a blackboard. Be especially cautious about bringing in fancy words like "exogenous." Even when such words are part of your organization's written vocabulary, they are jarring to listeners.

You'll have mastered the presentation when your pace is correct, your sentences are precise and clearly delineated and your voice sounds confident. Because someone engaged in presenting is usually more energetic than someone running through a rehearsal, you can expect your presentation to be even better than your final rehearsal.

Delivering Your Presentation

Your structure is tight, you know exactly what you want to say. Your rehearsals have made you comfortable with the material and words. Now you are ready to follow through with a strong delivery by taking steps to
- Alleviate nervousness
- Send appropriate nonverbal messages
- Involve the audience
- Establish rapport
- Speak clearly
- Use notes effectively

Alleviating Nervousness

A slight nervousness is normal for any management presenter, especially the first few times. Eventually, however, many presenters overcome the jitters (except, perhaps, for mild tension) and allow themselves to enjoy making a presentation. Their secret is not necessarily the confidence that comes from experience, although that helps, but a change in attitude: They have learned to shift their focus from themselves to the audience. We recommend that you concentrate on communicating your message to your audience rather than on wondering how you look to them. As soon as you get "into" your subject, most of your nervousness will disappear.

Nervousness has two sources. One is the constant stream of internal negative comments that nag the speaker when he or she begins to think about the presentation. ("I wonder how I'll come across this time?" "Last time I made a presentation, I was sure everyone was laughing at me when I had so much trouble with the projector.") The other source of tension comes from hyperresponsibility. The presenter feels that he or she alone is responsible for the reactions and well-being of everyone in the audience.

The first kind of nervousness tends to evaporate when you reprogram your thought process. If you have a logical argument and you're prepared, you can stop worrying about flaws in your reasoning and technical problems. Instead, you can focus on convincing the audience that your position is correct. Think about it this way: You believe in what you're saying. You're prepared. In fact, for this presentation, you're the only person who is so well prepared. Your audience needs to know what you have to say. With these thoughts in mind, you can proceed to change the words you say to yourself from negative messages to more positive ones. You can even list your concerns on a sheet of paper before the presentation. Then, for every negative message, substitute a positive one. For instance, if your negative message is, "I'm a nervous wreck," write, "I can channel this nervous energy into the presentation and give a more enthusiastic performance." This effort may take numerous repetitions, but eventually it works.

You can also overcome the second kind of nervousness — taking responsibility for everyone in the room. Come to terms with the fact that everyone in the room will not necessarily accept your ideas. It's not your job to please everyone. Your job is to get your message across in clearly understandable terms to the people who must have the information. Concentrate on the decision maker and on those who respond positively to you. Forget the others.

Many presenters also find that they relax as soon as the audience's attention is focused away from them, however briefly. If you are one of those presenters, and you find yourself getting tense or too self-conscious, try asking a question or engaging someone in the audience in a brief dialogue. For example, you might say, "You tried that in your department last quarter, Jack. How did it work for you?" or "Has anyone else encountered that situation? What did you do?" The audience will direct its attention to the speaker, and you will have a moment to take a slow breath, relax, and think about what you want to say next. (Do make sure, however, that the person you are addressing is actually paying attention to you and is happy to make a contribution. You don't want to put anyone on the spot.)

Because it is hard to counteract nervousness if you do not feel in control of the situation, take time before the presentation begins to put yourself in control:

- Allow plenty of time to check out the room and the equipment.
- Eliminate any physical barriers that stand between you and the audience. If you're scheduled to speak behind a table or lectern, plan to move away from it or have it removed.
- Greet people as they come in. Chat casually with people you know until it's time to start. If possible, shake hands with people, both those you know and those you are meeting for the first time. Physically touching another person through a simple handshake is often extremely relaxing.
- Start on time. Unless the decision maker is delayed, don't wait for laggards. Delaying will make you and your audience fidgety.

Sending Appropriate Nonverbal Messages

You're confident. You've rehearsed. You have a powerful, logical message. You're now ready to take on the task of presenting your points in such a way that you do not distract from your ideas. In management presentations, the drama should be in the content, not in the person. Once you're aware of the way people react to you, you can control the way you present yourself.

Leave the appropriate distance between you and the audience

Although a public speaker may be twelve to fifteen feet from the first row of listeners without being viewed as aloof and impersonal, a management presenter, who generally deals with far fewer people, should be no more than four to five feet away. If you're any farther away, the listeners may regard you as either stuffy or fearful. If you're any closer, people will become uncomfortable. When you're speaking to a group with whom you have had little or no personal or professional relationship, start speaking from a position farther away and move in slightly as the presentation progresses and as you build rapport with the group. But don't get too close. A tall presenter, for example, who approaches within inches of his listeners and leans forward, is expressing dominance more than friendliness.

To judge whether you tend to invade others' personal space, recall whether people ever inched away from you when you were engaged in informal conversations. Physical distance rules vary from one culture to another. Arabs want to be within inches of each other when they speak, whereas the Japanese expect even more distance than Americans. When you're in another country, the best way to learn the appropriate distance to put between yourself and the audience is to observe native speakers of approximately your status. (Chapter 14 provides more advice on global presentations.)

Stand up straight

Good posture gives the impression of authority. You can correct bad posture habits without difficulty by standing with your heels against a wall, bending your knees slightly, and pressing your spine flat against the wall. Unless you have abnormal curvature of the spine or other physical problems, constant repetition of this exercise will bring positive results. While you're making your presentation, make a conscious effort not to fold your arms. Folded arms seem to encourage slouching. To avoid slouching, slowly breathe in and raise your chest cage while keeping your shoulders relaxed and down. This will make you look more erect and confident, and will free your diaphragm for better breathing and voice projection. There is a difference between good posture and stiffness, however. If you march briskly to the front of the room and do not move for the rest of the presentation, you signal rigidity more than authority.

Consider your appearance

Psychologists have found that attractive people are more persuasive than unattractive people. They are not referring to a model's appearance. Anyone can cultivate attractiveness through good grooming and clean, neat, professional dress. A presentation is not the place to "make a statement" with your clothes — flashy clothes divert attention from your message. The standard business dress in many companies remains dark suits and white or blue shirts for men and conservative suits or dresses for women. In some corporations, even mild deviations from this standard, if tolerated at all, are considered the prerogative of only the very mighty. Although standards in nontraditional organizations may be more lenient, it is safer to stay on the side of conservatism. Anything too far from the norm will cause the audience to fix on the distracting feature rather than on your message. A good rule of thumb is to dress slightly more formally than your audience. If you are addressing a group on a "casual Friday" or at an off-site location, for example, everyone is expected to be in "smart casual" garb, that is, tailored linen slacks and expensive blouses or golf shirts. As a presenter, though, you're better off with some version of a sports jacket and a skirt and blouse if you're a woman, or slacks and a sport shirt if you're a man. Dressing this way will establish your authority as a presenter and alleviate nervousness.

Move with purpose and use natural gestures

A presenter who stays glued to the overhead projector or maintains a white-knuckle grip on the lectern is terrified, and everyone soon knows it. When you start the presentation, it's perfectly all right to begin by touching the podium (or the table, or the overhead projector) so long as you do not stay in that position for long. Touching something concrete is called "grounding," and can often increase a presenter's comfort level. You can get the same effect by picking up a pen or pointer, but remember to put it down as soon as practical. (We saw one presenter snap a pencil in half because he gripped it tightly with both hands.)

To give the impression of self-confidence, move about the room and use your hands as you speak. You may even convince yourself that all is well. Take advantage of your natural gestures, but avoid using one over and over. Some presenters, told that they need to add movement, adopt one gesture — raising an arm, for example — and use it repeatedly. At worst, such programmed gestures send the audience into a hypnotic state; at best, they're distracting. Tailor your gestures to reinforce your point. For instance, by bringing your hands together, you can assure your audience that your proposal "brings it all together." Similarly, you can refer to the ramifications of a problem by tracing ever-widening circles in the air. Because most management presentations involve visual aids, you can add movement by simply pointing out the most important features on the visual. Moving around the room is helpful if it does not deteriorate into the measured pacing of a caged tiger. Move with purpose. For example, move toward someone to answer a question, to the screen to point out a feature you're discussing, or to the projector to change an overhead. To guard against moving too much or pacing, stop each time you make a point. By pausing completely, you emphasize to your listeners the importance of what you are saying.

Control your facial expressions and mannerisms

Although we all know people who say "If you cut off my hands, I wouldn't be able to talk," very few people actually overdo gestures. Facial expressions, on the other hand, are difficult to control and often give an embarrassingly accurate clue as to how you really feel. Beyond checking yourself on videotape, the best way to control facial expressions is to make sure you're comfortable with your material and prepared to respond honestly and openly to any questions. Try to maintain an accessible, open presence. Remember that a smile breaks down barriers and does not, as many presenters seem to think, indicate that you're less than serious about what you're saying. When you smile at someone, he or she feels included and generally smiles back. As you talk, show interest in what you're saying. If you're not interested, how can your audience be?

Maintain eye contact

You will lose support faster by staring at your notes, looking only at the visual, or focusing on a spot high on the back wall than by any "mistakes" you may make in the content of your presentation. Similarly, if you direct yourself exclusively to the key decision maker in your audience, he or she will feel more uneasy than flattered, and others in the room will feel unimportant. Unfortunately, once some presenters learn that eye contact can make the difference between persuasion and failure, they fix one person after another with a piercing, unwavering gaze until the target looks away in discomfort. At some point in the presentation, try to look at each participant, with the goal of giving each, in turn, the brief message, "I can see that you grasp what I'm saying." Then, for your own comfort, focus on people who respond with a nod or smile, rather than on people who seem bored or hostile.

Involving the Audience

For a variety of reasons, today's audiences appreciate being involved. To the extent that you as the presenter can directly engage the audience, you are far more likely to be successful than if you adopt an "I talk, you listen" attitude. Even a simple device like asking a question and indicating that you want people to respond by raising their hands can be immensely effective. For example, you might ask a factual question such as: "How much do you think it costs to relocate a workstation, including telephone and computer services as well as actual furniture and dividers?" Most people will have an opinion and will venture numbers far less than the real answer (in one case, $5,000). The point is not only to direct attention to the importance of planning for moves (the original reason the presenter decided to use this device), but also to engage the audience.

Establishing Rapport

We've referred a number of times to the need for establishing rapport. There are various ways to do this. For example, people tend to believe those whose background, education, or belief system is similar to their own. Of course, that situation is not likely to occur 100 percent of the time, but you can always find ways to reinforce your common humanity with others. One management presenter we know has an invisible disability (inadequate depth perception) and always tells his audience at the outset that he has been known to trip over the projector cord. Not only does this assertion establish his rapport with anyone in the audience who has ever tripped or been clumsy, but, as he says, it also relieves his anxiety about tripping. If he trips, everyone has a good-natured laugh; if he doesn't, well, he's ahead of the game.

Another way of getting the audience on your side is to use "I," "we," and "you" appropriately. When you're relaying bad news about your department, say "I" and take responsibility. Don't say "they did it" and assign blame. (In fact, leave any suggestion of name-calling behind.) If you're presenting the work of a team, share the credit: "we found" or "we suggest." Also use "we" if you're including the audience in a joint venture such as problem-solving or decision making. When talking to clients or customers, always use "you" or the actual name of their companies rather than generic terms. To say "we provide custom-ized services to our clients" rather than "we would provide a custom-ized program for you," is offputting in the extreme. "You" is ideal for unifying members of the group. When you're saying something that may be obvious to some members of your audience and not to others, you can simply and effectively avoid creating "in" and "out" groups by using the phrase "as you know," and then continuing your statement.

Speaking Clearly and Conversationally

Strive for a conversational tone. Although courtesy and a degree of formality are important, stilted language is inappropriate. Not only is common language easier to understand, but the people are more likely to interact with a speaker who deals with them on equal terms. Printed words are separated by spaces. Sentences on the printed page are sepa-rated by punctuation marks. Paragraphs are marked by indentations. Since your listeners do not have that kind of visual guidance, they must rely upon you, as the speaker, to enunciate clearly, pause appropri-ately, provide verbal guideposts (such as "first, second, third"), and offer visual support.

You also help your listeners by varying the rate at which you speak. For complex material particularly, speak more slowly. If you have stud-ied a foreign language, you know how difficult it is to listen to native speakers conversing at their normal rate (what most non-native listen-ers want to say is "slow down!"). When you are presenting complex, technical, or unfamiliar (to your audience) material, it is as if you are speaking another language, and most listeners have to shift from "auto-matic" to "manual" in order to keep up with you. If you persist in mov-ing along at a rapid rate, your audience will tune you out.

You convey confidence when you speak at a moderate volume and pitch. A voice that's too soft is more often the problem than a voice that's too loud (although for some, nervousness leads to higher than normal volume). If you are presenting to a large group and using a microphone, ask before you begin whether everyone can hear you or whether your voice is too loud. Vary your pitch as you go along; an unchanging pitch becomes a drone. Lowering your voice is as much an attention-grabber as raising it.

A last suggestion: try for spontaneity. When you are talking to your friends and colleagues in normal conversation, you pause, comment on what you've just said, throw in anecdotes, war stories, and analogies, and in general "let things flow." If you can do the same thing during a presentation, your delivery will be much more interesting. Saying things like "I've got to be careful with my word choice here" or making comments about what you've just said — not in a self-deprecating manner, of course — will make people feel they are part of a relationship rather than a passive receptacle.

Using Notes Effectively

It's hard to imagine anyone trying to memorize a presentation word for word. Recall takes so much energy that you would have little left for relating to the audience. Worrying about not forgetting adds to your nervousness and, worse yet, if you forget a line, you might have to back up all the way to the beginning — every presenter's nightmare. Don't ever consider memorizing. Instead, learn to use notes, if you need a reminder, unobtrusively and effectively.

If you're forced to substitute for someone at the last moment, read through the material, eliminate any purely personal passages, absorb the meaning, and convert it into your own notes. You will be most convincing when using your own words. You will also avoid repeating the embarrassing experience of the substitute presenter who, before she realized her mistake, launched energetically into a first-person story about a combat experience as a U.S. Marine.

Many management presenters use their visuals as notes. If your overheads are not sufficient to remind you of the details, you can make notes on the frames. In terms of content, you may need notes for your opening remarks as well as your ending remarks, and for any statistical information that is too difficult to remember and will not appear on your visuals. Write down the name of the person who will introduce you and the names of key people in the audience — it's common to block on names when you're under pressure. For long presentations, your notes may go into more detail than is necessary for a short presentation. If you plan to use extensive notes, we suggest you underline key points or create a broad band of color with a highlighting pen that does not obliterate the words beneath. (Remember that these pens work only on typewritten material; handwritten notes in ink will bleed.) In either case, however, use only key words or short phrases; full sentences will cause you to read and thus destroy your phrasing.

Presenting While Seated

Sometimes the occasion or organizational culture demand a seated presentation. Sitting down makes control difficult. You'll have to adjust both body language and voice.

Eye Contact and Expression

Maintain eye contact, just as you would when standing. Around a table, everyone knows when you're not looking at them. Keeping a friendly, open expression and smiling from time to time is important because seated presentations are viewed as more informal than standing presentations. If you can't see everyone, mention the fact, and stand up.

Posture and Movement

Sit up straight on the front half of your chair with both feet flat on the floor. This will indicate your interest in the topic, help you maintain control of your audience, and present a professional image. Postures such as slouching over your arms (the "turtle" position), leaning back with your arms behind your head, or leaning back and rocking or swinging your chair can make you appear sloppy, indifferent, or lacking in confidence — all of which reduce your credibility.

Since you can't move your whole body to sustain audience interest, hand and arm movements assume much more importance. Put at least one hand on the table (keeping both hands out of sight makes people nervous) and use it to gesture. Pick up a pen and write on your copy of the handout if you can to direct attention to it.

Voice

Keep your voice strong. Go for projection, not volume. Because seated presentations are less interesting visually, varying pace, pitch, and tone is even more important than in standing presentations.

Using Visuals

Using Overheads

Using overheads smoothly makes you look professional. This means your equipment must be in good working order, and you must know how to use it correctly. Before anyone arrives, turn the projector on and off, check the focus, and make sure you have an extra bulb (know how to change the bulb if it goes out in the middle of your presentation). Always put your first overhead on the projector before the presentation (place it face up, as you would read it) and check that the projector is properly focused. Then turn the machine off until you want to show the overhead. With your first overhead ready to use, you will have a smooth beginning.

During the presentation, be certain that the visual on the screen amplifies the point you are making. If you finish the topic, and do not have a visual for your next point, turn the projector off. A glowing, empty screen is a major distraction, and a covered transparency with light leaking around the edges is almost as bad. Furthermore, by turning the projector off, you signal members of the audience to return their attention to you (and you are free to walk between the projector and the screen without the embarrassment of having your mid-section appear in the spotlight).

It is important to position yourself throughout the presentation so that you don't block anyone's view. After you project a transparency, move to one side and give everyone a chance to absorb the message. You can then move back to the screen to point to a message or to parts of a graph, or you can move up to the projector to point out something important. You want to become comfortable highlighting points on either the screen or the projector. Keep in mind that what appears on the far side of the screen is on your side of the projector. When you want to point to something on the screen, don't turn your back to the audience. Instead, stand near the screen and point with the hand nearest the screen; use a pointer if the screen is large or high enough to be out of comfortable reach. As a rule, you want to use your whole hand with the palm facing the audience rather than pointing with a finger — an open hand is a gesture of openness and willingness to discuss; a pointing finger is sometimes seen as a gesture of authority. Some presenters use telescoping pointers because they can close the pointer at will and because the closed pointers are easy to carry. A pointer can be very useful, as long as you remember that it is not a toy. Beating it on the screen or waving it in circles as you talk is unprofessional and distracting.

If you are near the projector, point on the transparency with a pencil or the closed pointer (your finger will look enormous and any nervous trembling will be greatly magnified) or, using a pen designed for the purpose, circle the concept you want to emphasize. Some presenters add information to a transparency while its image is on the screen. Marking the transparency during the presentation adds a sense of action to your talk and is a sign that you are in control. If you do write on the transparency, always stand to one side of the machine as you write, and then move away so everyone in the audience can read what you have written.

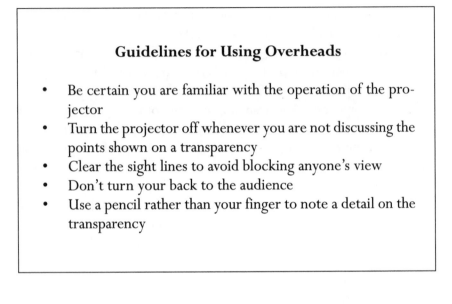

Guidelines for Using Overheads

- Be certain you are familiar with the operation of the projector
- Turn the projector off whenever you are not discussing the points shown on a transparency
- Clear the sight lines to avoid blocking anyone's view
- Don't turn your back to the audience
- Use a pencil rather than your finger to note a detail on the transparency

Using Slides

Since an effective slide presentation requires careful orchestration, conscientious planning and rehearsing are important. Check to be sure all the slides in the carousel or tray are right side up and in the correct order. When possible, use a remote control. If that is impossible, it is critical to rehearse several times with the projectionist before the presentation. If you have to say, "Next slide, please," you'll interrupt the flow of thought for both yourself and the audience.

Use a pointer to focus the audience's attention. Some presenters use a light or laser pointer, which allows them to point with a ray of light to a spot on the screen. If you use one, turn it off quickly after pointing, or the point of light will replicate a bouncing ball. Your dependence on yet another battery and bulb increases the chances of something going wrong; unless you have a very large, high screen, we suggest you use a conventional pointer.

Guidelines for Using Slides

- Check the position and order of the slides in your carousel or tray
- Control the projector yourself or rehearse with the projectionist
- Use a conventional pointer

Using Flipcharts

Before your presentation, be sure the easel is securely anchored on the floor, and the flipchart is firmly attached to the easel. If you are using an adjustable floor stand, set the height so you can comfortably grasp the page in the middle and flip it over the pad, and be sure the chart braces are secure to avoid having your charts slide to the floor as you speak. Determine where you need to stand to write comfortably on the flipchart, and make sure there is enough room for you to stand on that side. Since flipcharts are usually used interactively in a presentation, it is essential to write neatly and large enough for everyone in the room to read. If you must turn your back to the group to write, keep quiet while you are writing — the silence will not bother your audience, as they will be busy watching what you are writing. Use short phrases and abbreviations; turn to face the group before you resume speaking.

If you have prepared your flipcharts in advance, open the chart to the first blank page before the audience arrives. As you proceed from one visual to the next during the presentation, grasp and flip over the completed visual with the next blank page. Flip the visual with the hand nearest the flipchart as you face the audience. (If you are not ambidextrous, stand on the side most convenient for you, usually the same side from which you write.) If you do not have a visual for the next section of your presentation, flip to the blank page and move to another part of the room. As in any presentation, be certain to face the audience at all times.

Guidelines for Using Flipcharts

- Securely attach the flipchart to the easel
- Adjust the easel height before the presentation
- Stand on the side that permits you to write easily
- Grasp the visual in the middle to flip it
- Face your audience when you are speaking

Using Handouts and Presentation Books

We usually recommend against providing handouts or presentation books before a presentation because when someone has a copy of the presentation, he or she is free to roam through the document at will, paying little or no attention to you. Some audiences, however, demand copy in advance; for groups of two or three, "walking through" a paper copy may be logistically the most appropriate approach.

If you provide copies well in advance of the presentation so that the meeting participants can read the material before the presentation, you should consider the meeting a discussion and not attempt to take the audience through all the detail. You can speak to each summary page and ask for questions or comments about the material in the section. Be prepared to deal with the topics the audience wants to discuss. If you sense people have not read the material, you can then move quickly through each page. When people receive material in advance, the risk is that some will have read it and some will not. As always, you must focus on the decision maker and move at the pace that satisfies him or her.

If you are making a handouts-only presentation in which you provide handouts during the presentation, you should consider providing only one section at a time. If you are using a presentation book, sometimes called a "pitch book" or a "flip book," in a group of two or three, you might put your own copy in a notebook binder so you can use it as a substitute easel. In any case, at appropriate times turn your copy to face the audience and point to significant data in order to draw the audience's attention to you. Nothing is worse than presenting to a row of bent heads as everyone reads the book along with you.

Control issues arise when the audience has physical possession of the content. Always tell the audience what the book covers as you start the presentation. For example, you might say "The first section contains the material we'll cover today. Everything after tab 2 is a technical appendix." This may prevent some of the flipping through that takes place as the audience tries to figure out how you can possibly cover seventy-five pages of material in thirty minutes. Number the pages. That way you can direct people to the appropriate page if they seem to be getting ahead of you. It's far better to say "Let's turn to page thirteen," than "Go to the chart that looks like this [as you wave the page with the chart at them]. No, not that one, go back two pages …" and so on. Some people don't want to number pages because they are always inserting charts at the last minute and don't want to bother to renumber each time it happens. You can see that the tradeoff in control isn't worth it. Finally, even if you use presentation books, you might also use a whiteboard or flipchart to give yourself a reason to stand up and exert control.

Delivering a Computer Presentation

As we discussed in Chapter 5, designing a computer presentation can present some problems; however, delivery of such presentations differs only in minor ways from delivery of presentations using traditional slides or overheads. You do have a few additional possibilities, which if used well, will enhance the smoothness of your presentation.

The vital thing to remember is that, software manufacturers' advertisements to the contrary, your presentation program will not make the presentation for you. A computer presentation is simply another form of visual support — support for you, and for your message. All the guidelines for delivery in this chapter still apply. True, it is possible to set up a computer to give an automated "slide show" — but this gives you absolutely no way to read your audience or adapt the presentation to the decision maker's needs. Ideally, you should open with the projector off, then turn it on to provide support as you get further into the presentation. You may want to work in breaks for questions as you go, turning the lights up and the projector off each time. Finally, you should turn the lights up and summarize with the focus on you rather than on the screen.

Using a computer gives you the possibility of truly transparent presenting. Unlike other media, which involve switching overheads or darkening the room, computer presentations, with the right equipment, can run almost as if by magic — and with a good projector, even in ambient light. The secret, of course, is to know your equipment and your software.

Presentation programs are generally quite simple to use, and it's tempting to simply rely on pushing a button to move from one slide to the next. Nine times out of ten, this will be all you need to do. But what if somebody suddenly asks to take another look at the graph you were discussing ten minutes ago? You can make this kind of jump within a computer presentation quickly and easily — as long as you know the software. A number of programs allow you to jump instantly to any slide in a presentation by typing in the *number* of that slide (of course, you had the foresight to put a numbered printout of your slides in with your notes before the presentation began). Other programs have other tricks which can be useful in this kind of situation — make sure you know how to use them.

Almost every projector or panel comes with some kind of remote, varying from simple slide advancers right up to remote mice, complete with slide annotation and special effects features. If your equipment doesn't have the kind of remote you'd really like, chances are you can buy what you want. The first thing you should do, long before your presentation, is check out your remote to familiarize yourself with its controls. Most remotes are wireless; find out where you can stand in order to use yours. Sometimes you have to be almost directly in line with your projector, but quite often you can use the screen to bounce the remote signal to your equipment. This allows you to move freely as you speak. You may need a lavaliere microphone in a large room — you can run it through the same sound system as your computer audio if you wish.

If you have special effects on your remote, try them out and find out which ones will be useful. An image freeze can be a very valuable tool if you have to switch to another video source, or perhaps suddenly jump to another presentation. Just freeze the slide that's currently on your screen, move to your computer, and make whatever changes you need to while watching your computer screen. The audience will still have your last slide in front of them — as long as you keep talking, they'll hardly be aware that anything is out of the ordinary. Once you're ready to continue, just "unfreeze" the projected image and take up your presentation where you left off. A zoom effect can be very handy if you want to direct your audience's attention to a particular point on a complicated table or chart, and highlighters and an assortment of electronic labels and check marks allow you to annotate slides just as easily as you can an overhead acetate. Once you are familiar with your remote, a presentation with a computer is just like any other.

Evaluating Your Presentation

When you rehearsed the presentation, you anticipated what could go wrong and sought out your colleagues' advice. After the presentation, you need to evaluate your work. If the experience was unpleasant, you'll probably be tempted to distance yourself and forget it. Although that is a natural reaction, you can learn valuable lessons by carefully reviewing the presentation. If it was videotaped, brace yourself and look at it closely. If it was not, buttonhole someone who attended and ask very specific questions. ("How was it?" leads to unhelpful answers like "terrific.") Use the checklist below as a guide to what to ask yourself or selected participants.

Naturally, one measure of your effectiveness is whether you achieved the goal that motivated your presentation. However, it isn't the only measure or even the most accurate. On the one hand, a previous speaker, circumstance, or event may have affected how the audience received your message; on the other, your audience may have been so besieged by problems that it would have jumped at any reasonable proposal. It is equally possible that, despite overwhelming evidence and support for your plan, the key decision maker may choose to follow some flash of insight that has little or nothing to do with your proposal.

Checklist for Evaluating the Presentation

- Did I effectively communicate my main point? Does the audience know what the next steps are?
- Was the structure appropriate for the audience?
- Was I comfortable with myself? If not, why not?
- Did I respond to the concerns of the audience?
- Have I taken steps to follow up on any new issues that came up in the meeting?
- Did I use visual support effectively to enhance the presentation?
- Did I achieve my goal? Did the audience say "yes" to what I wanted?
- What would I change next time?

Since the process of gaining acceptance for a major proposal may take months, even years, don't invest too much in the success of one presentation. If you've followed our suggestions so far, you have gotten as far as you can this time, and you have laid the foundation for continual improvement of your skills.

SUMMARY

Rehearsing increases confidence and improves your delivery.
- Rehearse three times: alone, before a supportive but uninvolved friend, and before several co-workers
- Time the presentation and establish a sensible pace

During the presentation,
- Use strong, precise language
- Alleviate nervousness by thinking positively and by establishing rapport with the audience
- Send appropriate nonverbal messages to put your audience at ease and encourage them to respond positively to your message
  — Leave appropriate distance
  — Maintain good posture
  — Use natural movement and gestures
  — Control facial expressions
  — Look people in the eye
  — Speak conversationally
- Use notes, not written text
- Use visuals comfortably and professionally
  — Don't turn your back to the group
  — Don't block people's view of the visuals
  — Use the visuals; point, write on them

After the presentation,
- Evaluate each presentation soon after you make it
- Ask for feedback

9

Managing the Audience
Is Like "Herding Cats"

An experienced presenter recently told us that managing an audience in his company was like "trying to herd cats." We understand his frustration; audiences participate or contribute in a way that can seem quite random. Most often, those seemingly off the wall questions or comments result from frustration because the presenter is not meeting the participant's needs. Now that you've learned a system for organizing content to meet audience concerns, you'll be less likely to encounter that problem.

Questions and comments are important if people are to make decisions. In addition, people assess your competence by the way you respond to questions. A presenter who stays in control while encouraging positive discussion is a presenter who is likely to get action. Specifically, you should

- Prepare for questions
- Read the audience during the presentation
- Encourage interaction on your terms
- Handle questions with confidence
- Overcome objections
- Deal gracefully with interruptions and distractions

Preparing for Questions

Preparing for questions means breaking through the natural tendency to practice denial. People often freeze when they think about trouble-some questions, but "I hope they won't ask me about … negotiating fees … the recent litigation … the budget shortfall … our need to downsize …" is not useful. To prepare, a presenter should first con-sider how people's thinking styles may influence the way they will act, then second-guess questions and prepare answers based on the audience's concerns and thinking styles, and finally do a dry run to roleplay the answers well in advance of the presentation.

Consider Thinking Styles

In Chapter 2, we discussed one aspect of the Myers-Briggs Type Indica-tor (MBTI) that you should consider when developing a presentation (the difference between sensates, who want details, and intuitives, who want a bigger picture view). Considering such thinking styles provides insights into how people will behave in a presentation. Adjusting to different styles can make the difference between a successful meeting and an unsuccessful one. Your goal is not to make assumptions about people, but rather to recognize behaviors and respond to them.

Sensate or intuitive?

You hope you covered enough detail in the presentation, but the sensates may want to take you further into the detail and the intuitives further into the future. In addition, the sensates will want to follow the road map for the presentation; the intuitives are likely to ignore it, wanting to discuss only what interests them. The challenge for you, as the pre-senter, is to keep people on track without offending them. If the deci-sion maker wants to skip around, try to answer his or her questions briefly and return to the order you selected. You did check, after all, to get agreement to that order in your beginning. If someone wants de-tails that go beyond the scope of the presentation, try to answer the question briefly, comment if necessary that it isn't fully germane, and return to your presentation. (You may want to send details in advance to people you know want them.) Keep in mind that you do not want to be drawn too far from your plan by anyone except the decision maker.

Introvert or extravert?

In American culture, these terms have meaning that is quite different from the meaning in the MBTI. Introvert, which is literally translated as "inwardly looking," applies to people who draw their energy from within, and want to marshal their internal resources and come to a thoughtful conclusion before speaking. An extraverted person (notice the difference in spelling from American) is outwardly focused and draws energy from communicating with others. The extravert will talk to decide what he or she is thinking. During a presentation, the extravert may monopolize the discussion unintentionally. And the extravert is rarely bothered by an interruption if the discussion is a good one. The introvert, however, needs some quiet to come to terms with what to say, so that what comes out of his or her mouth is well considered and a full sentence. As a presenter, you'll have to monitor this behavior to make sure everyone participates in discussion, especially if you need consensus. And if you, as the presenter, are an extravert, do not assume that someone who is not talking does not understand what you are saying. Silence is difficult for an extravert, but necessary for an introvert. Wait for a response. Give people warning: "After we break, we'll want input from everyone" will let the introverts prepare.

Thinker or feeler?

Most presentations are organized on rational, logical principles, because the thinker style dominates business decisions (hence our focus on criteria in structuring content). An extreme thinker may decide that criteria relating to people are of relatively lesser importance than other criteria. A feeler, however, will focus on people-related issues. Because business decisions are considered to be "hard" issues, feeler criteria may not surface until the actual presentation. Recognizing a sudden question about how people will be affected and responding to it is important to get a feeler on board.

Judger or perceiver?

Judgers like to make decisions and move on to the next item on the agenda. Perceivers like to consider options and postpone decisions, sometimes on the chance that more information will become available. As a result, a judger may make a decision too soon and a perceiver may never make a decision at all. As a presenter, your challenge is to keep the judger from making a pronouncement before you have provided the options, if they are important, or the risks, if they are important. Once a judger has taken a public stance it is difficult to step back from it. A perceiver, on the other hand, needs a deadline. Always let a perceiver know when a decision will be necessary.

Second-Guess Questions

Presenters who are asked a question they haven't anticipated can be put on the defensive. Because your presentation was structured to raise questions in the decision maker's mind and then answer them during the presentation itself, you've already built answers to most questions into the presentation. Review your presentation; list any other questions you think may arise, including those asked by influencers or gatekeepers, using what you perceive to be people's thinking styles to guide you when appropriate. Write down the answer to each question, so you will not be caught with a weak response or, worse yet, no response at all.

Do a Dry Run

In Chapter 8, we recommended doing a dry run. Here's another reason to do one: if you have a colleague roleplay the decision maker and ask you nettlesome questions, you will have experience actually saying the responses aloud. Make sure the colleague asks realistic questions (true "off-the-wall" questions are permissible if the people in the audience can be expected to ask them). For some reason, having answered a difficult question out loud makes you more comfortable if you get that question during the presentation itself.

Reading Your Audience

Honing your ability to read your audience correctly always pays off. Since people are most comfortable with others who think and speak the way they do, you can do much to enhance your credibility in the eyes of your listeners by reflecting their language patterns, moods, and body language.

If you learn to listen for the pace of the questions or comments that come from your audience, you'll be able to adjust your own pace to match the questioner's. In a small meeting, it's easy to get an idea of the appropriate pacing by chatting with your group informally before the "real" presentation begins. If this is not possible, listen carefully when others speak during the meeting, and watch for signs of discomfort that might indicate you are speaking too rapidly or too slowly.

Another effective device is to listen for images or repeated speech patterns as clues. Most people are visual thinkers. They use phrases like "I see what you mean," and "that looks good." Some people are aural thinkers and use images like "it sounds good," "I hear you," or "can you amplify on that?" Kinetic thinkers are fond of expressions like "it feels right," "I wouldn't touch it," and "he rubs me the wrong way." It takes practice to hear these patterns and use them in your own speech, but it can be a very valuable, subtle way to break down a listener's resistance and put you both on the same side. If the decision maker appears thoughtful, slow down, soften your speech, and give her a chance to think about what you're saying. By contrast, is he looking impatient and seems ready to move ahead? Pick up the pace and move quickly to your next point.

Learning to read body language is also useful. There are many good books on the topic. Bear in mind, however, that these so-called signals can't be taken out of context. Most of us are aware of the most obvious body language "signals," like folded arms indicating resistance or defensiveness (but be careful — for many people, it's also just plain comfortable). But how many people realize that they can rarely get their decision maker to agree to act as long as he's leaning back in his chair, no matter how comfortable he looks?

Here are some of the most common body language "signals" you may encounter as a presenter:

- Someone who is receptive or agreeable
  — readily makes eye contact
  — sits in a relaxed, open manner, sometimes leaning forward
  — has unclenched hands
  — participates in discussions
  — nods and shows agreement through facial expressions
- Someone who is bored or frustrated
  — has a vacant, faraway gaze
  — fidgets
  — sits with her head in her hand
  — runs her hands through her hair or rubs the back of her neck
  — looks at her watch repeatedly
  — yawns, looks sleepy, or falls asleep
- Someone who is hostile or unaccepting
  — sits back and crosses his arms in a "show me" position
  — refuses to look at the presenter
  — scowls and frowns
- Someone who wants to interrupt or join in the discussion
  — leans forward
  — raises a hand
  — puts a finger to his or her lips

Becoming more aware of body language has another advantage: it enables you to mirror the decision maker's body language, which is a subtle way to increase her comfort and heighten her perception that you are a "good person." Just as wearing the appropriate clothes in a given situation makes both you and the audience more comfortable and increases the group's acceptance of you as "one of them," so does reflecting the physical styles you see around you. Is the meeting informal, with people leaning back with arms or legs crossed? If so, you may want to start there, but you'll want to sit upright or even forward on your chair before asking for a decision. Does the group seem to be more formal, with everyone upright and rather quiet? Their comfort level will be greater if you start the same way.

Encouraging Interaction on Your Terms

Managing your audience means getting people involved while maintaining control. Try to get people engaged early. While you may feel more comfortable in a "lecture" setting, you know from your own experience that presentations are more memorable, and move more quickly toward a decision, when the audience is involved and contributes to the discussion.

You may fear that by taking questions you will lose control of the presentation, or you may simply fear that someone will ask you a question you can't answer. In reality, each question gives you, the presenter, another opportunity to make or expand on your point, and may give you helpful information about the topic or the questioner. And only people who are interested ask questions. If you were in the audience, would you bother to ask questions or raise objections unless you were actively interested in what was happening?

When you postpone questions to the end of the presentation, some listeners "tune out" on what you have to say as they try to remember their questions; some people get lost because they need the answer to the question to follow what you are talking about; and more than a few may expend their energies wondering why you won't answer questions now. If people must make a decision based on your presentation, you want to be sure they understand everything as you proceed and they are listening.

How do you get people to talk to you? First, you need to give them permission to do so. Tell them what you want. Say something like, "I want this to be as interactive as possible, so I'd appreciate your asking questions when they arise in your mind." If the organization doesn't reward people who speak up, you may have to make this offer over the course of several presentations before people take you at your word. You can also plant questions by enlisting friendly members of the audience or members of your own team. To get the ball rolling, suggest they ask open-ended questions like "Could you tell us a bit more about the sales forecast?" or something similar.

If people aren't talking, model what you want. Use a conversational tone and pause often enough to give them an opportunity to interject. Say something like: "Many people ask at this juncture, 'Do these figures really mean that we need to rethink our costing procedures?'" or a similar reasonable question on the topic of your presentation. When you ask a question, your voice ends on an up note; doing this will signal that questions are permissible in this context.

When people do speak up, reward them. Don't frown or look away, even if the question is not the one you want. Looking at the questioner (even smiling) will let him or her (and the rest of the people in the room) know that you really do want questions. But don't fall into the habit of ritualistically saying "That's a very good question." The first person you say this to may feel rewarded; the others may feel condescended to. Moving toward the questioner is another method of reward, so long as you don't invade someone's personal space — coming closer than five feet is probably too close.

As the presenter, you're expected to maintain control of the discussion as well as control the people and the agenda. People who want to dominate the discussion and people who want to make statements rather than ask questions are a problem. Keep thinking styles in mind as you respond to people. Extraverts are not necessarily control freaks or hogs, for example. They need to talk in order to come to closure. If you're dealing with someone who really does want to hog the floor, you can simply say, "We need to hear from others on this point" or "Let's hear from the other side of the room." Always notice people's body language so you can look at people who may want to contribute and invite them to speak. You can also turn to someone and ask for input directly. Do make sure people you address are both knowledgeable and paying attention, so that you don't put them on the spot. In addition, don't let anyone interrupt or shout down other people in the audience. If someone is prone to making statements, you can comment on the problem politely by saying "Could you tell us what your question is?" or "That's a valid point [if that's true]. Did you have a question?" So long as you resist the temptation to be sarcastic, you'll likely succeed.

Handling Questions With Confidence

Answering questions easily and comfortably involves basic selling skills:
- Listen
- Probe (restate, rephrase, clarify)
- Answer
- Check

In neutral settings, this procedure works extremely well. The problem is following it when the going gets rough.

Listening is Difficult

Presenters are often anxious to get on with their presentation, and find it difficult to wait while a questioner finishes. (Extraverts are especially prone to interrupting.) As a result, they may not fully understand the question and therefore may not answer it, or they may leave the person who was interrupted feeling slighted. Always give the questioner a chance to finish, and concentrate on identifying what the question actually is rather than groping for an answer and only half-listening.

Understanding the Question is Imperative

Listening doesn't simply mean hearing the words. It also means trying to grasp the feelings behind the words. Probing for content — both emotional and rational — is a vital part of active listening.

To probe, the presenter also becomes a questioner, using open, focused, and closed questions to clarify the question and seek out any hidden meaning.

- Open questions are exploratory; they broaden a discussion:

  Could you tell me about your experience using the system to track options trading?

  What do you find most problematic about the way the process works?

- Focused questions pursue a line of thinking; they move a discussion from the general to the specific:

  You've raised the problem of communication several times; could you tell us why you feel communication is the major issue?

- Closed questions narrow the discussion; they require a yes or no answer:

  Are you recommending that we implement this within two weeks?

We're not in favor of ritualistic probing. When someone says she's happy to be there, we most certainly don't mean you should say "Are you ... are you really?" or that you should spend time probing a straightforward request for information. We do mean, however, that you should not leap to conclusions about what a question means.

Rephrasing the question is another form of probing. As with all communications, we tend to process questions in terms of our own expectations and beliefs. By rephrasing the question (that is, by saying it in other words), you give yourself time to think of the appropriate answer. Rephrasing also lets you narrow a very broad question, turn a statement into a question you want to answer, and defuse hostility. Don't feel rushed. If you pause before you respond, it is a compliment to the questioner, not a sign of indecision. Don't fall into the habit of simply repeating a question. It's silly to do this in a small group when everyone has heard the question.

Many managers feel a need to participate on some level even if they have no question to ask. Keep in mind that their statements do serve a function and often are supportive. They may register approval of what the presenter has said and, as such, are valuable in building consensus for a decision. Merely nodding your agreement to such a statement is not enough. Say something like, "I agree with you. It's vitally important that we …" (which gives you the opportunity to re-inforce a point or to move to your next point).

Answer the Question Forthrightly and Crisply

When you answer the question, maintain comfortable eye contact with the speaker. Give a concise answer. Don't start answering the question before you're ready; you'll tend to ramble, and a rambling answer may make you sound uncertain. Use the questioner's name if you know it, to make personal contact and to reinforce the message that the person's comments are important to you.

Check to Make Sure

Although some books recommend that you finish your answer by look-ing at other members of the audience to include them in the discus-sion, we feel you should end with a visual check that you've satisfied the person asking the question. If the person looks unfulfilled, you might want to check verbally, especially if the person is the decision maker.

How to Handle Difficult Situations

What if the question concerns something that you are planning to address later in your presentation?

Don't say "I'll get to that later." Give the questioner a short answer immediately and indicate that you plan to elaborate on it later in the presentation.

What if questions consistently arise at a point much earlier than when you planned to address the issues they raise?

Take time after the meeting to debrief. You know you failed to present your material in the order that would best address the group's concerns as they arose. Did you miss something when you analyzed your audience? Don't dwell on what went wrong. Instead, learn from the experience, and be sure you rethink any similar presentation you will be making in the future.

What if someone raises an alternative you have already rejected?

Acknowledge the questioner's intelligence before jumping in to show you have done your homework: "That's a good point. We did look at turnaround times, but we found ..." Never make your questioner look bad, and never get defensive.

What if you don't know the answer to a question?

Say so. Nothing can cause you to lose all credibility faster than someone catching you making up an answer or giving erroneous information. State a specific time you'll get back to him, if possible, and be sure you follow up. You can also turn this situation to your advantage by giving a partial answer or a range: "Although I don't have those exact figures, I can tell you that ..."

What if the questioner is upset?

Rephrase the question in neutral terms to defuse any hostility or change the focus. Repeating the original negative language will only reinforce it. Probe to find out the real source of the aggravation. Getting people to "talk it out" may be the only thing you need to do. Avoid becoming emotional yourself, or rational discussion will become impossible; if you need to, take a little time (and a slow breath) before answering. Resist the temptation to ask for approval to change the question's emphasis, and never ask "Does that answer your question?" unless you really want to know and are ready for the discussion to continue.

What if someone uses a question as the opportunity to "take the floor" and rattle on and on?

The most important thing is not to be rude or unprofessional — the audience's sympathies will suddenly go to your long-winded interrupter. Let her speak, and wait until she reaches a point you can address. As soon as this happens (either she gives you an opening, or she uses some phrase you can latch onto), take the reins and begin to address that issue. As soon as you comfortably can, establish eye contact with someone else while you continue to address the same issue. Then try to use that discussion to lead you back to an issue on your original agenda. Other strategies include turning the projector back on, changing slides, referring to the next page number in a handout, or reminding the audience of the agenda.

Overcoming Objections

Whenever you present a proposal to change, some audience members may be hostile or defensive, especially if it appears that what you're saying implies that they made a wrong move in the past. To avoid falling victim to the "shoot the messenger" syndrome, remember to stay objective and unemotional; be prepared to talk through the process that got you to your conclusions.

To avoid objections, never, never blindside anyone. Make sure anyone who will be affected by unpleasant information knows about it well in advance. Use your network to figure out who will be affected and how they will react, and keep updating this information as often as you can before the presentation. By checking with many people, you can test theories and findings from several different angles, and preserve credibility by showing that you have tapped those with specific expertise in the area to be discussed.

If someone does object, don't take it personally. People may seem to be attacking you personally, but they're most often exhibiting fear of change or some other emotional reaction. If you don't become defensive, you can turn what seems like an attack to your advantage.

Let's take some specific examples. What if someone flat out says to you: "You're wrong. You've completely misjudged the situation." Your temptation may be to quail in terror. Instead, take it as a gift. The worst thing is not an attack, but rather a situation in which people disagree but don't tell you. If someone says, "You're wrong," he is actually offering you an insight into the way he thinks and what he cares about, all essential information for you to persuade him. Your response should be a series of careful probes with open-ended, "content neutral" questions. "Could you tell me more ...? Could you help me understand ...? Could you expand on that ...?" — all these possible follow-ups will let you get more information about the issue without locking horns with the questioner.

What if you are asked a question that you simply do not want to answer? Perhaps you don't want to sound as if you are badmouthing someone else (or the competition, in a marketing pitch); perhaps you are ashamed of something you or your staff did. Whatever the ethics of the situation, trying to avoid answering questions usually doesn't work. If answering the question will hurt someone else, and the question is not central to your discussion, it's better to say something like "I'm not free to answer that right now."

What if a question or comment seems antagonistic? Keep cool. By handling objections comfortably and objectively, you establish yourself as a knowledgeable professional who is in control of the presentation. First, listen fully to the objection and acknowledge the other person's point of view (that's not the same as agreeing with the objection). Try to understand why he or she is raising the objection. Ask about the source of the objection — you may find that the real problem didn't even show up in the objection as it was first stated. Do not insist on having the "right" answer, since this automatically makes the other person wrong, an unacceptable standoff. Instead, try to create a spirit of mutual understanding, which may enable you to move toward agreement on goals or solutions that you can both accept.

Coping Gracefully with Interruptions Shows You Are in Control

If you present frequently, you'll be interrupted or encounter distractions sooner or later. These do not have to be terrible experiences; in fact, a "disaster" can actually form a sympathetic bond between you and the audience. It all depends on how you handle the situation.

The simplest kind of interruption occurs when someone tosses in an unrelated comment when you're in the midst of conveying an important idea. The key to handling this situation without losing your momentum in the presentation is to briefly respond to the question and immediately return to your train of thought. However, if there are a series of questions that are apparently unrelated to the substance of your presentation, something has possibly happened since the last time you did your audience analysis, something that is crucial to the client, and people want to know what you think about the issue. You might as well deal with it when it arises, because if you attempt to defer the discussion, people won't be listening to you anyway. The key is to be responsive while maintaining control. Your first attempt should be to gracefully summarize the discussion and segue back to the original agenda. If, however, the discussion becomes attenuated, indicate that time is getting short. Let the decision maker decide whether your topic or the one being discussed is more important.

Other common distractions include late arrivals, side conversations between participants, arguments between audience members, and noisy food service. If the late arrivals include key players involved in the decision-making process, quickly summarize (without visuals) what has happened so far and return to your train of thought.

Conversations between two members of the group can be annoying; it's your job as a presenter to control them. Your technique depends on whether you think they are talking about the subject of the presentation or about something unrelated. If you think they are talking about the presentation, you can try to draw them in by asking open-ended questions about the topic at hand. This works well if you know the people involved and have a close relationship with them. You can politely cut off unrelated side conversations by using one of several techniques. Calling on someone near those who are talking will attract their attention and often quiet them. Even subconsciously, they will sense that the rest of the group is looking at the person you are speaking to, and by extension, they are also looking in their direction. Using names is very powerful because it implies individual accountability. Individuals are better behaved than people who view themselves as part of an undifferentiated mass. If the distraction continues, move nearer to the talkers; they will sense that others are now looking in your direction, and in their direction as well. Don't move so close that everyone else becomes uncomfortable, though. That smacks too much of your fifth grade teacher towering over you, sneering "Is there something you'd like to share with the rest of the class?" Usually, with even a modest invasion of their personal space, the talkers will fall silent.

Unexpected comments or questions can arise in any informal presentation. But one day you may encounter an interruption that falls under the category "acts of God" — for example, when the power goes out, or a jackhammer starts up just outside the window. Don't try to compete with the distraction or pretend it didn't happen — that just makes you look insecure, and perhaps a little foolish. Some "acts of God" require quick thinking and considerable improvisation. But when you handle the situation graciously (open windows for light and use flipcharts, or call a break until noise stops), your audience will rally to your side.

Then there is the moment every presenter dreads: you're halfway through your remarks when an assistant comes into the room and whispers a message to the key decision maker, who then tells you he must leave in three minutes to fly to the site of a new oil discovery in the North Sea. As long as you've prepared well, you'll be ready. Go to the summary text visual and calmly review your main point and major support points (branches). Finish by indicating the next steps or any action required. Ask for agreement (if appropriate, and you're near the end) or reschedule the meeting (if there is major unfinished business). Your ability to deal with upsets and surprises of this sort speaks well for your managerial skills as well as your skills as a presenter.

If you create a well-structured presentation that reflects your audience's concerns, including its need to take action, you'll have a leg up on managing participation. Once you're actually in the presentation, staying in control and using some simple techniques will take you the rest of the way.

SUMMARY

People judge your competence on your ability to manage interaction.
- Prepare carefully for questions
  — Consider how different thinking styles influence behavior
  — Anticipate questions and prepare answers
  — Do a dry run out loud
- Watch and respond to audience cues
  — Mirror language
  — Respond appropriately to body language
- Encourage discussion throughout the presentation; ask for questions
- Use questions to reinforce your message
  — Listen carefully
  — Probe and rephrase
  — Answer crisply
- Overcome objections without becoming defensive
- Debrief after the presentation. What worked? What didn't?

10
"Who's On First?"
Coordinating and Delivering
Fluid Team Presentations

Much of the work in businesses today is done in teams. As a result, more and more presentations are team presentations. To make a successful team presentation, you'll need to

- Recognize the pros and cons
- Organize
- Plan for introductions, transitions, and conclusions
- Decide on fielding questions
- Present as a unit
- Debrief

Recognizing the Pros and Cons

Team presentations have four advantages. First, the person who did the analysis and/or thinking usually presents that information, and someone who "owns" the content is more confident and fluent than someone who glances at the pages or the visuals half an hour before the presentation. Second, in a marketing presentation, the client or customer can evaluate what the presenters are like to work with by observing how they work with each other during the presentation. Third, a team may produce a better presentation than an individual, because a team can be more creative, and because team members may give each other objective feedback. Finally, changing presenters reduces any audience boredom by providing stimulation.

In the first two editions of this book, our research caused us to come out very strongly against team presentations. Sometimes conflicts within the team are played out in front of the audience. Some team members fail to take responsibility for the final product, and teams may often neglect dry runs for the expediency of slapping together presentations on the airplane or on the way to the meetings. We have seen instances in which people failed to introduce each other or made awkward transitions (or no transitions). Occasionally, we have seen team members look helplessly at each other when the time came to end the presentation, because they hadn't designated anyone to conclude. These problems still exist. However, as people have become more and more familiar with teamwork, we have seen many more riveting team presentations, and we feel comfortable with the form.

Organizing to Present as a Team

Some presentation teams already exist as a unit for some other purpose in the organization and presenting is their subsidiary purpose; some form for the explicit purpose of giving a presentation. Of course, checking process issues in existing teams is always a good idea, even if members have apparently worked out issues such as assigning roles and establishing trust. But it is true that existing teams may have more time to focus on presentation content, visuals, and delivery because some of the "garbage" may have been eliminated.

Teams that form solely because they need to give a presentation have more work to do. For example, if investment bankers want to give a new business presentation to a client, the relationship manager may choose to assemble a team of product specialists who can present specific solutions to the client's problems. The members of the team may be based in different locations, and only assemble in the same location immediately before the presentation begins. In these cases, serious problems can arise. The leader may not be able to exercise enough direct power over the other members of the team to coordinate the process efficiently, and a breakdown in communication may lead to a disjointed presentation. Organizing in this case involves both process and content issues.

Lead the Team ("Who's in Charge Here?")

To bring a team presentation together when you have limited positional power is no simple task, especially when you are dealing with raging egos or insecurities. Everyone has demands on his or her time, and the need to work out the nuts and bolts of the presentation may be far down the list of priorities.

As the leader, you'll need to first scope out any underlying group process issues. This takes time, especially if you have to pursue team members around the country or the globe to get their input; but it's important to work these issues through. Make sure you consult everyone involved. Don't assume that people will go along with whatever the team agrees to, just because they've done so in the past. If you ignore someone, his unspoken resentment may cause him to retaliate in passive-aggressive ways, like "forgetting" to get the figures for an important chart, or failing to proofread. Even worse, disgruntled team members may "act out" in the presentation itself, with snide comments or rolled eyes. It may seem hard to believe that people could react in this petty manner, but we've seen it happen.

Agree on the Purpose and Schedule

Getting agreement on the purpose of the presentation (a surprising number of team members will erroneously view the goal as "creating the slides" rather than "getting the decision maker to act") and on the roles each member will take is necessary in order for the presentation to flow smoothly. Once you negotiate these issues and get the group to commit verbally to all the relevant issues, you can use our process to retain control as you structure content (see Exhibit 10.1).

The team should first agree on a schedule, preferably by working out a flow chart or Gantt chart. Meetings software is helpful here, as is

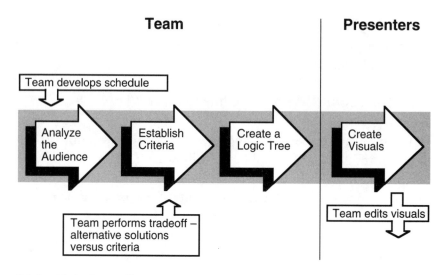

Exhibit 10.1. Process for structuring content as a team

groupware like Lotus Notes. It's common to keep massaging content until the very last minute. Doing so is not a good idea. Decision makers will never know if you left out one computer run, but they will definitely know if you misspelled the company name or scanned the logo and made it the wrong size and color. It's important to build in time for production and quality control (proofing the visuals, dry runs, preparing for questions). Most of the major mistakes in presentations come in the final days before the deadline, and errors compound as people become more rushed and anxious.

The first pieces of the process should be undertaken as a team, with the team coming to closure on each step. If the team is in different locations, communicating by e-mail and fax can work so long as the leader follows up by phone, although it is less likely that the brainstorming part of the process will be as successful as in a face-to-face meeting or videoconference.

Because they want to avoid conflict or simply for convenience, team members often decide to let each member present the results of his or her research (a decision that guarantees a disjointed topical structure), or else use editing as the sole vehicle for reaching agreement on content. Both methods are inefficient, ensuring that material will be created that is ultimately jettisoned as unsuitable or, worse, that material is included simply because some team member worked hard to put it together. A better method is to use the tree to get agreement on structure before writing. Having objective criteria for excellent structure (the tree) means that everything included will meet the needs of the audience. Using the tree also helps ensure that people will contribute equally throughout the process, saving endless bickering the night before the presentation, as team members find to their horror that the results of hasty assignments have not resulted in a coherent whole. If you are working with team members who are not familiar with tree terminology, you can still use the method by getting agreement that the presentation has to be focused on a specific audience, and then "working the process" by asking the audience analysis, criteria, and logic questions in a nonthreatening way.

We've seen team presentations deteriorate when people did not feel that they were well-treated when the assignments were delegated. To avoid dissention within the group, you should first agree on the relevant criteria for making the assignments and have a reasoned discussion. Usually, the person with the most rapport with the audience (the relationship manager, for a sales presentation) should provide the introduction and possibly the conclusion. After that, each branch of the tree should be presented by the person with the most comfort and knowledge about the point being made. While it is important that anyone who attends the presentation has a role, everyone does not have to actually present. Some members of the team can serve as resource people, answering questions fielded by whoever is presenting that portion of the presentation. A good rule of thumb is to never have the number of team members outnumber the audience.

Resist the temptation to use the presentation as a training device for more junior people, unless there is plenty of time to rehearse. Presenters must totally control and be comfortable with their material. Remember the audience will not take into account the difficulties involved in team presentations. They will evaluate the presentation on all the same dimensions as an individual presentation.

Planning For Introductions, Transitions, Conclusions

We've talked about the importance of introductions elsewhere. Nowhere are introductions more vital than in team presentations. Most often, the people in the audience know only one member of the team — the person with whom they have the relationship — and you cannot assume they've read anything in advance, even if you sent it to them. In the beginning of the presentation, as you follow all the rules for getting the audience engaged, be sure to slowly and distinctly introduce each member of the team by name, and give some indication of the role he or she will play in the presentation. For example, "I'm George Serra and I'll be setting the stage and summarizing our presentation. To my right is Constance Banker, who will show why dog toys are the most attractive market ...."

The team members should also use names when transitioning from one segment to another, for example: "Now that we've seen how profitable dog toys can be in the United States market, I'll turn the floor over to Gene Buccelli, who will show you why the global possibilities are ...." Using names is always a good policy, but when the audience is trying to deal with more than one presenter, it's vital. People often skim through the transition in their eagerness to pass the baton to the next presenter. Remember that although you've been living with the material for some time and know exactly where you're going, the audience needs all the help it can get. If a member of the team forgets to make the connection to the next section clear, the next person should pick up the slack, and summarize what's just been said as well as preview the next message. Team presentations are, almost by definition, longer than other presentations, and long presentations demand more guideposts if the audience is to keep up. If you're using chained logic, as many consultants do, you'll need to spend even more time highlighting the links, whether they are causal or sequential.

Always decide who will conclude the presentation. Usually it's the same person who opened — the person with the strongest relationship to the audience. The issue of who will field questions is particularly important, because control issues get played out during the question period more often than in any other portion of the presentation.

Fielding Questions as a Team

Since people look at the way team members relate to each other as an indication of what they are like to work with or as a general measure of their competence and professionalism, the way the team handles questions is vitally important. In addition, people in the audience may try to play team members off against each other. The most common complaints from team members are these:

- The team leader answered before I had a chance to
- The team leader contradicted me
- The presenter was dead wrong, and I didn't know how to correct him or her
- The presenter asked another team member to answer the question without visually checking to see whether he knew the answer

Decide in advance how questions will be handled. Normally, the presenter of a specific section of the presentation fields the questions during that section. That does not mean answering every question, but referring questions to other team members who may be more knowledgeable. Rather than looking around helplessly and asking if anyone knows the answer, visually check with your team members, see whether their body language indicates they'd like to respond, and say something relatively neutral like "James, would you like to respond to that?"

Allocating responsibility for fielding questions should eliminate some wails of "she tromped on my lines." However, some team members (extraverts) really like to talk. They may not be upstaging the presenter on purpose, but rather because they feel the need to add information and provide follow-up answers. Talk about the issue in a neutral fashion during the debrief; don't cast blame. It may take a few times to extinguish a habit of gross interruptions, especially if you have let it go on for some time in the past, but it is well worth the effort. The same applies if someone openly contradicts the presenter. If you feel the presenter has said something that is incorrect, evaluate how important it is. If it is a minor error, you might let it go (so long as the handouts or pitch books are accurate). If it is something that will cause major problems later, however, you'll have to take action. Start with something neutral. For example, "I'd like to expand on that ..." (the tone here is that you are asking permission to interject, so you won't be construed as interrupting). At some point, you can work around to a more accurate interpretation of what was just said.

What if the presenter is losing control because he or she is being needled by a questioner? As a team member, you should help out. Perhaps you can do some probing, or answer the question in a slightly different way to defuse the situation. Tact is extremely important. When you have made your contribution, the presenter should say something like this: "Thank you for that point, Bret. Now I'd like to point out ...." Always keep the control firmly with the presenter, especially if it's a junior person. If the audience perceives a power vacuum, they may start directing questions to the more senior team members, and the cohesiveness of the team will be destroyed.

Delivering the Presentation as a Unit

Egos have no place in team presentations. The audience expects people to work together to create an intelligent case for a point of view. During the dry run, try to establish whether there is a major discrepancy in delivery styles and try to adjust so that extremely forceful people are tempered, and less powerful presenters are given air time and supported. Videotaped dry runs can help you work on a unified "look," although you may choose not to go to these lengths unless you have an extremely important audience.

Pay close attention to your team members when you are not presenting, even if you have heard the pitch and the witticisms a hundred times before. You cannot expect the audience to be interested if you are gazing off in space, marking time until you can get back in the spotlight. To keep yourself involved, take notes of what the audience says. In addition, note anything team members are doing well or anything they need to do to improve. These notes can provide a helpful memory jog during the feedback session.

Debriefing the Presentation

Schedule time for a debrief immediately after the presentation. No one should be surprised when they receive feedback; rather, it should be an accepted way of improving work as a team. The team should assemble to consider what went well and what didn't. Often, people only give negative feedback, taking for granted anything that went well, but this is usually counterproductive. Make a serious effort to recognize specific things that went well (a smooth transition, an apt answer to a question). If you offer negative feedback, make sure that it refers to something within the person's power to change.

One major debrief question is: "Did we achieve our goal? Did we get the action we wanted?" Focusing on the ultimate goal will put everything else in perspective, especially if you were successful. One team leader then opens up the discussion with the question: "How can we do it better next time?" This kind of open-ended question will usually encourage individuals to engage in a kind of self-critique, especially if the team leader starts with himself or herself. The focus should be on solutions, not problems, so if a concern is raised, people should immediately try to generate potential solutions.

The need for this discussion may be easier to sell if the team works together on projects other than presentations, but it's important to come to closure even if the team was assembled for the sole purpose of presenting. Everyone needs immediate and concrete feedback. The end product of the debrief should be a list of at least three things to improve, and the leader should keep track of these goals and review them with the team just before the next presentation.

SUMMARY

To be successful in a team presentation,
- Agree on purpose
- Create a schedule with production time
- Work through the group process issues
- Use the tree system for getting agreement on structure
- Deliver the presentation as a unit
- Field questions smoothly
- Debrief to capture the experience and work to improve it

11
Meetings, Negotiations, and Informal Interchanges

Many of the techniques for making formal presentations also apply to

- Participating in meetings
- Negotiating
- Getting action through telephone calls, voice mail, and informal interchanges

Participating in Meetings

Many managers hate meetings, often with justification:

"I spend most of my time in meetings. I can't get any work done."

"We listen to the same arguments time after time, and we never make a decision."

"Jim (Jane) blathers on interminably. He (she) doesn't know when to stop."

Meetings, like presentations, are action-oriented. For a meeting to be effective, it must have a single, clear objective. By focusing on that objective and using the techniques for developing a logical argument for a specific audience, leaders and participants move together toward a useful conclusion.

Since most of a manager's time is spent in meetings, those that are focused and well-prepared can be a welcome relief. People resent having to attend three-hour meetings that accomplish one hour's work; on the other hand, they are inclined to work more productively for a leader who knows how to conduct a tight, well-managed meeting.

Leading or Facilitating the Meeting

Chairing a meeting means more than taking the seat at the head of the table. You need to understand your role, assemble people who can take action, make sure that they are properly prepared, keep the discussion focused and moving, and arrange for the implementation of any decisions.

Clarify your expectations

If you're the senior person (the boss chairing the weekly staff meetings, for example), decide who will make the final decisions and then let people know. Although most people these days pay lip service to collegial management styles and decisions made by consensus, it's unfair to assemble people, suggest that you will accept the decision of the group, and then, if things don't go your way, reserve the decision for yourself. It's far better for everyone to know that the decision is yours than to change the rules in midstream.

Establish the objective

In order for a meeting to be useful, the discussion must be focused. If you inform the participants in advance about the purpose of the meeting, they can come prepared to contribute. Advance notice does not stifle creativity; instead, it helps get everyone on the same wavelength — a necessary step toward using the meeting time to advantage.

To state the purpose of the meeting clearly, you must think about it on two levels. First, in a broad sense, consider where your meeting falls on a continuum between information sharing and decision making; most fall somewhere near the middle. For example, a meeting called to review progress on a project includes sharing information to bring everyone up to date, as well as problem-solving to deal with both anticipated concerns and anything else that crops up during the discussion. Second, once you know what you want to achieve on a broad scale, decide more specifically what you want to happen as a result of the meeting. The person who calls a meeting, just like a potential presenter, should be able to state the objective clearly in one sentence, as in the following examples:

> Coordinate division plans for next month's move and design a contingency plan.
> Decide whether to construct a new plant in South Carolina.
> Review second-quarter sales and make any necessary changes in third-quarter marketing plan.

Each of these statements is specific and complete. In the last example, if the leader had said simply, "Review second-quarter sales," some participants might have assumed that the discussion would focus on adjustments to the third-quarter marketing plan, especially if second-quarter sales had taken a dive, but they would not necessarily have thought about a specific course of action.

Even weekly staff meetings should have objectives, so that they do not become tedious and unproductive rituals. In general, staff meetings should focus on change; that is, on identifying existing problems, anticipating potential problems, or looking for opportunities. Recitals of routine activities, the standard fare of many staff meetings, guarantee boredom and resentment. Regularly scheduled meetings seem to have a life of their own. It's a good practice to think about whether *any* regular meeting is necessary.

Can a meeting have more than one objective? As long as everyone attending has a stake in every topic, and as long as you can deal with each topic quickly, meetings with multiple objectives can be successful. (When you circulate your preliminary agenda, double check the level of interest in each topic. If only two people need to discuss an item, delete it from the agenda and have them meet separately.) Keep in mind that problem-solving is difficult in a group of more than eight, and no one should be present at a discussion in which he or she has no reason to participate. Furthermore, a person's capacity for unbroken concentration is about an hour and a half. If you know it will take longer than that to reach all your objectives, schedule several short meetings instead of one long one. If the agenda is lengthy and people have come from out of town to attend the meeting and can't be reassembled easily, a meeting may run several hours. In this case, schedule a fifteen minute break every hour and a half, with refreshments.

Prepare the agenda

The agenda items should relate directly to the meeting's purpose. For example, if the purpose is to "decide whether to recommend adding production capacity in our trimming department," each agenda item should refer to a specific step in the problem-solving process:

1. Establish criteria for decision making
2. Review five-year production figures
3. Estimate short- and long-term demand
4. Review construction cost estimates
5. Evaluate potential short-term use of excess capacity

The leader starts the problem-solving process by isolating the pieces of the problem and putting them on the agenda. The agenda items must be so specific that participants can consider the issues in advance and be ready to contribute to the discussion. Notice that in the example above, the meeting's purpose calls for a recommendation. Whether you're working alone or as part of a team, your first order of business when making a recommendation is to establish the criteria against which to measure the possible solutions. Therefore, the first item on the agenda is to formulate these criteria.

Select the participants

Developing the invitation list for a meeting is an art. On the surface, it is much like drawing up the list of attendees for a presentation: only those people who will participate in making the decision or who have a vested interest in the outcome should attend. But what should you do when you want to invite people whose interest is not great, but whose contribution to part of the discussion is valuable? It is insulting to invite someone to provide information and then summarily dismiss him after he has said his piece. If his contribution is worth hearing, he should be invited to stay for the entire discussion. If confidentiality is an issue, schedule another meeting without him. In a similar vein, if someone with both substantial organizational power and a stake in an issue cancels at the last minute, postpone discussion of that item to another time. It's probable that any decision that's made in the person's absence won't hold, and the whole issue will have to be reopened later.

Consider your purpose in selecting participants. The closer your purpose is to the decision-making end of the continuum, the more homogeneous the group should be. In a highly hierarchical organization, the best results occur when no more than two levels in the hierarchy are present. Lots of posturing, but poor problem-solving, may take place in a group that includes the staff, the boss, and the boss's boss. If the meeting is largely designed to share information, the homogeneity of the group is less significant. If the invitation list begins to read like the company's softball league roster, however, go back to the agenda, narrow the objective, and prune some of the topics.

When planning meetings, it is a good idea to keep in mind that most people concentrate best in the morning and like to do their individual thinking early on. Scheduling an important meeting for the middle of the morning breaks into their routine and may spoil their day. If you suspect that to be the case, start an afternoon meeting at about 2:00 p.m. with an ending time of 3:00 or 3:30 p.m. so that participants can go back to the office and handle any pressing matters before they leave for the day. If people are coming from out of town, afternoon meetings or luncheon meetings are preferable to morning meetings to allow for inevitable transportation delays.

Determine the order of the agenda

Sometimes the order of agenda items is predetermined by logic; the agenda mentioned earlier is a good example. If the meeting includes several disparate topics, however, review the public positions of those attending the meeting, or try to divine their preconceived ideas, and deal with less controversial agenda items first. If you begin with a subject on which there is general agreement rather than conflict, you'll set a positive tone for the rest of the meeting.

Decide who should conduct the meeting

If you initiate a meeting, you'll usually also lead it. Sometimes, however, you may choose to delegate the job. If you've called a meeting to consider a problem in which you have a large stake and a strong position, choose a competent person to direct the discussion — one whom other participants view as impartial. At times, a relative outsider may serve as a leader to ensure impartiality. For example, someone from the human resources department may lead a meeting in the finance department. Whatever the circumstances, the leader's purpose is to facilitate problem-solving or decision making and to keep the discussion on an even keel. He or she is not a participant and should never dominate the meeting. In addition, the leader should understand what contribution each participant can be expected to make and on what issues a consensus must be reached.

Distribute material in advance

Well in advance of the meeting, the leader should distribute a written notice that includes the time, the meeting's purpose, the agenda, a list of the participants, and any pertinent written materials (see Exhibit 11.1 for a sample preliminary agenda). The agenda should include a time estimate for each item so that participants can judge the level of detail they're expected to go into. Always include the time the meeting will end, since people tend to be much more concise when they know the time limits. Some managers like to include on their agenda a synopsis of the decision each item will require. If the group has sufficient trust in the leader, or if the leader has sufficient clout, these directions

Preliminary Agenda
June Production Planning Meeting

Date: June 18

Time: 10:00 a.m. to 11:30 a.m.

Location: Meeting Room B

Objective: Decide whether to recommend additional production capacity in
               trimming department

Attendees: Joe Fischer
               Stan Sussman
               Eric DeRenzie
               Jane Coleman
               Lewis O'Neil
               Betsy Zerlow

Agenda Item	Purpose	Allotted Time	Presenter	Material to be read in advance
Establish criteria for making decision	consensus	15 min	–	–
Review 5-year production figures	information	10 min	J.F.	figures
Estimate long- and short-term demands	decision	20 min	J.C.	–
Review cost estimate	information	15 min	S.S.	estimates
Consider potential short-term use of excess capacity	decision	20 min	B.Z.	estimates

Exhibit 11.1. A useful agenda includes assignments and time estimates

promote quick closure on each point. Keep in mind, however, that it's rarely possible to achieve enthusiastic, unanimous agreement. As the leader, you must be prepared to accept less than total consensus; that is, you must be satisfied if those present simply agree not to block a decision or if they agree only to try a course of action.

Naturally, the leader should give everyone who is to make a presentation sufficient lead time to do a credible job of preparing. Less obvious, the leader should alert any participant expected to contribute more than general comments. Failure to let people know that they'll be called on for information puts them in an uncomfortable position.

Control the process

Protect the meeting from outside interruptions. Never let people take calls except in cases of dire emergency. Unless you've had problems in the past with how participants relate to one another, let people sit wherever they want. Participants usually distribute themselves around the table in a manner that makes them feel relaxed, and their feeling of relaxation usually improves the openness of the discussion. If you do anticipate problems, try to make adjustments. For example, you won't want two people who have locked horns in the past to sit opposite each other (people are more likely to argue when they can establish good eye contact). One technique is to ask a confederate to station himself opposite one of the antagonists, but this may be excessive except when serious conflict is expected. If the meeting is formal, it is acceptable to provide tent cards that assign seats. If certain participants frequently interrupt with side comments, try to break up the clique by assigning seats or by assigning one of the individuals the task of making a presentation. The presenter will be so busy concentrating on his or her presentation that there won't be time for by-play.

As the participants enter the room, try to read any nonverbal cues that give you insight into each person's mood. Although managers pride themselves on their objectivity, they are inevitably influenced by personal factors. If you are relying on someone to carry the discussion but her mind is clearly elsewhere, you may not achieve your goal.

Always start on time. Begin the meeting by restating the purpose (remember, some people do not read their mail), and guide it to a successful conclusion by insisting on discipline, encouraging participation, summarizing the discussion, and providing transitions between agenda items. During the discussion, don't permit side conversations, in-jokes, innuendoes, extended war stories, or anything else that might destroy cohesiveness. Don't compete with the other participants for "air time." To stimulate clearheaded discussion, ask open-ended questions (that is, questions requiring more than a simple yes or no answer). You can ask these questions of the whole group and have people volunteer answers. If you have people in the group who need time to think before answering, you might write the question down on a whiteboard or flipchart to provide the necessary thinking time. If it is not threatening to others, you can take the answers from several participants and point out how they compare or contrast. Keep people on track politely but firmly. Should someone begin a major digression, try something like, "That's an interesting point, but we're getting pretty far afield. Let's get back to the agenda for now and talk about that next week." It may help to keep a running tab of items that need to be discussed at a later date on a flipchart. If adding an item to a future agenda can be turned into an action step at the end of the presentation, the person who brought it up will feel attended to.

If discussion of a particular item takes much longer than you planned, assign someone to look into it further and report at the next meeting. As we have said, consensus on all items may not always be possible — for instance, if your discussion has turned up information gaps that must be filled, or if a conflict is too deep. You should be able to demonstrate consensus on at least some items, however, or participants will leave discouraged. When you reach agreement on an item requiring action, write out what the action is, who is responsible, and when the task should be completed (see Exhibit 11.2). At regular intervals, clarify and summarize to keep participants from ruminating too long on one topic and to help them move on to the next. Properly done, summarizing serves not only as a reminder but also as a way of checking to see that everyone is on the same track. Its function is simi-

ASSIGNMENTS

Meeting Objective: *DECIDE WHETHER TO RECOMMEND ADDITIONAL*
PRODUCTION CAPACITY IN TRIMMING DEPARTMENT

Meeting Date: *JUNE 18*

Decision Adopted: *RECOMMEND ADDITION TO FACILITIES*
(SIZE TO BE DECIDED)

Action Plans:	**Action**	**Person Responsible**	**Completion Date**
	DEVELOP NEW EXHIBITS SHOWING DEMAND BY SECTOR	*J.C.*	*JUNE 22*
	PUT TOGETHER TABLE FOR SENIOR MANAGEMENT SHOWING BEST, WORST, MOST LIKELY CASES	*S.S.*	*JUNE 21*

NEXT MEETING SCHEDULED FOR JUNE 25

Exhibit 11.2. Once a decision is reached, an assignment sheet serves as a reminder

lar to previewing and reviewing in a presentation.

Always end on time. Never ask the fateful question, "Does anyone have anything else to discuss?" Someone will, and chances are it won't be anything you want to deal with. If you've managed the meeting appropriately, you'll never have unfinished business. At the end of the meeting, summarize the discussion, state items on which there is agreement, review all the action plans (state the name of the person responsible for implementation and the date by which completion is expected), and thank the participants. After the meeting, you may want to provide additional reinforcement by sending a memo that recalls this information.

To improve your leadership skills, review the meeting in your mind as soon as it ends. Use the following checklist to help you evaluate your performance.

Checklist for Evaluating Yourself as Leader

- Was the agenda appropriate to the purpose?
- Was consensus reached on a sufficient number of items?
- Did I prepare participants adequately?
- Was everyone who could provide vital information included?
- Did I encourage participation?
  — Did I cut anyone off too soon?
  — Did I keep people from rambling?
  — Did I call on everyone who wanted to speak?
- Did I let someone else control the meeting? If so, why?

If you lead a group that meets regularly, it is equally important to set aside five or ten minutes at the end of the meeting to discuss how the meeting went. This debriefing lets the group members share their concerns and suggest ways to improve the effectiveness of the group as well as increase their sense of responsibility.

Being a Participant

A friend of ours has a wonderful poster tacked on her door. It says, "Don't just talk — say something!" It's the best advice we can give to anyone acting as a participant in a meeting. As a participant, your responsibility is to listen actively, to consider new ideas, and, most of all, to make an intelligent and positive contribution.

One way to stay with the topic is to draw on the presentation skills you learned in the earlier chapters. Use a logic tree as a structure for note taking. If you're lucky, the speaker will open with his or her main point. Write it down and then listen to see how the point is supported. If no main point is apparent, jot down ideas as they're presented and connect them as relationships emerge. This technique forces you to listen critically and to see both the strengths and weaknesses in the argument. A few sessions of listening to illogical or pointless arguments will also teach you to pay attention to your own presentation skills. You'll soon find yourself silently asking "What is my main point? What is my support?" before you speak.

If you intend to respond with a significant argument rather than a simple comment, quickly sketch a tree to remind yourself of your support points. If, for example, your group is reviewing last year's production to estimate expansion needs, and you believe the figures for one item are not representative of production capability because a severe winter and a trucker's strike caused delivery delays, the temptation may be to say: "We shouldn't use these figures. They're not realistic." Far better, however, to stop and ask yourself: "What exactly do I want to accomplish?" and "What do I want these people to do?" Presumably, you want any decision to be based on accurate projections, and you want the participants to accept your view. By knowing what you hope to accomplish, you can avoid fueling a heated personal debate, and concentrate on advancing the discussion.

Once you've decided that your remarks will make a contribution, decide how much you absolutely need to say for people to understand your position. In other words, analyze the audience before you make your tree. Then jot down your main point: *We should add 2,000 pieces to the figures.* Your notes might look like this:

Speak to your main point first. If you begin by voicing your disagreement, people will begin to think about a rebuttal and stop listening. Continue with your support points and then stop. Most of us, once we start talking, enjoy the sound of our own voices. Listeners, however, appreciate conciseness. Often, those who say the least at a meeting are listened to most.

Stay until the end of the meeting. As we mentioned, agendas are often arranged to leave the most controversial items for last, on the theory that there will be quicker agreement if only the most interested participants remain. If you find such an item toward the end of the list and the meeting is running late, try to negotiate a postponement until the next meeting.

Checklist for Evaluating Yourself as a Participant

- Did I concentrate on the argument?
- Did I add anything new to the general understanding of the problem?
- Were my contributions stated in positive rather than negative terms?
- Were my remarks complete but concise?

During the meeting, concentrate on issues, not on your performance. After the meeting, however, take a few minutes to review the quality of your participation.

Negotiating

So far we've talked about meetings in which, ostensibly, everyone has at least a basic interest in proceeding toward a solution to a problem, or in taking advantage of a strategic opportunity. In what we traditionally consider a negotiation, however, the participants often view themselves as adversaries — they believe the discussion will end with one side a winner and one a loser. That need not be so if you consider negotiating as problem-solving. We all negotiate many times every day. We negotiate such simple issues as where to have lunch, and such complex ones as when our child should have the use of the car and what to do about the offer to buy the business. We negotiate in every meeting.

To be successful in a negotiation, it is important to remember that any discussion influences a relationship. In other words, the discussion is one in a long string of discussions. Driving a bargain so hard that the other side will bear a grudge and take every opportunity to get revenge will be counterproductive in the long run. Identifying shared goals and seeking ways to achieve those goals help create the atmosphere you need to have a win-win situation.

There are many books devoted solely to negotiating. Here are some guidelines, based on the principles laid out in this book, that we think will help you.

Preparation Is Key

One theme of this book is that you can't overprepare for any important communication. Because of the fluidity of the process, that precept is especially true for negotiations. Many people practice avoidance because they fear conflict, but the result is often that the other party dominates the agenda. Preparation for any important negotiation should include the following:

- Determining the goals that you believe are important.
- Determining the extent to which you are willing to give up some of those goals.
- Determining your counterparty's goals and what he or she can live with.
- Seeking common ground (Remember you are still considering goals, or criteria). Try to settle at the outset how both of you will measure whether a solution is acceptable. Often you will find that the other person's criteria are similar to your own or, at least, not in conflict with them. For example, in negotiating budget allocations, one person may want his or her allocation for production to be commensurate with that in other firms and, to that end, cite an average figure of $2.6 million. You, on the other hand may want to allocate $750,000 to research and development to keep that division in the forefront but consider other goals less important. Both you and your counterparty may be able to get what you want.
- Seeking creative ways of reaching those goals. You should generate ideas with your counterparty, rather than relying only on those you brought to the meeting.

Notice that these steps preclude any discussion of prior positions. If people have a position in mind, they will argue for the position rather than seek ways of reaching a goal. Never back anyone into a corner by insisting that he or she take a position for or against an issue. Instead, try to spell out as many options as you can that meet both parties' criteria.

It is always better to ask about someone's goals than to speculate. People are often willing to tell you what they want. But if you can't get information, use your best judgment and try to read responses during the negotiation. In essence, then, a sensible negotiator relies on analyzing the people, their thinking styles, and their criteria, and practicing problem-solving techniques to reach agreement.

Recognizing How Negotiators Communicate

When is an "attack" really an "attack?" Some people see hostility and aggression in every statement the other party in the negotiation makes. The words "What do you mean?" can be interpreted as a request for definition or as a challenge. Tone of voice influences the interpretation. But sometimes even the most innocent question is misread, leaving the parties farther apart rather than closer together. The other person's perception is the reality you live with. If you want a successful conclusion to any negotiation, be careful of your language and tone and don't jump to conclusions about the other person. It is also helpful to recognize some of the common techniques adversarial negotiators use, and to consider how best to respond to them.

Nibbling

People will attack a proposal in small bits, in an attempt to get you to change your approach or to wear you down. In response, focus on the criteria and the goals.

Referring to a higher authority

Some negotiators will insist they cannot make the decision. In response, seek a meeting with the decision maker.

Playing good cop, bad cop

We all know that approach. One member of the other team takes a hard line; his partner intercedes, offering a concession. Focus on the apparently more conciliatory person and discuss criteria.

Coming to the table with a give-away

This is the most common device of all. It is the equivalent of asking for $20,000 when you really want $10,000. It may be a good technique if you are never going to do business with that person again. But the concept that the first offer includes a give-away makes many people uncomfortable because they don't know what the "real" offer is. In most business settings you do better to make it clear from the beginning that you are not playing that game and you don't expect others to play it.

How do you know when a negotiation has been successful? Ask yourself these questions:

- Does everyone involved feel like a winner?
- Does each party believe the other side was fair?
- Would I enjoy dealing with this person again?
- Am I better off after the negotiation than before?

Getting Action through Informal Exchanges

Telephone calls, voice mail, and short conferences that take place either in the hall or in someone's office are by far the most common forms of management communication. Individuals differ in the way they choose to communicate — some people are more effective in person than they are on the phone, whereas others view the telephone as an extension of their right arm. Too often, though, people make the mistake of launching into a discussion or reaching for the phone without thinking through what they want to accomplish. "Thinking on your feet" is a skill everyone admires, but wise managers try to avoid relying on it.

The strategy for both unplanned meetings and phone calls is similar to that for more formal presentations. Start with some preliminary questions such as those in the following checklist.

Checklist for an Informal Conference

- What do I want to accomplish?
- Am I talking with the person who can make that happen?
- Is a phone call or face-to-face conversation better?
- What does the person know about the situation?
- What preconceived ideas might he or she have?
- Do I need any data before I go into this discussion?

Once you've decided that it's appropriate to get ahead with the conversation, organize your ideas, just as you would for any presentation. Consider this transcript of a phone call between Joe Seymor, the comptroller for the Midwest division of a manufacturing company, and Jane Thomas, the head of corporate planning. After some initial pleasantries, Joe began:

> Listen, you know we've been having this problem in district 5. Well, I was talking to Brette the other day — you know her — she's the one who started in corporate personnel and now does something in human resources for the Eastern division. She said she knows some consultants who have a lot of experience with that sort of problem. She thought I should call them. Before I do that, though, I want to check with you.

> (Silence, while Jane wonders: What is "this" problem? Why do I care who Brette is? Who does he mean by "some" consultants? What is he checking with me about? WHAT DOES HE WANT FROM ME?!)

Joe committed two major errors: he left out important information and he told Jane a good deal she didn't need to know. This vagueness and lack of preparation, although common in telephone calls, is nonproductive. Had Joe organized his thoughts and asked himself before he made the call, "What do I want Jane to do?" and "What is my objective?" this call would have proceeded quite differently. Joe's objective would have been to request approval to hire a writing consultant for the senior staff in district 5. His notes would have looked like this:

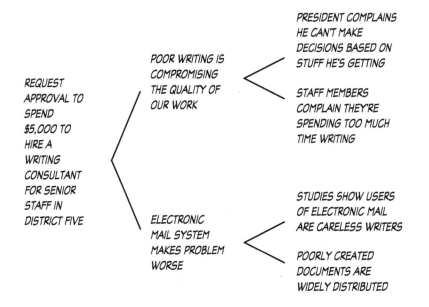

Making notes before picking up the phone is absolutely necessary, particularly in the game of telephone tag, in which you and your target keep missing each other's calls. When the person finally reaches you, you most likely have your mind on something else. If enough time has passed, you even may have forgotten why you called. Worse, you may not remember who the person is. An abbreviated tree, written on a scrap of paper and taped to the phone, will help you enormously. Should you need or want a record of the discussion, you can add to your notes during the return conversation.

Voice mail is used so often that people take it for granted and treat it extremely casually. People leaving messages often sound as if they are surprised that the person is not available, and ramble on and on before they get to the point. You should always be prepared either to hold a live conversation or to leave a message. Some tips to remember:

- Say your name and telephone number distinctly. Spell your name if it is unusual.
- State your main point first. If you don't, people may fast forward right past it because they think you don't have one.
- Indicate any true urgency as quickly as possible, and state the reason for the urgency. "I need to know by Tuesday" is a useless statement, unless you add something like, "because the grant proposal is due the following Monday at 12 noon."
- Use the same conversational and upbeat tone you would use if you actually got the person on the phone. Whom would you rather call back, someone who sounded confused and depressed, or someone who sounded upbeat and cheerful?

Face-to-face conversations often go the same way as unplanned phone conversations — full of vague references, lacking a proper beginning to orient the listener, and rambling on without clearly disclosing the purpose of the conversation. When you corner a person without warning, it is especially important that you follow the rules for a good beginning and a well-organized argument. Your listener has no idea what to expect, and no time to reconstruct past events. If you are buttonholing a person who works in another department and doesn't know you well, the best way to start is by introducing yourself and mentioning your title or function. Obviously, you would not approach an informal face-to-face conversation with notes in hand. At the same time, it is unwise to have an important conversation if you haven't planned it. But if you are caught off guard and can't play for time, keep these guidelines in mind:

- Limit the discussion to those topics that will help you reach your objective
- In choosing what to say and the order in which to say it, remember the listener's concerns (criteria) and knowledge of the subject
- Be concise
- Ask questions if you don't understand

When you get in the habit of following these guidelines, your conversations, both in person and on the phone, should be more fruitful and more efficient.

SUMMARY

To present your views effectively,

- In meetings,
    — Polish your leadership skills

        Establish an objective

        Prepare a concise agenda

        Select participants carefully

        Control the meeting

        Start and end on time

        Summarize and debrief the participants

    — Be an active participant

        Follow the discussion attentively

        Concentrate on issues

        Be open to new ideas

        Make constructive contributions

- In negotiations,
    — Think of negotiating as problem-solving

    — Begin by considering goals; know what you can live with

    — Seek shared goals before considering solutions

    — Think "out of the box" when looking for solutions

    — Recognize techniques, but negotiate as a partner

- In telephone calls, voice mail, and face-to-face conferences,
    — Plan ahead

    — Clarify your purpose

    — Consider your listener's concerns and knowledge

    — Be concise

12
Speaking
in Public

As you rise in the organization (or if you have to sell your firm and yourself as an entrepreneur), you'll have more and more opportunities to address outside groups. To do this effectively you should know how to

- Decide whether or not to accept the invitation to speak
- Introduce the elements of drama and humor
- Adapt your presentation techniques
- Write and read a speech
- Serve on a panel
  - As moderator
  - As panelist

Although most management presentations involve no more than eight to ten people, when you speak in public you are likely to be addressing larger groups. For the most part, preparation, organization, and rehearsals for these occasions require techniques similar to those we discussed in earlier chapters. You'll still have to focus on one main point and support it with logical arguments; and you'll still use an open, objective, businesslike tone. However, there are differences.

Deciding Whether or Not You'll Accept the Invitation

Your first decision is whether you should speak at all. It's always an honor to be asked, and you should treat it as such. Furthermore, the kind of exposure public speaking gives you is priceless in terms of advancing your career, and will help your organization as well. One head of a consulting firm finds that his main source of new clients, apart from referrals, is the "rubber chicken circuit." Find out whether the speech must be given on an assigned topic. Often, the program chairperson or conference coordinator has something in mind when he or she calls you to ask you to make a speech. If your talk must fit in with those of others on the agenda, you need to know in advance. You should definitely speak if you are familiar with the topic and you can come up with a sustainable point of view and an enlightening discussion that will allow you to establish credibility with the audience. If you are simply being used as a "placeholder," for example, because they asked someone else and that person canceled, consider your response carefully. The risks may outweigh the rewards. Instead of a flat-out "no," see whether you can find a connection between the topic the coordinator wants and one you can deal with gracefully.

Introducing Drama and Humor

Pick a gripping title

Even if someone else set it up, you'll need to "sell" your speech to its potential audience — generating excitement for your remarks in advance will help gain a positive reception. The place to start is with an enticing title. Forced humor is usually a failure, but imagery works very well, especially in combination with a more straightforward description. One presenter, when asked to speak about strategy in the retail industry, chose this title: "Can't See the Socks for the Fibers: The Failure of Strategic Thinking in the Rag Trade." Another idea is to skewer jargon or euphemism. The title "It's Time to Right Size Executive Compensation" does both quite nicely. Apart from puns and other word plays, a good way to come up with a hip title is to invent a phrase that would explain your main point to a reasonably alert high school student. Uncensored brainstorming will serve you better than rational thought in this endeavor. If all else fails, make sure your title states your main point, your point of view. At least then the audience will not come dreading an hour's worth of dry data or methodology, or worse yet, utter fluff or a thinly veiled sales pitch for your company or product.

Adapting Your Presentation Technique

Once you have done the set-up for the speech, the major adjustment will come in your delivery style. Although you should always be yourself when you present, you'll have to project your personality with a bit more theatricality and energy when you speak to a large group in an echoing auditorium than when you talk to a small group in a conference room. A light touch is more important in a speech designed for general consumption than it is in a formal presentation, although wit is appreciated in almost any communication. Don't try canned jokes unless you are a comedian, and don't make fun of anyone, even yourself. The following guidelines will help you speak successfully in public.

Warm up the audience

When you make a presentation to people you know well, you don't have to spend time warming up the group. For a large group, you'll have to take time for the preliminaries. Starting with an anecdote or a story provides a good introduction. A historical anecdote is also a safe way to introduce a light note — but be sure it makes a point. That way, if the audience doesn't laugh, the anecdote still serves a useful function. Lengthy introductions, especially those involving complicated anecdotes, make people fidget. Something to get the audience's attention: "How many of you own mutual funds? How many of you are wondering where the market will go next?" plus a transition into your main point and a quick recap of the major supporting points ought to suffice. If you are genuinely glad to be there, say so, but also say why, if you expect to be believed. Don't dwell on anything unpleasant, such as the trip from the airport, the slides that didn't arrive, or your nervousness — no one will know any of this if you don't tell them.

If you have a regional accent that is markedly different from that of most of the people in the audience or if English is your second language, make sure you give the audience time to become familiar with your speech patterns before you launch into your main point.

Assert your authority

When you speak in public, people expect you to exercise the authority that comes with the role of expert. Apologies, slumping shoulders, and poor posture all signal a lack of confidence. And when a speaker appears ill at ease, most listeners let their minds drift rather than vicariously experience the speaker's discomfort. Others may take signs of nervousness as an opportunity to attack. Either way, you lose. The opposite problem, pomposity — assuming that your high position in some organization entitles you to a hearing — is equally dangerous. Your success in public speaking must stem from your personal qualities and expertise more than from your role. No audience will accept what you say if you don't inspire respect and trust.

Use gestures

When you can't move about freely (in many formal situations, you will find the microphone permanently attached to the lectern), gestures are the only way to hold the audience's interest and relieve your own physical tension. Used well, they intensify the meaning of what you say. Paradoxically, people who find gestures easy to use in small groups often freeze in front of a large audience. They feel "everyone is looking at me" rather than "everyone is listening to me." As we have recommended previously, any time you find your energy invested more in nervousness than in the content of your talk or your audience, try to find a way to make your anxiety work for you. In this case, you can discharge some of your tension through gestures.

Most people are aware that their usual gestures are too small in scale for a large auditorium or banquet room, but they do not know how to scale them upward. Here are some do's and don'ts:

Do ...

- Gesture with your whole arm rather than your hand and wrist. By using the whole arm, you'll make your gestures more forceful and they'll be more visible from the back of the hall. When you use a full-arm gesture, resist the temptation to pull your arm back quickly as if the gesture were a mistake. Comfortably hold the gesture for a moment, then slowly bring your arm back in. Practice this in front of a mirror until it feels and looks natural.

- Gesture with both hands. When you use both hands, you appear more confident (because you seem more in control of your body) and more expansive. To improve your use of gestures, notice how professional presenters handle themselves when they address a large group. Then evaluate yourself on videotape.

Don't ...

- Assume a relaxed, hands-in-the-pockets pose. It's too easy to play with keys or loose change (besides, you'll look like a kangaroo).

- Park your hands on your hips (you'll remind people of their sixth-grade teacher).

- Clasp your hands behind your back (you'll look like a military person or a deacon).

- Clutch the podium, if you have one (you'll look like you're trying to shield yourself from a barrage of tomatoes).

Make yourself heard

When you're not accustomed to addressing large audiences, the tendency is to start off too softly, inviting petulant cries of "louder" or "we can't hear you" from the back of the room. These kinds of interruptions diminish your authority in the eyes of the audience. The secret is to test the strength of your speaking voice before the event begins, preferably with a colleague in the room in which you will speak. After a few trial runs, you'll become comfortable with a tone and pitch that at first might have felt unnatural. Practice will also give you the opportunity to work on projecting your voice. If you have any doubts about whether people can hear you, ask the audience if your voice is reaching the back of the room. If you're using a microphone, test it before the audience arrives to see how far you can move away from it and still be within range. It may be farther than you think. Although inexpensive microphones can't pick up a voice more than eight inches away, professional equipment has a greater range. If you plan to use a lavaliere, practice with it ahead of time.

Look at people - the back of the room doesn't have eyes

In large groups, you cannot look at everyone, especially if you're tethered to a podium. But you can look at one individual in each section of the room to assure everyone that you are aware of their presence. Don't look over everyone's head and gaze at some spot halfway up the back wall. Some presenters think this makes the entire audience feel included, but it is more likely to give people the impression that something in the rear of the room is more important than they are. A perfunctory effort at eye contact is not sufficient. You cannot cast sidelong glances at individuals or make a series of darting eye movements without unsettling the audience.

The only kind of eye contact that successfully establishes the feeling of connection with members of the audience is a reasonably long, in-focus look at specific individuals. At first it may be difficult to do this with a sea of faces. Eye contact can help to ground you and to eliminate the fantasy of a hostile, threatening mob. You'll find it immensely helpful to look for someone you know in the crowd. If you can't station a supportive friend in one of the first few rows, look at the person who introduced you as you thank him or her, and then turn your attention to finding someone responsive out in the room. If you can arrange it, move into the crowd at some point during the speech, à la talk show host — if at no other point, then during the question period. Your eye contact will automatically improve.

Use notes, not a script

Even though the solemnity of the occasion may seem to justify it, we recommend that you do not read a prepared speech unless you are dealing with a highly controversial issue and your remarks may be reported in the press. It's very difficult to read a speech with any feeling. When you use notes, on the other hand, you indicate that you are in control of the material and have no need to be overly careful about what you say — that you can be spontaneous.

Don't use alcohol or relaxants

Although alcohol provides an initial high, it may make you feel unpleasantly out of control and anxious, encouraging you to be flip, and inducing you to make inappropriate remarks. If you drink far enough in advance of the presentation, the ultimate depressant effect will damage your ability to speak forcefully and can play havoc with your timing. In any case, the self you feel internally will be at odds with the one you are projecting to your audience — a dangerous state. Alcohol also dries your mouth, exacerbating the dryness caused by nervousness. Relaxants slow you down and make it difficult to speak resolutely or respond to questions with wit and intelligence, skills very important in external presentations. If dinner is served just before the presentation, avoid eating heavily (perhaps not too difficult, given the quality of most catered meals). Too much food will make you sleepy.

Defuse Hostility

There may be occasions when hedging is legitimate (if the questioner is overtly hostile, for example, or the facts as currently known suggest one conclusion, but you know that additional information, which is not public, points to another). Sometimes, stung by loaded questions and lulled by the certainty that no one could possibly check it out, presenters are tempted to falsify the facts. Don't succumb to this temptation. Once you are caught distorting the truth, everything you say will be open to question. In short, you'll lose all credibility with this audience, and possibly with future audiences, especially if the press is around to record your misstep. Even if you're not found out, it isn't worth the anxiety of thinking you might be.

Be open in answering questions. The best way to avoid blurting out something when you're on the defensive is to train yourself to pause before you answer any question. It's perfectly acceptable to say you don't know (if you don't). It is also acceptable to say, "I don't have those figures with me." If it's important enough, you might offer to find the answer or have someone on your staff find it. The person asking the question then has a channel for getting the information later.

If you can't avoid an answer, and the answer may seem damaging, always put the response in context. For example, one speaker pointed out before she responded to a question, "There's a tendency for people to believe there's a solution for every problem. If we could just sit down together, they say we could work it out. I'm here to tell you, though, that most problems can't be solved — the best we can do is try to make the consequences of the problem less negative." Don't be trapped into answering a request for "a simple yes or no answer" — almost nothing is that simple. By taking something to its logical limits, you can show the absurdity of either/or thinking.

Look for logical flaws — not to embarrass the questioner, but to deflect the question. For example, we heard one speaker respond to a loaded question by saying, "I can't agree with you because I don't agree with your major premise, which is that all oil companies are dishonest in reporting their profits."

If you're truly concerned that your audience will be unfriendly, get a friend to roleplay the question-and-answer period with you. If you've heard a question before, you'll be much calmer when you respond.

Finally, don't get angry and don't lose your sense of humor. One speaker, after a barrage of leading and hostile questions, finally paused, looked at the last person to offer a question, and said, "Could you rephrase that? I haven't got it in a form I want to answer yet."

Writing a Speech

If you must read a speech, take special care to write it or have it written to be spoken, and then rehearse carefully. One new CEO, whose command of the English language had been honed by years of academic training, was in the midst of reading a lengthy sentence in his text when he suddenly stopped and said, "I don't know how I got into this thought, but I sure as hell am willing to admit that I don't know how to get out of it." It was amusing, but he could have avoided the situation by writing his words to be spoken, not read. The following guidelines will help you write a readable speech.

Choose simple sentences

Impromptu speakers don't usually load up their sentences with a great many dependent clauses. It's hard to visualize a manager running into an office shouting, "The Thomas computer file, on which I was working thirty minutes ago, has been erased!" More likely you would hear something like, "I was working on the Thomas file just thirty minutes ago, and now it's been erased." You may also freely eliminate "that" in sentences like: "It's conceivable that we'll be in the black by 1992." Better yet, just write: "I predict we'll be in the black by 1992."

Use verbs rather than nouns

Rather than "there's a belief among managers that," it is more effective and less wordy to say "managers believe that."

Eliminate long connecting words

Most people never use words like "nevertheless," "furthermore," "additionally," and "therefore" when they speak. Including them in a speech meant to be read will distance you from your audience. Substitute "that's why" or "so" for "therefore" or "thus;" "but" or "all the same" for "however" or "nevertheless," "then" or "and" for "furthermore."

Emphasize your Ideas with repetition

Consider the strength of this phrasing: "Why should we adopt this budget? Because it's fair. Because it's feasible. And because it's going to guarantee us a competitive edge for the next four years." Repeating "because" emphasizes the link between the points. Repetition and parallel structure allow the speaker to build the case with growing drama.

Imitate spoken speech

Use short, simple words. Use contractions like "you'll" or "we're." Use "I" when appropriate and "you" whenever you can. Leave prepositions and clauses at the ends of sentences. Use everyday words and phrases like "sticking to your knitting" rather than "creating corporate clarity."

Use stories to make your point

We've recommended starting with an anecdote (one that's to the point and not too long). We also recommend using stories during the speech itself. It's part of the convention of speechmaking and people will appreciate the effort. Don't wander into the land of sexism or ethnic slurs, though. It may seem obvious, but relating stories pointing up such things as alleged national or ethnic differences can be extremely offensive.

Develop a resource library

Audiences expect to be entertained, if not by jokes, then by learning something new and interesting. Although you must always confine yourself to ideas and thoughts that bear on your main message, checking through a library that includes books on historical anecdotes and misquotes by famous people can spice up your speechmaking.

Take command

You may be a self-effacing person in your normal business life, but as a speaker, you're in charge. Keep the audience with you by telling them directly what you want them to think or do. Give your ideas maximum impact by saying, "Think about that for a minute" or "Remember, we've been working on this idea for two years" or "Your support is vital to the success of this plan."

Ghostwriting a Speech

If you're the ghostwriter, make sure you talk frequently and pointedly with the person who will give the speech, and then follow all the rules for good speech writing. Writing for someone else requires talking with that person long enough to get a sense of his or her speech patterns and vocabulary so the final product will sound like that person, not like you. If a third party has given you the assignment, consult with the ultimate speaker. You are inviting disaster if you operate with second-hand information.

From the beginning, make sure that you and the speaker agree on the main point. Make a logic tree and get preliminary agreement on the organization of the speech. That way, you can keep a coherent focus even when the person giving the speech tries to throw in irrelevant ideas. Most people are insecure about having someone else write for them, because they feel an intense ego involvement with the content of the speech. If the speech is important enough, the person giving it certainly will talk to many other people to confirm that he or she is on the right track. Each of those people will have suggestions (almost no one who's asked for advice refuses to give it, even if he or she has nothing original to say). Your task is to make sure that, at least while you're still responsible for the product, nothing extraneous is included. You need not be stubborn or insist on your own ideas over those of the person giving the speech; rather, you need to work with the person either to find a logical way to include the idea or to persuade him or her to hold the idea for another occasion.

Guidelines for Ghostwriting

- Consult frequently with the person giving the speech about
  — Audience analysis
  — The main point
  — The organization
  — The tone
- Don't substitute your ideas for those of the speechmaker
- Make sure the person giving the speech knows who's responsible for arrangements

---

Finally, find out who is making the arrangements for the speech itself and, when you deliver the final version, include a summary of those arrangements as well as the name and telephone number of the person responsible. If you're the only person with whom the speaker has talked, he or she may incorrectly assume you're in charge of the whole effort. It's far better to dispel this illusion in the beginning than to explain later that you weren't responsible for some misadventure.

Reading a Written Speech

Review every written speech by reading it aloud and taping it. If you stumble over certain passages, stop. Then put what you're trying to say into simple phrases. Once the speech is printed out (either double or triple space), underline or highlight stress or emphasis points and pauses. Even if you wrote the speech yourself, rehearse by reading it aloud several times. If someone else wrote it for you, this step is especially important. Nothing is more damaging than reading a speech in such a stilted way that the audience thinks you're seeing it for the first time.

If you work with a speechwriter, make sure you talk to the person several times. You want to convey not only some sense of your position on the subject, but also a sense of your vocabulary and the cadence of your speech. If the speech doesn't sound like you, you won't be able to read it with grace, no matter how much you rehearse. You can save yourself time by talking at length with the speechwriter — before he or she outlines the speech, after you've read the outline, and after you've read the first draft.

In the last analysis, quality control is your responsibility, even if someone else wrote the speech. We were once told a marvelous (if apocryphal) story about President Lyndon Johnson, who decided that he no longer needed his "Rose Garden" speechwriter — the person who wrote routine speeches welcoming groups like Scouts or Texas constituents at informal gatherings in the White House Rose Garden. He gave the speechwriter his pink slip along with a final assignment. On his last day, the speechwriter delivered note cards for the speech to President Johnson, who strode out to the Rose Garden, welcomed the assembled delegation, and started to read:

My fellow Americans:

Some say we cannot have full employment and a low rate
of inflation.

I believe we can and I will tell you how ...

Some say we cannot have true equality of treatment
and a society that rewards merit.

I believe we can and I will tell you how ...

Some say we cannot protect our national security and open the door to negotiations with the Soviet Union.

I believe we can and I will tell you how ...

LBJ then flipped to the fourth card, which read:

Okay, Lyndon, now you're on your own.

The rest of the cards in the pack were blank.

Serving on a Panel

Executives are often called upon to moderate or participate in panel discussions. Some of the techniques used in these situations differ from the usual presentation techniques.

Moderating a Panel

As a moderator, you are the leader of the group and, even though you are required to remain in the background far more than when delivering a presentation, you are responsible for attending to a number of seemingly minor but crucial details.

Pay attention to people's names

Although most people, to be polite, laugh off mispronunciations of their names, they often hide their true feelings of offense. This basic reminder may seem simplistic, but even professionals seem to need it. Once you've got the names right, memorize them, and as extra insurance write them down somewhere as well, just in case you have to refer to them. However, don't read the names directly from cards. Doing so signals the audience that the panelists are not particularly important to you, and therefore needn't be to them.

Introduce yourself and the panel members

In your concern for others, it's easy to forget yourself. A simple, "Good afternoon, I'm Harry Newsom, the moderator of our panel on changes in corporate planning policies" is usually enough. In introducing other members of the panel, use the same guidelines we established in Chapter 5. Don't get carried away describing a person's credentials. Confine your remarks to the panelist's expertise on the subject of the discussion.

Set the stage

A good moderator, like a good presenter, creates an appropriate environment for the panel discussion at the outset. Tell the audience what the panel is about, why it is important, and what the format will be. Your tone, your manner, and your professionalism set standards for the panelists and establish rapport with the audience.

Set time limits

It is good practice to note at the beginning the importance of adhering to a schedule. (One moderator complimented each panelist when he or she finished on time.) The wise moderator will set up, in advance, some system for cuing the participants that their time is up and will make sure that everyone understands the ground rules. If a panelist does start to run over, you will need to intervene with some comment like, "We appreciate your detailed discussion, but we need to move on to Mr. Thomas." If you don't control garrulous panelists, tension will start to build in the audience, among the panel members, and particularly in the person who will speak next.

In most cases, it works best to take questions after each panelist has completed his or her remarks. If you ask the audience to hold questions until the end, you run the risk of people forgetting what they want to ask or, worse yet, of spending the entire presentation thinking about their questions. Your job as a moderator also includes limiting the time spent on questions and answers. The early and final remarks tend to get the majority of questions, so your greatest problem will be to elicit remarks during the middle.

Maintain a sense of dignity

Even if you know all the members of the panel on intimate terms, the audience does not. "Chatting them up," as one British manager describes it, can devalue the whole enterprise. It's far better to be straightforward in your transitions from one speaker to the next and to save informal remarks and in-jokes for another situation.

Provide transitions

A typical transition statement links the speakers together. For example, "Thank you, Ray. Mike Stern will now tell us how the purchasing system Ray described compares with systems in the midwestern region." Be specific. Rather than say, "Mr. Anthony will now talk about the financial implications," say, "Mr. Anthony will now explain how this proposal will affect the standard of living of most Americans."

Know how to close

If a controversy is raging at the end of a discussion, try to start "decompressing" the participants about five minutes before the time is up. You can do this either by switching to a less controversial topic or by starting to summarize each person's point of view on the issue. At the very end, allow yourself time to make a general summary and a concluding statement, then thank the panelists for their participation.

Participating in a Panel Discussion

As a participant, you have a responsibility to yourself, to the panel, and to your organization. Although you are only one member on a panel, you still make a presentation whenever you make a statement. Therefore, all the presentation rules apply. If you can, call the other panelists, introduce yourself, and find out approximately what they are going to address. Pay special attention to anyone scheduled to speak right before you, and create an appropriate transition if you can. At a conference on various aspects of university administration, one panelist followed a discussion of the need for decisiveness that began, "We need to act, although ..." (the talk covered the various obstacles to acting decisively) with a fund-raising segment that began, "We need to give, because ..."

Follow these guidelines as well to help you participate with quality:

Create your own transitions

Sometimes the moderator doesn't provide a transition. In this case, create your own. Generally, it's easier to build on whatever the preceding speaker said than to try to provide a transition to the person who follows you. You can usually draw upon some thread in the previous speaker's remarks and show how it relates to what you're going to say.

Avoid sending negative messages

First of all, don't show boredom by examining your nails, tugging on your hair or earrings, closing your eyes, sighing heavily, or yawning. (It's rare to see a panelist actually fall asleep, but it has happened.) Also, don't show your hostility with flashing eyes, raised eyebrows, rigid posture, or a glare at the speaker. The lack of control reflects on you.

The behavior of the panelists, even those who are not speaking, sets the standard for the audience's behavior. As members of the panel tire of looking at the speaker, their gaze wanders or they stare into space, and that is disconcerting to the audience and to the speaker. Attentive observers in the audience check the panelists' gestures, facial expressions, and posture, and look for unspoken disagreements or conflicts. You can assist the speaker by being an active listener. Look at the person speaking, nod or smile at the appropriate points, keep an open, easy expression, and take occasional notes to show your attentiveness.

In general, serving on a panel, like delivering any other public presentation, gives you an opportunity to sell both yourself and your organization. It's something you should learn to do with style and grace if you're going to advance in the organization.

SUMMARY

Speaking in public is good for you and your career; say yes if it is a topic you can speak about credibly.

- Use humor that makes a point
- Look and act the part
  — Stand up straight
  — Use large gestures
  — Speak with authority
  — Use notes, not a script
  — Stay away from caffeine, heavy food
  — Be open in answering questions

When you must write out a speech, write it to be spoken, and read it naturally.

- Choose simple sentences
- Use verbs instead of nouns
- Use everyday language
- Emphasize ideas with repetition

Serving on a panel effectively requires attention to details.

- As a moderator,
  — Set the tone
  — Provide substantive transitions
  — Summarize
- As a participant,
  — Create transitions
  — Avoid sending negative messages

13
Videoconferences

Videoconferences have already replaced many face-to-face meetings, and all managers should expect someday to both orchestrate and participate in them. To take full advantage of the opportunities offered by this medium, you'll first need to know how it works and then how to

- Decide when a videoconference is appropriate
- Prepare
- Manage the technology and the people as conference leader
- Make an effective contribution as a participant

What Is Videoconferencing?

Videoconferencing is any specialized aid that allows people to share information electronically, in a visual and spontaneous way. Here's just one example: imagine you are the marketing director for the Sizzling Soda company and you'd like to add a guava drink to your product line by next summer. You need feedback from Harriet Sloan in Hawaii. You turn on your PC, click a few buttons, and she appears on the screen. You brainstorm for a couple of minutes, then decide to seek advice from Fred Jones in Florida. Fred thinks the idea has merit, but turns on a video database to look up data on consumption of guava drinks, focus group records, and the availability of the production line for new products for the coming year. Within seconds you're watching a recorded videoconference in which the head of production cautioned against overextending bottling capacity in the new southern plant this year. In only twenty minutes, you have the information you need for a decision — defer the plan until next year.

Videoconferencing is a practical, natural, and effective supplement to the meetings that businesses routinely conduct in our global society.

What Are Videoconferences Good For?

It's not enough to just hear words spoken over a telephone; you need a context, a connection to someone and something. You need to know that "yes" means "yes, I agree" not "yes, I understand you." Videoconferencing can help identify the nuances. The written word can't match demonstrating a hard-to-describe mechanical problem for engineers working in Detroit, Mexico City, Tokyo, and Munich under production deadlines. Computer-supported interaction enables colleagues to share information across oceans and time zones.

Videoconferences have a number of advantages over the conference calls they are rapidly replacing in many companies. With a good system, you can pick up the kind of body language cues that would otherwise only come with a one-on-one meeting. The costs involved in arranging one-on-one meetings, such as the expenses of both travel and loss of productive time, are often prohibitive. Many executives find that to avoid these meetings is worth the cost of setting up the complex systems that videoconferencing requires. Document and application sharing during videoconferences is now a common feature; this means the participants can actually do work in the meeting, not just talk about it. And of course, with true videoconferencing, participants can use visuals to get a point across, an advantage in any situation, and especially so if the meeting involves crossing language barriers.

Of course as with any evolving technology, there are some disadvantages to videoconferencing as well. Small body language cues, such as a raised eyebrow or a quick glance, can get lost, especially if the videoconferencing system is a lower-cost one, with less smooth video transmission. This is still the major problem with the current video technology; video is choppy with all but top-of-the-line systems. An additional problem is the discomfort new participants may feel from constantly being under the camera's eye. However, the advantages usually make it worthwhile to endure these inconveniences.

The Technology

Because of the wide variety of videoconference forms, publicity in the business press has not yet dispelled the confusion that videoconference terminology creates among nontechnical managers. Manufacturers' advertised descriptions of videoconferencing systems often add to this confusion. The options involved in any videoconferencing system range greatly in complexity and in price. "Videoconference," in the sense we're using the word here, can range from an audioconference supplemented by shared document markup, through true application sharing (where participants can actually access the program that created the document), and finally to full-motion black-and-white or color video with any number of accompanying aids, such as electronic whiteboards or computer interfaces.

In-house or outside facilities?

Any corporate management wanting to experiment with videoconferences has at least three choices: setting up in-house facilities, renting equipment to use on the premises, or contracting to use outside facilities. High-quality, in-house facilities are still expensive to construct and maintain; however, the current proliferation of desktop (PC-based) videoconferencing systems means that a basic setup is now within the reach of most companies.

Executives responsible for in-house videoconference facilities believe that managers are more likely to use this medium when the facility is on site than when they must arrange for outside services. In addition, they believe that having in-house equipment improves the quality of a videoconference, because it allows participants to rehearse presentations beforehand. Security is also of less concern when videoconference facilities are in-house. Although "scramblers" may be employed to encode and then decode messages, using outside facilities inevitably involves dealing with nonaffiliated technicians and camerapersons, and their presence increases participants' concerns about information leaks.

Some companies have chosen to rent videoconference equipment on a per conference basis; some have chosen to lease it, installing it in-house on a semipermanent basis. However, leased equipment is believed to be less reliable than permanently sited equipment. On the other hand, with leased equipment, if the state of the art changes drastically, the equipment contract can be canceled. Money invested in a permanent facility is a sunk cost, and with technology changing all the time, a company could quickly find itself saddled with some outdated equipment.

As an alternative to owning, renting or leasing equipment for in-house use, an organization can rent videoconference facilities off premises. Several companies are in the business of setting up audio or videoconferences. These companies arrange for satellite time and will usually also perform some standard housekeeping functions, such as checking visuals to see that they are in order. They may even develop the presentation visuals. This takes some of the burden off the meeting participants and puts it in the hands of the experts.

Choosing a videoconferencing system

The first question when considering the purchase of a videoconferencing system is this: room system or PC-based? Apart from the cost, which varies enormously between these two forms, the other important issue is the size of the groups who will be participating. Desktop systems are ideal for one-on-one situations, but if the system will be used for synchronizing group meetings at two or more locations, then a room setup would be more appropriate (see Exhibit 13.1).

While full-motion video certainly is the most impressive form of videoconferencing, it is not the only solution to your meeting needs, nor is it necessarily the ideal one. Shared document markup is another option; financial analysts can see and annotate a shared document im-

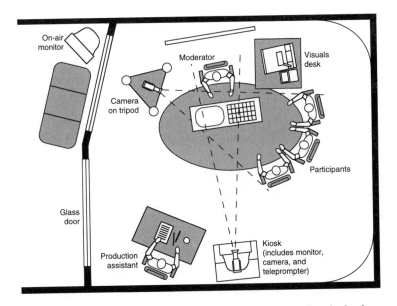

Exhibit 13.1. For group meetings, a customized room setup is the ideal solution. This diagram, provided by Small Planet Communications, shows a two-way audio and video setup that uses two cameras at each location. The moderator has access to visual display equipment which can send visual support images directly to the screen.

age (i.e. spreadsheet) on their computer screens, while discussing it over a standard conference call. This can be a very convenient fix for some situations. The catch, however, is that participants are only working on an image of a document. Someone still has to make all the changes to the original document at the end of the meeting. The next step up, application sharing, is usually a better solution. Here, one participant is running a program that can edit the document being discussed — but everyone participating in the meeting can directly access that program and make changes to the original document itself. This can save time otherwise spent in reediting.

In many situations, true videoconferencing is the best solution. However, systems vary immensely in quality, and it is important to look very carefully before you settle on one. Even if you only plan on using the system internally, with each unit linked to other units of the same kind, other systems may at some point have to be linked in. Therefore, it is wise to consider only systems that support an industry-standard protocol as well as their own proprietary communication system, and that have dialup capability (and do not rely on having a dedicated digital connection). If you have an internal computer network, you may want to look at systems that can run using your existing network wiring. However, you may well find that you start running into network bottlenecks — all that data running down wires that were just not designed for such heavy use can really slow down the system.

It is important to find out what bandwidth a system runs on. Higher bandwidth translates into higher quality and higher dollars. However, it is possible to find systems that are optimized to run at a lower bandwidth setting, and that therefore have a comparable picture to the more expensive setups. Frame rates can be confusing as well. You want the highest frame rate you can afford, since a high rate means a smoother, less jittery image. However, frame rates quoted by manufacturers are often dependent on bandwidth; while a specific system may be capable of transmitting at up to thirty frames per second, for example, your budget may restrict you to using a narrower bandwidth, and therefore to a much slower frame rate. Once again, the moral is: try before you buy.

Sound quality is of vital importance when selecting a videoconferencing system. Think about it for a moment — if you lost either video or sound during a conference, how easy would it be to continue? Without video, you could at least keep working — you would have the equivalent of a regular telephone conference call. Without sound, your meeting would be over. Good sound quality can make the difference between a videoconference that works and one that doesn't. You should consider a full-duplex sound system, which allows more than one participant to speak at any one time, and thus eliminates the awkward breaks and drop-outs caused by voice-activated microphones. This gives you the closest possible approximation to a regular meeting, and puts participants at ease.

Designing an ideal videoconferencing environment

In the "old days" of videoconferencing, say three or four years ago, most videoconferencing facilities were either in-house or off-site studios — in either case, facilities that were carefully constructed by videoconferencing professionals for the best possible results. With the increase in popularity of portable and desktop videoconferencing systems, however, there is an increased likelihood that you may be required to choose the room to be used for a videoconference, and to specify how it should be set up.

The popularity of "Rollabouts," or portable videoconferencing units, might lead to the impression that any conference room can now be effectively used as a videoconferencing studio. Unfortunately, this isn't the case. Considerable thought still has to go into the room setup if the videoconference is to both look professional and provide a comfortable environment for the meeting participants. For example, participants feel more relaxed when they see the entire room at the other location than when they see only a close-up shot of the person talking. It is even better when the two rooms are similar enough to look like extensions of each other.

Because people tend to freeze when they see a camera or a microphone, it's desirable to hide both these items. Using just one or two omnidirectional microphones is easier and more efficient than using individual microphones for every participant. Good room acoustics are also very important to ensure that participants feel comfortable. Though acoustically padded "dead" rooms might seem like a good idea to cut down on problems of room echo, carrying on a normal conversation in such rooms is very hard. A better solution is a room with a certain amount of natural echo, which can then be controlled electronically when the audio signal is transmitted.

Good lighting can play a vital part in making your videoconference look professional. Many meeting rooms use fluorescent lights, which tend to give participants' faces a sickly, greenish cast. Halogen or incandescent lights will make everyone look a lot more natural. Backgrounds should be as simple and uncluttered as possible, and colors should be kept neutral.

You have additional points to keep in mind when you are setting up a one-person desktop system. You should ensure that your camera is approximately at nose level, and that your face appears at the appropriate size on the screen; that is, your chest should be at the bottom of the frame, the top of your head near the top of the screen, and your eyes about two-thirds of the way up. You should, if possible, have one light placed to illuminate your face, but be careful how you situate it. Too high, and you will look like you have bags under your eyes. Too low, and — well, you remember how kids look when they shine a flashlight under their chin to tell spooky stories at night. It can be tricky to get everything just right at first, but if you take time to experiment with lights and camera positioning, you're sure to find the setup that makes you look your best.

Deciding When a Videoconference Is Appropriate

Any electronic meeting must be carefully planned. For a videoconference in particular:

- The purpose must be suited to the available technology
- The costs — in time, money and human energy — must be justifiable
- The key people must be willing and able to participate

Is the Purpose Suitable?

Many videoconference veterans are convinced that people reach informed decisions more quickly during a videoconference than when they are in a conventional meeting. Studies have shown that because of the concern about seeming unprepared on camera, participants in videoconferences tend to arrive better prepared than they would for traditional meetings. On the other hand, some experts feel that people hold back from participating during such conferences because they don't want to prolong the agony. The two keys to success seem to be whether or not the people involved in the videoconference know and trust each other, and whether the person who arranged the meeting has devoted substantial time to preparation. This is true even if the primary purpose is marketing (cross-selling), for example. It's impossible to envision a videoconference "cold call." Whatever the case, not even the most ardent advocates claim that electronic meetings will replace face-to-face meetings for all purposes.

Problem-solving meetings

Since problem-solving is a major component of most business meetings, the usefulness of videoconferences for this purpose is a major concern. Participants accustomed to conferences using full-motion, two-way video report that, once they adjust to the limitations imposed by electronic conversation, both problem-solving and decision making are quite possible in a videoconference setting. Some even believe that the constraints of the medium's rigid time limits — imposed by demand for the facilities or the high costs of running overtime — create a healthy discipline that could improve conventional face-to-face meetings.

Some managers argue that videoconferences are not appropriate for problem-solving because the medium prevents them from reading nonverbal cues. But full-motion conference set-ups, in which the entire conference room and all the participants are visible at each location, may not interfere significantly with a person's ability to see facial expressions and read shifts in attitude. Depending on the size of the screen, the camera's ability to focus on a participant may even enhance some nonverbal cues.

One plus in using a videoconference for problem-solving is that it allows you to relax one of the general rules about meetings — that all participants be at about the same hierarchical level in the organization. Even though peers may still find it easier to have an open exchange, something about communicating at a distance seems to make discussions between top management and middle managers easier and more productive. As one person put it, "If I say something that makes the vice-president mad, at least I've got a 3,000 mile head start."

Other generalizations about making problem-solving meetings work — that participants know each other, that they have about the same level of knowledge of the problem at hand, and that they be equally familiar with the problem-solving techniques used in the organization — are as important, if not more important, in videoconferences as they are in conventional meetings. Even with everything in its favor, though, a videoconference cannot promote successful problem-solving in all instances. In fact, for major projects that involve assembling a task force of people who know each other but do not normally work together, it's usually worthwhile to hold the initial meeting with everyone in one room. At this meeting, you work out the preliminaries and divvy up the tasks. You should then use videoconferences during the middle stages of the project to keep the participants focused on the goal. At the end, it's a good idea to bring everyone back together for the final report and debriefing. ·

Another meeting that isn't appropriate for videoconferencing is one that covers highly sensitive issues, either very confidential matters or issues that would arouse intense emotions. Such issues embarrass people and are unlikely to resolve themselves quickly. In general, any topic dealing with promotions, firings, or performance evaluations falls in this category.

Screenings and interviews

As companies have increasingly sought candidates around the globe as well as across the country, some have used videoconferences to screen applicants or consultants instead of footing the bill for an airline ticket. These uses, however, border on what we have categorized as "sensitive" and, at least at this stage, cannot be described as an unqualified success, except perhaps for a very preliminary screening. It's anxiety-provoking enough to be in an interview without the added burden of having a camera put you on center stage. As a result, this form of interview may not provide an accurate reading of individual talents. On the other hand, should it become a commonplace procedure among large organizations, people will, as they always have, learn to adapt.

Formal presentations to a number of locations

One-way video, two-way audio systems are designed to permit people at one location to talk to and be seen by people gathered in as many as a hundred locations. The presenter's picture and voice are transmitted and, while members of the audience can participate by making statements or asking questions, their pictures are not transmitted. Some firms have this equipment at their corporate headquarters with receiving locations at various divisions scattered around the country. These firms use their videoconference systems mainly for employee meetings and training sessions.

This set-up works well when communicating with external audiences who do not need to participate in making a decision. Automobile companies have used it to introduce new models or to relay changes in parts prices, and drug companies have used it effectively to introduce new products. It has proved to be an extremely efficient way to disseminate information companywide. One advantage of this kind of videoconference is that everyone knows that major expenses are involved, so they are instantly aware that this is an important issue, and are more likely to participate in the conference.

Technical problem-solving

Engineers and technical people, such as computer programmers and systems analysts, frequently call a meeting when something goes wrong to establish the dimensions of the problem, make a stab at determining the cause, devise strategies for solving it, or allocate pieces of it to each person to solve. For such groups, the capability of transmitting visual data (engineering drawings, for example) to several locations simultaneously makes videoconferences tremendously productive. Shared document markup is a very useful feature in this kind of situation; application sharing even more so.

Will a Videoconference Be More Economical than a Face-to-Face Meeting?

The expectation, almost always, is that videoconferences will save significant amounts of money. Therefore, they are usually considered when the potential participants are separated by great distances or when travel arrangements are difficult to make. The true cost of any meeting involving travel, however, goes beyond simple monetary considerations. Maximizing the productivity of the participants frequently weights in favor of a videoconference. After all, time wasted making airplane connections could be spent making executive decisions. And, while many people work in the airplane, some find it difficult to do so. Others find that crossing time zones so disrupts their bodily rhythms they cannot work for hours, or perhaps even a full day, after a long trip. The cost and inconvenience of long-distance travel is not always at issue, however; some companies use videoconferences simply to link offices scattered around a metropolitan area. They find it cuts down on the general wear and tear involved in travel, even when the distances are relatively short.

Are All the Key People Willing and Able to Participate?

Sometimes, circumstances make a videoconference seem like the only solution. A key participant may be unable to leave home base because of a pressing business or family problem, or there's a crisis that demands immediate response from several persons at different locations, or several participants have so many competing demands on their time that an electronic meeting is the only way of getting them together. In addition, some CEOs virtually demand videoconferences to save themselves travel time. However, there are managers who simply won't agree to a videoconference. One CEO we know, when approached to participate in a videoconference, snorted, "I don't need to see a person to get him to agree to a decision — I just pick up the phone and the problem is solved." If you work for someone like this, forget the videoconference, no matter how appealing the idea — a meeting without all the key decision makers is a wasted exercise. Others, who have no concrete reasons for objecting to a videoconference, may be afraid of the technology. Trying something new makes most people anxious about making fools of themselves in public.

Objections to videoconferences may come from middle managers as well as executives. In addition to the usual fears, these managers may see travel as a "perk" — a reward for reaching a certain level in the organization. If participants view a videoconference as depriving them of a privilege, their suppressed resentment may express itself as unwillingness or failure to engage in discussion, and, at worst, as subconscious sabotage. Not surprisingly, engineers and other technical people are the least likely to object to videoconferencing on anything other than objective grounds. Their participation can usually be taken for granted.

Preparing for a Videoconference

You need to prepare for any presentation, and preparing for your first videoconference requires additional effort. Your first experience can influence all your subsequent encounters, so you'll want the experience to be positive. Whether you're to be a participant or a leader, you'll need to understand how the system works, how to signal the leader, if you are a participant, and how to manipulate the equipment and signal the participants, if you are a leader. Besides understanding the mechanics, it is important for you to

- Dress for the camera's eye
- Establish a relationship with the other participants before the conference
- Create special visuals

Dress for the Camera's Eye

The medium of a videoconference imposes some limitations on what you can wear. Any strong pattern is out — its lines will be translated by the camera into a wavy movement, and the garment may actually appear to be jerking slightly. Wearing white is a less obvious pitfall. Too much white tends to make your facial tones very dark, or the white will bleed into a light-colored background. Red also bleeds into some backgrounds. Neutral tones, such as a beige or gray suit with a neutral colored shirt or blouse, are preferable.

You should be aware that in close-ups, or with a one-person desktop setup, only your face will be visible to the other participants. Wearing loud ties (for men) or fussy blouses (for women) and lapel pins or large jewelry, including exaggerated earrings, chokers, and large brooches, reflect light back into the camera, draw attention away from your face, and will diffuse the power of what you're saying.

Establish a Relationship with Other Participants

Relationships are easiest to establish and maintain if everyone can see everyone else, talk and listen face-to-face, and give each other immediate feedback. Most people need to spend time together before they can work together effectively. Getting to know other participants is especially important before a videoconference, in order to compensate for the possibility of missing the subtle cues that give you insight into someone else's true attitude toward a proposal or another person. If it's impossible to meet people face-to-face, try to call them on the phone and establish the relationship that way. If that isn't feasible, pay special attention to the audience analysis questions in Chapter 2.

Create Special Visuals

Since the capability of transmitting visuals is one of the reasons for going to the expense of holding a videoconference rather than an audioconference, making effective graphs and charts always pays off. The design principles we cite in this book generally apply to visuals for a videoconference as well. Because some distortions are inherent in the transmission process, concentrate on keeping text brief and graphics simple.

Many videoconferencing systems now offer "screen sharing," which allows you to show full-screen computer graphics, exactly as they would appear on your own computer screen, to all participants in a meeting. This is the best possible way to share visuals, and offers a welcome break from the usual videoconference fare of "talking heads." However, if your system doesn't offer this option, you'll need to find other ways to display your graphics.

If your videoconference studio has a camera with a zoom lens, or if you are using a one-person desktop system, you can use a simple 3 x 5 inch card as well as a large flipchart. In fact, the television camera is more successful at blowing up than reducing visuals. Cards can be prepared easily, either by typing (using a strong pica type as opposed to a fine-serif elite) or by neatly lettering with black felt-tipped marking pens. If you are meeting in a videoconference room equipped with an overhead camera, you might find it desirable to create your visuals with felt-tip markers on 8-1/2 x 11-inch tablets. The speaker can then simply place the visuals on the table and focus the camera on them. For flipcharts, letters should be at least 1-1/2 inches high, but 2-1/2 inches to 3 inches is better. The 3:4 screen ration demands that flipchart visuals be designed to be horizontal rather than vertical, which is not the conventional flipchart shape. For overhead transparencies, the proportion used should be 2:3 (close to the 7-1/2 x 9-1/2 inches usually prescribed), otherwise part of the graph or chart will be lost when projected. If you are preparing graphics in color, stick to the middle of the color spectrum — blues and yellows usually transmit well. For more ideas on effective use of color in graphics, watch news shows on TV. Their video equipment is capable of much higher quality transmission than yours, however, so keep it simple.

Although blueprints or engineering drawings are too large to transmit in their entirety, it's possible to cover parts of them and focus on the remaining segments. Photographs, particularly Polaroid prints, can be transmitted by most systems. Three-dimensional objects can be situated in front of a tripod camera and shot that way. In general, use originals rather than copies of your visuals, since the text in copies may be too light to transmit well.

If you intend to develop visuals during the meeting, perhaps as a way of keeping track of decisions or new ideas, try to get into the studio ahead of time to experiment with different kinds of pens, letters, and colors. Although facsimile transmission may be viable, using it during the conference creates the same problems as distributing handouts during a regular meeting.

Managing the Technology and the People as Conference Leader

Leading a videoconference is much like leading a face-to-face meeting.

Handle the Details

Although the technical part of the job continues to get simpler, some room videoconferencing setups can still present problems, especially if you are using off-site facilities. As conference leader, you should always arrive at the conference site early enough to check out the equipment and make sure that the cameras are able to pick up the visuals.

At commercial videoconference studios, personnel are available to help you with the equipment. Nevertheless, be sure to try everything yourself — watching someone else do it isn't enough. If no technicians will be on the scene during the videoconference (and they may be asked to leave if the conference deals with proprietary information), find out whom to call should something go wrong. Even if you're an inspired tinkerer, you shouldn't count on being able to get things running again on your own, and you cannot afford this kind of disruption.

Limit the Agenda

People tire more easily in a videoconference than they do in a face-to-face meeting. Whether this is because of the unfamiliar surroundings, the stress of focusing on a screen rather than a group of people, a fidgety concern about the cost per minute, or some combination of these factors, it appears that fifteen minutes and three topics is about as much as people can effectively handle at a stretch in this medium. In setting the objective and the agenda, keep this in mind.

Brief Participants

Each participant should be notified of the videoconference well in advance, and notification should include time, date, and place of the videoconference. For a problem-solving session, participants should also be sent any data or background information they will need. In addition, depending on the circumstances and the degree of familiarity the participants have with the technology, they should be sent such advance materials as:

- A letter introducing the moderator (or leader) and a photograph
- Biographies of the participants, with photographs
- The agenda
- A diagram of the room layout
- Instructions for operating any equipment, or pictures of the control console

If you're using an outside facility (or even an internal one not familiar to most participants), include a map that shows how to get there.

Monitor the Process

Most face-to-face meetings are preceded by some informal talk and banter. This social warm-up is perhaps even more important before videoconferences. The more closely your videoconference resembles a face-to-face meeting, the more relaxed participants will be. Arrange for informal talking time if at all possible. If the conference includes a presentation of some kind, be sure the person making the presentation familiarizes himself with the facilities, and his visuals are appropriate to the medium.

Introductions, always important, are vital in a videoconference. At minimum, open the meeting by calling on each person and transmitting his or her picture to relieve participants of the feeling that they are talking into a void and to give everyone a face to go with the voice. At this time, you may say a few words about the participants or ask them to identify themselves. They should also introduce themselves each time they speak. Even though it seems somewhat contrived for Joan to say, "This is Joan in St. Louis" before talking, it is immensely helpful to others in keeping the discussion from getting bogged down. Introduce everyone present in the studio, even those who are observers, and call on each by name rather than by location. If someone is called away during the meeting, mention the departure to avoid the embarrassing situation of having a participant address someone who is no longer there.

During the conference, you must juggle the details of the discussion as well as the electronics. Given the expense of videoconferences, the techniques of summarizing, repeating, and staying on a time schedule (see Chapter 9) are even more important than in a face-to-face meeting. Make sure that new and complex ideas are given sufficient discussion time. Talking about anything complex is more difficult electronically than in a face-to-face meeting, even when you have sent advance materials. Participants may fight the technology in some way or be so eager to finish and get off camera that they'll pretend to understand when they do not. In this setting, asking for questions may not elicit them, so summarizing at regular intervals is especially important. Some videoconference consoles allow the moderator to hit a pause button and talk privately with others at her site. It is hard to imagine a situation in which using this method of excluding others would be advisable. Those left out are guaranteed to feel insulted.

The moderator is also responsible for soliciting feedback, both during the conference itself and afterward, possibly by distributing written forms. In the early stages of introducing videoconferences to an organization, obtaining feedback can make the difference between having people collaborate and having them resist the technology and spread their negative reaction through the organization.

As leader you must be certain there is a host at each site — someone who can introduce participants to each other and take care of details. This is especially important with large videoconferences to multiple locations. The host may also have responsibility for coordinating breaks between segments. The fifteen-minute rule still applies here, so a major companywide meeting may even start to take on the character of a TV show, with portions of entertainment every fifteen minutes or so.

Making an Effective Contribution as a Participant

If the videoconference will be held in-house, you will be able to try out the equipment in advance and become comfortable with the surroundings, the way your voice sounds over the microphone, and the way you look on the television monitor. Once you're familiar with the equipment, participating in a videoconference is less intimidating. It will probably take several encounters, however, before you will be comfortable enough with the form to truly concentrate on the substance of your contribution. Some tips to follow:

Try to keep a friendly expression

If you're speaking, use as much energy as you can muster, since some of it seems to get lost in the transmission. If in a group videoconference you suddenly notice that you're on camera, don't stare fixedly into the lens. Instead, try to look both at the camera and at others in your location. Viewers in other locations don't appreciate glassy-eyed stares. As in any presentation, remember that the viewers will look at the entire group, not just the speaker.

With a one-person desktop system, keeping your expression natural presents even more of a challenge, as you are the only "real person" in the room. Try to imagine that the camera itself is one of the participants. Don't keep looking aside, or down at your notes, or you risk appearing untrustworthy to other participants. Keep vital notes taped to the side of the camera lens where you can see them, and keep smiling.

Don't engage in conversations with others at the site

This isn't good practice in any meeting, but in videoconferences with voice-activated microphones, the side conversation will trigger the mike and ruin the audio transmission for the speaker. For the same reason, try to keep casual sounds to a minimum — nervous coughing and clearing the throat will also activate your microphone.

Use good judgment when taking notes

If you're a doodler, be aware of the overhead camera. Keep caricatures of other participants or pithy written comments out of camera range.

Listen carefully to what others are saying

This advice seems obvious until you consider that you cannot take advantage of the nonverbal cues you're accustomed to in normal meetings and you are likely to be distracted by the setting. Listen to the words and the meaning behind them. Using a desktop videoconferencing system gives you an advantage here. The camera and monitor are located close together so you have the feeling of talking to the other person rather than to the camera. In a room setup, you will have to concentrate more to overcome the distractions of the technology.

Rehearse

If you know that you will be making a contribution during a planned videoconference, do all you can to get ready for it. It may be hard to prepare for the "on-air" feeling; if you are using a desktop system you may at least have a chance to practice your presentation in front of the (disconnected) camera until you feel a little more comfortable. If you will be using a room system or facilities off-site, rehearsing may be harder. But as long as you have prepared your content thoroughly and are familiar with your material, you will be in good shape to deal with whatever surprises the technology throws your way.

SUMMARY

To participate effectively in a videoconference, you'll need to know how the equipment works, and how to

- Decide whether a videoconference is appropriate by judging whether
  —The objective of the meeting fits the medium
  — Most of the factors that lead to successful meetings are present
  —The cost is less in money, time, and human energy than a face-to-face meeting
  —The key people will participate
- Prepare for a videoconference by
  — Dressing for the camera
  — Establishing a relationship with the other participants
  — Creating appropriate visuals
- Manage the technology and the people as the conference leader by
  — Handling the mechanical details
  — Briefing the participants
  — Monitoring the process
- Make an effective contribution as a participant
  — Introduce yourself
  — Keep a friendly, open expression
  — Don't engage in side conversations
  — Listen carefully
  — Rehearse

14
Presenting Globally

More and more people are making presentations to people from other cultures, whether they are actually going abroad or presenting to clients who come to the United States. You can increase your chances of success if you

- Adopt the right attitude
- Prepare, prepare, prepare
- Adapt structure and delivery
- Manage interaction and avoid confrontation
- Use visual support
- Work with an interpreter effectively

Adopting the Right Attitude

We would never recommend that you try to be something you're not, but everyone has a range of behaviors to choose from, even when they operate in their own culture. One cross-cultural expert we know suggests becoming a "150 percent person." Essentially, you're striving to add another 50 percent of possible behaviors and communication styles from the other culture to your core 100 percent, and to use that extra 50 percent when interacting with someone from the target culture. You only add the new styles; you never subtract from your own style. The dividend of adding the other 50 percent is that it will make you a better problem solver and communicator in any setting, because you'll find it much easier to see things from a different point of view.

We can't provide a compendium for dealing with all the dos and don'ts of the cultures and subcultures you may encounter. There are literally hundreds of books on dealing with Japanese business people, for example. We can, however, give you some insight into the right attitude to take and how our system can help you do a better job of presenting. Bear in mind as you read this chapter that our advice also holds if you are presenting to people from different subcultures within the United States.

People in the United States can often escape experiencing cultural variety on a personal basis, despite continuing efforts by the media and the educational system to increase exposure. The country is vast; our insularity is historically immense. In addition, the global march of popular culture means that you can pop into a McDonald's in Tokyo or buy a Mickey Mouse doll in a Disney store in most European countries. And in most countries, Western business suits are the norm in commerce. It's sometimes tempting to give in to the fantasy that "people are the same everywhere." Acting on this assumption, however, can cause problems. On the other hand, hypersensitivity to the differences among cultures can be paralyzing. Some people resist going global because of the fear of embarrassing themselves in ways they may not even realize. As usual, a "golden mean" should prevail. Presenting successfully in another culture involves adopting the right attitude, specifically,

- being open to new experiences
- respecting varying communication styles

Be Open to Learning about Other Cultures

Perception is selective and determined by your culture. You are biased. You are the product of your particular upbringing just as your hosts are. Because so much international business takes place in English, people sometimes assume, incorrectly, that cultural issues are irrelevant in international business presentations. It will seem draining at first, but your approach should be openness to different values, behaviors, and perceptions. Resist the attempt to evaluate others' behavior in terms of your own norms and values. Are your opposite numbers being "obstructionist?" Perhaps they have a different sense of time, or they believe that they can use your impatience to their advantage. It's not an issue of right and wrong behavior, even if it's easier for you to define it that way. Taking the attitude "I'm going to learn about them, their needs, and their ideas before I can earn the right to share my own," will gain you much more respect and make it more likely that you will ultimately be successful. A little knowledge is a dangerous thing, however; don't assume you know everything because you've visited a country before. Remember to "know what you **don't** know." If you develop a theory about why certain behavior is happening, check it out with someone in the culture. Assume that people are different until you can prove that they are the same.

There are numerous resources available. If you live in a major city, the travel section of any large bookstore will provide a good start. It will provide enough information to ask some educated questions and introduce excellent conversation starters. For example, one presenter found that merely stating something like "I'm anxious to see the Tivoli Gardens, because I've read that it was Walt Disney's inspiration for Disneyland" can open up a conversation in Copenhagen. The local university may offer courses, or a professor may be willing to talk to you. If you work for a large corporation, the training department may be able to refer you to outside courses that are relevant even if there are none offered in-house. You might listen to language tapes if you studied the language of the country in school. The effort won't make you fluent, but it may bring your command of the language back to the point where you can offer more than a few pleasantries. You may also find that reading the local language newspaper will bring back the vocabulary. (When you visit the country, by the way, it doesn't hurt to be caught with the local language newspaper, provided you can actually read it. It's another indication that you care.) At minimum, even if you have not studied the language in the past, you should learn the appropriate phrases for greeting and taking leave of others, as well as the words for "please" and "thank you."

Most major cities have restaurants that specialize in the cuisine of the country you are going to do business in. Not only will taking meals there acclimate your palate to some of the more unusual taste sensations, but the people who serve you may be able to give you some cultural advice (providing they aren't busy and they are actually from the country involved; don't make this assumption, ask). If you may be entertained in a banquet setting (as, for example, is common in China), it is good to know what to expect and to learn about any specific cultural norms. In China, for example, you should never finish the rice that comes at the end of the meal, because that indicates that you were not given enough to eat. Why call attention to your boorishness if you can instead indicate that you respect the customs of the country?

When you are actually in the country, go out with your hosts. Try to taste everything you are served; if you don't like it, don't comment on it. Ask questions about everything you see or do. Do not comment on differences in a way that suggests that the "American way" is better. Never criticize. And when outside the United States in North or South America, do not refer to something from the United States as "American" when you are comparing it to something local — other cultures on the continents are American too.

Finally, remember that there may be numerous significant subcultures coexisting within a country or a larger culture. Take the example of Arab culture, where one can drink alcohol in a very few countries — the United Arab Emirates, to take one example — but not in most, like Saudi Arabia. Don't generalize from your experience with one subculture to another.

Be Respectful

You should always be respectful when dealing with people from another culture. People are quite rightly proud of their cultural heritage, and you should take things as they come. In the former Soviet Union, people are acutely aware of their former superpower status, and a Russian executive with rough handouts can find it highly embarrassing to be contrasted with someone from the States with his color laptop. In other cases, North Americans have deeply offended people by asking that they meet in the hotel rather than in the person's basement office because they think it will provide a higher standard of service.

Recognize that directness may be regarded as rude in many other cultures. Sometimes you can adjust your phrasing easily. Instead of saying "I want you to do X," you might say "It would be very helpful if X were done." Take your cue from the phrasing you hear around you. Don't forget your goals, but recognize that there is more than one way to achieve them. Similarly, categorical statements and insistence on "right" or "wrong" choices won't get you as far as flexibility.

Preparing

Unless you immerse yourself in the culture or live in a country for an extended period, you can't hope to understand all the nuances involved. Total knowledge is not your goal. Demonstrating that you have empathy and that you care a great deal about communicating on the other person's terms is what you're striving for. Here's how to start.

Find a Cultural Informant

When preparing to do business abroad, many business people consult a "cultural informant," a colleague or acquaintance who can provide information on how people in the target culture share information, what people expect in presentations, whether information should be written or spoken, and so on. Most often, people will be delighted to share information. Don't take their responses literally, though, especially in cultures where an effort is made to "tell you what you want to hear." If something isn't clear to you, ask again later, rephrasing the question to get additional information.

Ask for specifics on how Americans are frequently perceived by the other culture, and how these perceptions relate to nonverbal behavior, communication style, and appearance. Dress is especially important in Europe, for example, where things like wearing a Hermes tie or carrying a Lancel briefcase are noticed as a sign of prestige or wealth, and contribute to a perception of higher status. France and Italy especially are style conscious — avoid somber, ultraconservative suits in Southern Europe.

Your cultural informant may be an expatriate, preferably one who has had many years of experience living in the country. He will have made plenty of mistakes and can tell you in detail what to avoid. But do some gentle probing to find out whether or not your informant has actually immersed himself in the culture. A person can live in a country like Spain or France for years and only use the language to order food and do basic shopping. Such a person is less useful to you as a source of information.

Observe

If you can, when you get on site, take some time to observe. While you're in the foreign culture, watch the behavior and communication styles of the people from your host culture. Are they animated? Do they use their hands often to emphasize? Or do they listen quietly and reflect on what the other person is saying before making a statement? Of course, we can't generalize here on "cultural behaviors." However, if you observe several interactions, you might just see some patterns of communication that may help you. Watch the local television channel. Even if you can't understand the language, you'll pick up a little of the flavor of the typical interaction, particularly if you compare different kinds of shows, such as news, soap operas, and game shows, to their United States equivalents.

Now, let's go back to our system for preparing and structuring a presentation. In our research and experience, we have found that the system we have described, with a few modifications, will help you create and deliver effective presentations to audiences from various cultural backgrounds.

Gauge the Audience's English Language Ability

We've found that simply asking the question, "How well do members of the audience speak English?" does not provide helpful information, since the answer is usually some version of "very well" or "not at all," regardless of the actual skill level. Try to get specifics as to education, travel abroad, and the like. Ask your contact whether the audience has attended other presentations in English and what their reaction was. Since you may well be socializing with members of the audience before the actual presentation, pay close attention to whether they seem to disengage after a period of time and start conversations with others in their native language. In that case, assume a slightly lower level of fluency and subtract about 25 percent from the time you intended to spend presenting.

Adapting Structure and Delivery Style

Although you'll always need to use our system to prepare content, think about some alterations to meet the needs of other cultures, especially in terms of the beginning of the presentation. In Japan, for example, the audience may need more detail up front to allow them to assure themselves that the presenter has done his or her homework and to allow them time to digest the information.

There is no such thing as immutable logic (one culture may think something is totally logical, while another would consider it totally illogical). When you use Western logic — whether parallel or chained — in a presentation, always check afterwards to see how it was received. In European countries like France, chained logic is much more common than it is in American presentations (although this is changing as American business techniques become more prevalent). Hold fast to the idea that the main point should be up front, however, regardless of the type of logical structure you choose. Listening in a language other than your own is always difficult, and knowing where the presenter is going is always helpful.

Sense of time and urgency vary also. In Latin America, and in some Mediterranean cultures, people may be prompt, but generally the clock is not the tyrant it is in the United States. Arrive on time, but be accepting if things start a little late. Adjust for the eventuality that you'll have less time than planned when you decide how much to include in your presentation. To take another example, people in sub-Saharan Africa and many other cultures "love to sit and talk," not because they are taking the whole thing casually, but because they may be more comfortable making decisions by "gut feel" rather than analytics.

In some cultures, people from the United States are viewed as much too hurried and their attempts to leverage their air travel time by packing as much as possible into a presentation are not appreciated. People need time to "munch on the material." Trying to rush them will be counterproductive. North Americans are also seen as much too stressed out about events over which they exercise little or no control. If something unfortunate happens in Thailand, for example, the Thais may be much more inclined to accept it rather than go to extremes to try to change it or find a way out.

Consider the level of persuasiveness and "selling" that is culturally acceptable. In Japan, overt persuasion is not the norm. Sharing details that provide evidence that you did the necessary research or examining all perspectives and alternatives is common. Trying to force people to make a choice between supporting and rejecting your recommendation will result in no choice at all, then or later. In Finland, modesty is valued. Overpraising your product, service, or firm will win you few friends.

Adapt Your Delivery Style

Adjusting your delivery style means adjusting both the way you speak and the way you act.

Adjust your speaking patterns

It's exhausting to listen to a language that is not your own. Build in more time for breaks. Shorter, more frequent breaks are better than one long one. You'll get through less material in a presentation than you would in the United States.

Sadly, the stereotypical exchange in which an executive from the

States progressively talks in a louder and louder tone (as if the audience is deaf) is not uncommon in intercultural presentations. Another habit people have is speaking English in the accent of the people they are presenting to — this sounds ridiculous at best, condescending at worst. If you have the slightest suspicion that you fall into either of these habits, have someone on your team monitor you and give you honest feedback.

Mirroring (without aping) the delivery style of native speakers can get you started in adapting your own style. When in doubt, go for more formality than you would ordinarily. Slow down and speak in a normal tone, especially in the beginning, so that the audience can get used to your voice patterns and style. It's difficult to cue yourself to "speak more slowly." Instead, remind yourself to pause more often, and use cue papers in between your overhead transparencies or write "slow," "pause" on the pages of the flip books. When using slides or computer-generated presentations, train yourself to pause in between visuals by rehearsing and pausing for the count of three each time you change. Pausing when you switch from one visual to another will be especially helpful to your audience because when listening to a foreign language, people find it very difficult to read and listen at the same time.

Articulate

Remember listening to audiotapes in the language lab when you studied Spanish (or French or Russian) in college? You could understand some native speakers readily while the dialogue of others was impenetrable. The ones you had difficulty with might have been speaking too quickly, or they might have failed to enunciate. To be understandable, you need to say every syllable and emphasize the consonant sounds. Demosthenes practiced with a mouthful of pebbles; you might try clenching something between your teeth and trying to make yourself understood. If you really have a problem in this area, you probably should consult a voice coach. The exercises he or she prescribes will help you present to English speakers as well.

Repeat and repeat again

Repetition is not rude; it is vital to understanding. Restate the point in different words. Use visual imagery with culturally neutral allusions (for example, most businesspeople have coped with plane travel, so you might try to explain a point with a reference to airports).

In some cases, repetition is necessary to provide emphasis. In some countries in sub-Saharan Africa, saying something once and then moving on will merely signal that whatever you said was not very important. Repeating the information is vital. In some countries of the former Soviet Union, the people you present to are accustomed to operating in a system where they were not rewarded for retention. Once you've talked, talked, talked, talk some more. Ask the same question at least three times (if they notice you are repeating the question, say you're looking for clarification). Because people may have been at risk if they had the wrong kind of knowledge, they may actually forget things more easily. Repetition is also helpful in certain Arab countries, where everyone must attend the presentation at one point or another, but individuals arrive and leave in random (to you) fashion. In fact, the whole idea of privacy (one-on-one meetings with the decision maker) is not relevant. Judicious repetition and summarizing is crucial in these instances.

Put it in writing

After talking, put everything in writing, in as much detail as possible. This is actually good advice any time you are working with people whose first language is not English. Sometimes, for example in China, the senior people will meet before the rest of the team gets together. If nothing about this initial meeting has been put in writing, the other side will be inclined to say, "But our senior people agreed to this." This is not nefarious, simply a bargaining device.

Use proper English grammar and usage

Even if you cannot bring yourself to use the subjunctive, as in "We *should* very much like to open a market in Singapore," you can avoid gross mistakes like "Between you and I, this is a good deal." (It's "between you and *me*.") Most people who know English as a second language are more familiar with English grammar and usage than are native speakers because they studied the subject formally much longer.

Remember, too, that slang is ephemeral. Many people studied English idioms in textbooks written long ago. They may be quite fond of saying things like "it's raining cats and dogs," and "let us make hay while the sun shines," as one decision maker did in a meeting in Southeast Asia. But that doesn't mean they can cope with recent moronic and over-used phrases like "cut to the chase." Slang and jargon are used by groups to indicate solidarity within the group. Using words others do not understand creates this solidarity at a cost, and it creates a distance between you and members of the other culture. Remember, too, that in many countries, the educational system stresses British rather than American English usage, and be aware of the differences so you can adapt as necessary. Use simple sentences, that is, sentences in which the subject is followed by a verb, and sometimes an object. Use nouns rather than pronouns when you can. Don't use the passive voice if English language skill is tentative because people will find it harder to understand. Don't use prepositional verbs like "get through" or "finish up."

Use formal manners and forms of address

The general decline of manners in the United States should not blind you to the fact that politeness is still extremely important elsewhere in the world. Neither should the egalitarian mode and the crunching of hierarchical structures here allow you to ignore the proper way to work with people in other countries. Treat everyone with extreme courtesy. Show appreciation in culturally appropriate ways for their kindness in hosting you in their country. In general, don't address anyone by his or her first name unless specifically asked to do so. Don't even say, "May I call you Hans (or whatever)" because that will put the person on the spot. If you've been practicing a few polite greetings in an unfamiliar language, make sure you're aware of different "you" forms — such as the French informal "tu" compared to the formal "vous," or the German "du" versus "Sie" — and be sure to use the correct form for the situation.

Most people in Latin America prefer formal manners. Use titles or last names, and remember that most last names include the names of the mother's family. For instance, in person you would address Juan Gomez-Galmez as "Senor Gomez" (using his father's family name), but in writing you would add Galmez, his mother's family name. You will find people with advanced degrees addressed as Doctor or Professor, even if they have no academic position. It's a way to indicate respect. Follow suit.

Pay special attention to appropriate methods of business card exchange in Japan and other Pacific Rim countries. Have your cards printed with English on one side and the relevant language on the other. If you are making several calls in various countries, take care to keep each set of cards separated. Under pressure, you may hand out one with the wrong language because you are unable to discriminate among them.

In any society, find out in advance who is most important in the hierarchy and provide that person with more attention. The others will take their cue from the senior person. Usually, no one will ask a question or interject unless the senior person does so first.

Adjust the way you dress

Dress formally. People from other cultures may be shocked by some American preferences for T-shirts and the like. Always dress conservatively until you have a chance to observe enough situations in the culture that you know what dress is appropriate. It's better to be on the safe side and to choose long sleeves rather than offend people. Women should usually wear long (not mini) skirts or dresses rather than pant suits. Ask your cultural informant if you have any doubt at all.

Adapt to conventions for eye contact, gestures, body language, and personal distance

In almost all cultures in which we have worked, with an audience of five or more, the presenter is perceived as more professional when standing. In very small groups, and in someone's office, standing is less important, unless you are illustrating a point on the screen, board, or flipchart. When standing, hands in the pockets are almost always taboo. This body stance conveys a posture that is too relaxed for most audiences, especially if this is the introductory presentation.

In general, hand gestures that indicate size, distance, and trends (up or down) are reasonably universal and can contribute to understanding. However, inappropriate gestures can get the presenter in trouble. It's a good idea to learn from your cultural informant which gestures are appropriate and the meaning of various gestures. Similar hand gestures have different meanings in different cultures. For example, the OK hand signal, the thumb and forefinger curved and touching, means "money" in Japan, not OK. In some countries in Latin America, the OK symbol means something unspeakably crude. Whenever in doubt, limit questionable gestures. In Japan, keep hand gestures to a minimum. Fewer gestures make you appear composed, mature, and professional.

Pointing with a finger is considered ill-mannered in Sweden and in other cultures, just as it is in the United States. Use either a pencil or a pointer when appropriate; we have been told that using a laser pointer in groups smaller than sixty is considered "overkill" in some cultures, and a presenter would hear snickers in the audience if he or she used this method.

Avoiding eye contact is taken as a sign of "shiftiness" or "uncertainty" in the United States, but many cultural taboos revolve around the use of eye contact. In Japan and other Asian countries, direct eye contact is "too direct," considered confrontational and rude, and should be avoided. Short and discreet looks at each person are important, but focus on the necktie knot or neck area when focusing on an individual for a short while (thirty - fifty seconds). On the other hand, direct eye contact and "visiting with" all members in the audience is important in Finland and Sweden.

Personal distance norms vary widely. In certain Mediterranean cultures, people tend to stand very close to each other when conversing, much too close for the average North American. In Southern Europe, a presenter doesn't run much risk of invading personal space, but in other cultures we have seen it happen. In one case, the audience member actually moved his chair backward to escape — not once, but twice — as the presenter kept inching forward. Do not touch people unless it is clear that they welcome this kind of physical contact. Americans tend to overreach when it comes to touching, with some men

---

Guidelines for Delivery to Audiences for Whom English Is a Second Language

- Use simple English: subject + verb + object sentences, and remember that some non-native speakers' English reading ability is often better than their verbal ability — provide written support
- Speak slowly, pause often, and enunciate clearly
- Indicate your transitions clearly between topics, using words like "first," "second," and "finally;" it helps to show the transitions on a slide or overhead
- Ask for questions frequently, allowing sufficient time for your audience to formulate and translate their questions in their minds
- Use gestures (but be sure to check the "cultural taboos") to illustrate your points
- Avoid using idioms, jokes, sports talk, and American analogies
- Relax and enjoy yourself — the audience may be evaluating WHO YOU ARE as much as what you say

expressing friendliness by putting their arm around people. This can be a major embarrassment. Of course, it works the other way as well, especially if you are in a European country and have established a relationship with someone. They may customarily exchange kisses. Be prepared. If you are a woman in an Arab country, be aware that men may not be allowed to have any physical contact with you and wait until the man extends his hand to shake hands.

Managing Interaction and Avoiding Confrontation

People from the United States tend to be more interactive in meetings and presentation settings than people in other countries, even in the United Kingdom. In the United States, a presenter is likely to be interrupted during his talk with questions, and much discussion occurs after the presentation is finished. However, in some cultures interruption is considered rude. We've heard managing directors in the United Kingdom object, for example, that an American's presentation was rambling and that the presenter had not been briefed appropriately because the presenter asked a number of checking questions at the beginning of the presentation.

Cultures vary. In Japan, for example, the listeners will show respect for the presenter by not asking questions early on, and will ask very few at the end. Junior people who attend the presentation and say absolutely nothing may call you afterward and ask a myriad of questions.

In Finland, listeners may come to hear and receive something that they will simply accept or not accept. Finnish listeners don't feel an obligation to participate. Questions will be carefully considered and well-founded. Any questions that are asked call for real answers, as do objections. However, it is not worth chasing after questions. Listeners in Finland need to first form their own opinions about 1) the presentation, 2) the manner in which the subject is being handled in each case, and 3) the presenter. If the Finnish audience accepts these three, questions begin to arise.

In Sweden, as in the United States, one might receive more questions, and as the speaker, you must establish in the beginning whether
you want to be interrupted or prefer to take questions at the end. In
some situations, the non-native English speaker may be hesitant to speak
in English among his peers or colleagues. Anticipate a lack of questions
and prepare some of your own to help direct a more interactive session.

Telling people that you would like to take questions may encourage the audience to ask more questions. Be aware that the presenter is
often perceived to be the expert and that if you answer questions in a
tentative way or admit you don't know the answer, you may confuse
the questioner. Be prepared.

When speaking in any non-English speaking environment, it's best
to give plenty of pause time after asking for questions from the audience. The listeners need time to digest the information and form their
thoughts and questions in another language. Count slowly to twenty or
twenty-five after soliciting questions or comments, giving plenty of
extra time for people to develop questions. Though some presenters
may be uncomfortable with this "long silence," the audience will not
be. At all costs, avoid asking, "Do you understand?" It's very difficult
for this to sound like anything other than a criticism of the audience's
language ability. If it seems comfortable, you can have someone in the
audience repeat what you've just said so you can check for understanding. Sometimes you can pose a question in a problem-solving session,
and split the group up into teams and have each team select a spokes-
person to report back to the group. This works well in Asian cultures in
which issues of "face" are important.

Understand Cultural Views of Confrontation and Conflict

Americans often misread the "subtext" involved in presentations and
meetings, even in the United States. Americans fare even worse in countries where, for social or political reasons, people will rarely disagree
in a public forum. Often, lack of response does not mean lack of un-

derstanding. In actuality the message is more like this:
I understand
… I don't agree
… I can't tell you that I don't agree.

In the former Soviet Union, people will defer to the head person in attendance at the presentation. In Pakistan, as well as in many other countries, people will not disagree in public, but will come up to the presenter later in private to register an opinion. In one fascinating case, twenty-eight physicians, when asked for approval of a logo for an ad campaign, gave superficial acceptance. Every one of the twenty-eight asked for a private meeting afterward to express their view that the logo was offensive.

Using Visual Support to Increase Understanding

"A picture is worth 10,000 [not 1,000] words" is a *Chinese* proverb. Visual support will help the non-native English speaker follow and understand your spoken message much more easily than just listening to the words. Seeing the key words or concepts in a clear, easy to understand visual, whether text, conceptual, or graph, will enable the listeners to read the key message rather than struggle to hear your explanation. Using message headings is especially helpful.

Don't use prepackaged multimedia presentations. It's tempting to take that expensive sales presentation on the road, but the pace is usually much too fast for non-native English speakers, and they may find the invitation to interact extremely stressful. In addition, if you have to dim the lights, you'll find that you'll lose your audience. When in doubt, low-tech is better.

Consider using a flipchart to illustrate concepts if you see that your audience is losing the thread. Writing on the flipchart is also guaranteed to slow your pace to one that is more easily understood by the audience.

Additional advice on visual support includes the following:

- Don't overuse the map of the world, either as a background or a stand-alone page or slide. Don't *tell* the audience you're global — *show* them by sharing your knowledge of their culture and their concerns.
- Use simple pictures that are meaningful to the target culture. Use simple English declarative sentences with a minimum of dependent clauses as your message heads.
- If possible, translate slides into the target language and include them in the handout. At the very least, have a translation on the facing page of the book.
- Avoid comics and humor in graphics. Once again, humor is the hardest thing to translate, and comics will be seen as overly casual.
- Use the currency and the measurement systems of the target culture in charts. For example, unless you have a specific reason not to (like maintaining consistency so that you can compare data across countries), convert miles to kilometers, pounds to kilos, and so on. It seems like a small point, but anything you do to reduce the appearance of ethnocentrism is well worth it.

Using an Interpreter Effectively

If you need to speak in a language that is not your native tongue, unless you are fluent in that language, you'll want to use an interpreter. If you do need a translator, here are some tips to keep in mind.

- Don't depend on members of your business team to act as interpreters. Language interpretation requires 100 percent attention; your team member will not be able to contribute to the content or monitor the flow of discussion if he or she is concentrating on translating.
- Meet with your interpreter before the presentation. Clarify roles and expectations. Share your overheads, documents, and handouts with your interpreter. Emphasize important technical terms or ideas.
- During the presentation, speak directly to the audience, not to the

interpreter. Do not say things like, "Ask him if we can have 20,000 goat puppets shipped by next week," because that is what will be literally translated. Ask the question directly, "Mr. Soohoo, can you ship 20,000 goat puppets by next week?" If culturally appropriate, make eye contact with the decision maker, but in any case, do not make eye contact with the interpreter. Similarly, extend your polite remarks to the decision maker. You should only speak directly to the interpreter if you need to confirm your understanding of something the decision maker has said.

- Realize that your interpreter is communicating your words, not your intentions. Speak clearly and simply. Use standard English and clarify and summarize frequently. Avoid idioms and jokes. Often, the interpreter will merely indicate that you have told a joke and alert the decision maker to laugh at an appropriate juncture.

- Slow down your pace (especially if you are from the Northeastern section of the United States where machine gun pacing is prevalent). Pause frequently, after two or three sentences, to allow time for the interpreter to translate and verbalize your comments in the other language. If you go too fast, the interpreter may miss portions of what you are saying or forget to convey something.

- Recognize that interpretation will literally double the length of the presentation. Even if the cultural norm is to have extensive polite exchanges at the beginning of the discussion, try to limit the time spent in these niceties. The norms of an interpreted presentation are slightly different from a standard presentation. Once into the meat of the discussion, don't say more than absolutely needs to be said. (Because you will have used a tree to structure the presentation, you'll be ahead here.)

- Often, the person you are presenting to understands some English. In some cultures, people prefer not to speak in English because their pronunciation is not perfect and perfection is the only acceptable standard. Resist the temptation to talk to your colleagues or to the interpreter "off the record" in English.

- Your interpreter can be a good source of cultural information. Ask about his or her impressions of the discussion. Don't rely on your own interpretation of the decision maker's body language. If he nods, ask the interpreter to confirm with him verbally that he means "yes" rather than "I hear you."

- Be patient.

SUMMARY

To present successfully to people from another culture,

- Keep an open mind
  — Be ready to learn
  — Be respectful
- Research to prepare
  — Find a cultural informant
  — Observe
  — Gauge your audience's English language ability
- Adapt your presentation's structure and your delivery style
- Deal with questions appropriately, and be aware of cultural views of confrontation and conflict
- Use visuals to increase understanding
- Work with an interpreter effectively

Women Presenters Abroad

In a study quoted in Training & Development in April 1994, 20 percent of women managers considered that being a woman was a disadvantage abroad; 42 percent said it was an advantage.

Most of our informants say that a woman businessperson's success abroad is a function of her sensitivity to cultural issues. Dealing with people in cultures in which women are not typically in a leadership role demands extra sensitivity and much more attention to audience analysis. Acceptable dress is very important. As one person said, seeing a woman walk down the street in a short skirt in some parts of Pakistan is the equivalent of someone walking down Fifth Avenue in his or her underwear. Naturally, if you're operating in a major city (Karachi or Islamabad, in the case of Pakistan) you can push the limits a bit more, especially if you have taken the time to observe the Pakistani women who may be members of your host group. But you should always have options — a scarf that matches your outfit, long-sleeved blouses, baggy pants — to cover your limbs and your hair if necessary.

That said, in many countries, women are seen as foreigners first, women second. They are not expected to act like local women. In some cases, expatriate women may even be treated better than their male counterparts because of the novelty. There is an assumption that because women are still relatively rare in business, they are the exceptional ones. In sales and marketing, being a woman provides additional visibility and memorability. And if a woman has stronger interpersonal skills, this can be a major advantage in a situation demanding sensitivity and receptivity (e.g. a foreign culture). One woman reported, "My clients talk more to me than to my male counterparts. And 50 percent of my effectiveness is based on volunteered information."

Our own experience is that people look at us as experts and foreigners who happen to be women. Gender has always seemed irrelevant. Professionalism and competence are always respected, no matter what form they come in.

Index